LIVING OPERA

LIVING OPERA

Joshua Jampol

2010

OXFORD
UNIVERSITY PRESS

Oxford University Press, Inc., publishes works that further
Oxford University's objective of excellence
in research, scholarship, and education.

Oxford   New York
Auckland   Cape Town   Dar es Salaam   Hong Kong   Karachi
Kuala Lumpur   Madrid   Melbourne   Mexico City   Nairobi
New Delhi   Shanghai   Taipei   Toronto

With offices in
Argentina   Austria   Brazil   Chile   Czech Republic   France   Greece
Guatemala   Hungary   Italy   Japan   Poland   Portugal   Singapore
South Korea   Switzerland   Thailand   Turkey   Ukraine   Vietnam

Copyright © 2010 by Oxford University Press, Inc.

Published by Oxford University Press, Inc.
198 Madison Avenue, New York, New York 10016

www.oup.com

Oxford is a registered trademark of Oxford University Press

Library of Congress Cataloging-in-Publication Data
Jampol, Joshua.
Living opera / Joshua Jampol.
p.   cm.
Includes index.
ISBN 978-0-19-538138-2
1.Opera—interviews. I. Title.
ML1700.J35 2010
782.1092'2—dc22   2009027687

1 3 5 7 9 8 6 4 2

Printed in the United States of America
on acid-free paper

For Sophia,
who, so far, likes Rossini . . .

Acknowledgments

You can't—obviously—do a book like this alone, unless you make it up. I didn't. Many people helped it into life, including the interviewees, and I thank them all.

The interviewees first. It's not easy corralling a group like this, nailing them down to specific hours and precise places—even the media-savvy, the well agented, those who adore exposure or simply like to talk.

I'd like to thank the *International Herald Tribune*'s Creative Solutions team, led by Véronique Feldmann: Linda Healey, Reine-Marie Melvin, Marnie Mitchell, Kathleen Gray, Perry Leopard, and Greig Stevens.

I also thank Pierrette Chastel, Opéra de Paris; Rita Grudzien, Royal Opera House, Covent Garden; Ulrike Hessler and Suzanne Lutz, Bayerische Staatsoper; Louise Pedersen, Royal Danish Opera; Aude de Jamblinne, EMI/Virgin Classics; Véronique Le Guyader, Universal Music/Philips & Decca; Gabriele Schiller, PR2 Agency, Cologne; and Florence Riou.

Preface

The interview, especially when it enjoys the luxury of lingering, as these do, will reveal a personality—call it the voice. The point of the interviews here was to get to the voices of these twenty opera professionals and to get them to disclose something about their work and why they do it the way they do.

Hearing insiders explain it would, I thought, interest other opera outsiders besides me. How Seiji Ozawa's approach differs from William Christie's; or how Waltraud Meier's style is distinct from Natalie Dessay's. Remembering things they said, we in the audience could watch for them the next time they appear onstage, or match what they said with things we recalled from previous performances. And thus, though still outsiders, move a bit more toward greater understanding of opera.

I also wanted to give an international take on the subject and a vision across generations, which is why the interviews take place in Europe's top houses with both younger and older professionals. Equally important, I've kept the flavor of the language of those who are not native English speakers —a good two-thirds of this book's cast.

But living opera is as much about communicating as it is about singing, conducting, producing, and designing. Call it an audible subtext. It's about how people so often hidden behind makeup and masks speak about their lives and livelihoods when those masks are off—or how they don't, or can't.

Who you are, and what you do all day can be difficult to express in words, particularly if your usual means of communication is more abstract. You may find that not all twenty clearly communicate in words, or that their passion for what they do is the only clear message you get. Decide for yourself. How do you think these interviewees performed as communicators?

It's intriguing that not everyone who communicates professionally onstage can repeat the performance off, in front of a single reporter, microphone, or camera, without the trappings, costumes, stage directions, rehearsals, and colleagues. The goal is the same, of course: performance, persuasion, and, in the end, seduction. Offstage, however, though you're still playing to a public: you're playing yourself.

Not everyone gets the same questions, which would have produced interviews with interchangeable answers and no voices at all. For the most part I followed the voices—both in the sense of letting them roam and in the sense of pursuit. A few questions are repeated often enough to give readers a compass—and a yardstick to measure how different voices handle the same query. Compare James Conlon or Samuel Ramey on "What quality do you need to do your job?" with Heidi Grant Murphy or Robert Carsen, for example. Or Pierre Boulez or Kent Nagano on "Does twelve-tone lack the more traditional elements of musical communication?"

The idea was to come away with a more intimate feel for the twenty people who so kindly played the game, but also with some understanding of communications techniques, too—both on the reporter's and the subject's side. This could even come in handy one day. Because performing and persuading are part of the communications package we all use, every day, in our personal and professional lives. For, unlike opera, when it comes to communications, none of us is an outsider.

Contents

© Philippe Gontier

LIVING OPERA

Pierre Boulez, or "The Incorruptible"

We begin in Paris, where we shall return after touring several of Europe's top opera cities.

The vast spaces of the Cité de la Musique, in the north of Paris, are a rather recent addition, and an even newer one is planned, for this is where the capital's future concert hall will soon be built. To hear professionals talk about it, the city sorely needs one. Pierre Boulez talks about it. He also speaks of Berg, Schoenberg, Kandinsky, and other favorites.

The Cité de la Musique is the seat of the Ensemble Inter-Contemporain, the group he founded in 1975, entirely devoted to the performance of new music. You are in his second-floor, end-of-the-hall office in late afternoon. Outside the door is his name on a red plaque. The long, cozy room has a mirror and makeup table on which sits a blue bowl with wrapped teabags. A beige couch floats on a soft carpet, a big black piano broods in the far corner. You sit at a small, round table in the middle of all this. Behind him, folded up against the wall, are three black music stands.

In constant movement, he's not the easiest person to get an appointment with. But Boulez is in Paris for a whole month just now. The curator of the Louvre Museum has invited him to be Guest at the Louvre, a series which offers personalities outside the museum (writers, dancers, musicians —Toni Morrison was one) a chance to take a fresh look at the Louvre's collections. Guests devise a program for the public of films, conferences, and concerts. Boulez, who has written extensively on music and the visual arts, was a natural.

He is smallish and smiling, in a jacket and sweater, gray pants, buttoned-up knit shirt, blue socks, black shoes. At eighty-three, he looks back over a long career—though one short on opera, as he will admit. He remains nonetheless a dominant force in contemporary music, a controversial figure in the past—one who still speaks his mind, as you'll discover—and a French icon today. His eyes sparkle, and he smiles when you quote him in your questions. The interview, begun with a joke, goes by rapidly.

The joke was that I had been delayed ten minutes at Reception (Entrée des artistes)—where Boulez must go in and out every day when he's there—while the man and woman at the desk flipped through their internal phone-book, trying to find his number, because neither of them knew who he was.

I thought I'd start with this and switched on the tape recorder before we sat down.

I have news for you: they don't know who you are at Reception.

[*Laughing*] That's nothing. Once I went to Chicago. The customs man looked at my passport and said, "What is your business in Chicago?" I said, "I'm going to conduct the Chicago Symphony Orchestra." He said, "What is that?" [*laughs*]

That's America. This is Paris. Chez vous.

[*Waving a hand*] It's the same.

Let's start with someone who does know you, then. Last week I saw Waltraud Meier and mentioned I'd be seeing you. I asked if she could think of anything I should ask. This is what she said. Not a question, a comment, and I'd like your reaction: "What can I tell you to ask Pierre Boulez? He is such a miracle in this music world who was and is always incorruptible in his music making. He gives more answers than you can ask questions." Does that please you when people—colleagues—call you "incorruptible"?

No. I don't want people to think of me that way. Because you know what politician here in France was called "The Incorruptible"? Robespierre [*laughs*]. He was incorruptible and cut off quite a lot of heads. That's not at all my intention, to cut off heads. If by "incorruptible" she means sticking to one's ideas and not being disrupted by any kind of difficulty, then yes, for sure. Because I have a personal view of music but don't impose it on anyone. But I want to express it, certainly.

Has this personal view changed at all over the years? Earlier in your career you were known as wanting to "disturb" the public and shake up systems.

Not really [*laughs*]. There is a proverb in France that says, "Only idiots never change their minds." From this point of view, I'm the perfect idiot. Because I think I was, in a way, oriented very precisely, when I was already twenty or twenty-one. Now I'm less . . . not sharp—because I hope I still have a sharp mind—but I don't want to cut up everything, like before. Now I say, "Okay, this exists. I don't care very much for it. But it can exist. I don't mind." But for the essential part of my thinking about music and about composers generally, of this century and the past century, I have really orthodox tastes—I mean, like everybody. I ask myself this question: "Without this composer, would music have been different?" Without Schoenberg, would twentieth-century music be different? Yes, it would have been different. Would twentieth-century music be different with or without Hindemith? I say no. That's my kind of judgment, for myself. I have reasons for it, and I know the reasons. It's not just a fancy or a taste which changes from time to time. My choice of composers was very deep and deeply thought. And felt. You cannot change the value of these people.

You say, "oriented precisely when you were twenty or twenty-one." Did these values come from Olivier Messiaen?

Messiaen was an influence, certainly. [René] Leibowitz also. Messiaen was not really much aware of the importance of the Second Viennese School. He knew two things: *Pierrot lunaire*, because it was performed in France in the '20s, and there was a lot of discussion about it. And he knew the *Lyric Suite* by Berg. Apart from that, he didn't know Webern at all. And with a reason, because he was never performed. There was also this attitude in France of, "German culture is good for Germans. But for us it's of no importance."

So if I were to ask if different aspects of music or opera matter to you more, or less, now than twenty or thirty years ago, what would you say?

Not much. I have changed my mind about Berg, not because of Berg himself, but because of the environment. Berg, at this point, in 1945, '46 or '47, was considered as the only composer because he was attached to the post-Romanticists. For us today, if we say Berg is only attached to the post-Romanticists, that's not very important or not important enough. I studied Berg, the *Kammerkonzert*, *Wozzeck* and the *Lyric Suite*, and discovered what he was, really. And the complexity of his thinking. And the kind of emotion which goes for the filter of formal invention. That's when I found him really interesting. But I discovered that later.

So, to use your yardstick, music would not be the same without Berg?

That's for sure.

I have some questions on twelve-tone music. Some people say it's no more than a footnote in musical history. It lacks the emotional connection that traditional music has—repetition, tension, suspense, resolution. People don't seem to find that in twelve-tone.

Twelve-tone was a chapter—the illusion of Schoenberg, who said, "I have fixed the future of music for one hundred years." He said something like that at one point [*laughs*]. First, it's too much like Hitler, with the Reich of one thousand years. I don't like this type of person who says, "I've fixed the future." I can imagine his reaction, because his music was not accepted, he had difficulties surviving even, there was anti-Semitism, too. So it was difficult for him, simply that. There was a period in his life when his thinking was . . . theocratic, do you say? For him he had the order, and it was like the Creation. God did it in six days, and on the seventh, he rested. It was exactly that: just organize twelve-tone, then everything will follow. But at the same time he was constantly checking the value of his twelve-tone with old formulas. *Variations, Opus 31. The Suite, Opus 25. The Suite, Opus 29.* Menuetto, gavotte, gigue, and so on. All these old forms. How can you really be new, even with a new technique, if you just check if it is valuable through old forms? That was the contradiction. He even lost some of his genuine invention along the way. On the contrary, in *Pierrot lunaire* or *Erwartung,* you find the kind of free inspiration which is much more interesting. It's the same with Kandinsky. In 1910, 1912, 1913—in his Murnau period—Kandinsky's invention was absolutely extraordinary. But at one point, Kandinsky, like Schoenberg, was afraid he would dissolve into chaos. So both wanted order. For Kandinsky, it was the Bauhaus period, with the circles and squares and geometrical figures, very simple. I can understand that at one point they were afraid. But they cut off their own wings, in a way.

So to people who say twelve-tone has really nothing to do with the greater flow of music—

For me, it's a tunnel. You have to go through the discipline, to know what it is, really. You cannot imagine Bach writing canons all the time. Strict music. He wrote the *Musikalische Opfer* or the fugues. The fugues were sometimes very strict. But he also wrote *Preludes*, which are very free—inventive, but free. It's the same for me. You can have moments of music which are absolutely determined, and moments of music which are, on the contrary, absolutely dominated by freedom. And that's the kind of dogmatism of Schoenberg. He could have invented the kind of musical moment completely under control. Because you cannot get this type of feeling otherwise than through a very severe technique. But I mean, there are other ways of expressing yourself.

You do a lot of teaching. Have you found a formula to explain to the lay person what twelve-tone music is?

Yes. Twelve-tone music is being completely under the very strict rules of tone row where nothing is repeated. I mean nothing is repeated in the tone row, but you can organize the tone row divided, you can have harmony with the tone row. You can also have segments of the tone row. Four segments of three, three segments of four, two segments of six, and so on. As a kind of arithmetic formula, it's very simple.

And people understand it?

Yes, but that's not what's interesting. What's interesting is the invention from that point of view. And if you are too dominated by that, you lose a kind of spontaneity. My twelve-tone period was one year and a half, something like that. Then it was finished. But I went through this discipline and even exaggerated this discipline, applying it to other characteristics of the sound, like dynamic, duration, and so on. And I saw that it was practically as absurd as total chaos. But I took this lesson. And if I hadn't gone through this period, I couldn't have conquered my freedom as I did.

You have a background in mathematics. How important is that for a musician?

It's nothing. You know, my background in mathematics was just after my baccalauréat. I was finishing my studies; I had one year at university. That was it. And I was already detached progressively, because I wanted to be in the musical world.

Some people say it's important to be mathematically minded if you're in music.

Not at all. I will tell you an anecdote I've told many times. I was professor in the Collège de France, which is higher than the university. Each year, there is a book, and all the professors give a kind of résumé of what you did the previous year. I still receive this book. Sometimes I look at the mathematicians' résumés, and *I don't understand a single word.* I don't! My level in mathematics was one of a very young student, no more. That's a legend. Because people think, "Well, he organizes things, so he's a mathematician."

That's what people say.

You can take the fifty-year-old woman who goes into a shop to buy things and adds up the prices. That's about my level of mathematics [*laughs*].

You said—I think it was in the 1960s, "The most elegant solution for the problem of opera [Boulez begins to laugh] is to blow up the opera houses."

Yes. That was very strange, because there was the . . . how do you say . . . *schlagzeile* . . . the headline, which was, "Blow up the opera houses." But what I said precisely, and you just said it, was, "The most elegant solution to get rid of the routine would be to blow up the opera house—but that's a solution that is very impractical." I added those words, immediately after.

They don't use that part.

Exactly.

I heard that remark is still causing problems. Is it true that after 9/11, it led to a dawn raid on your hotel room by Swiss police?

Yes, in Basel. I never knew why. That was a *Spiegel* interview in 1966 or 1967. Forty years before September eleventh, so I don't think it had any relation. But they never gave me an explanation for that.

You don't work with a baton, do you?

No. I began conducting chamber groups. Very small, six or seven musicians, like *Pierrot lunaire*. For this kind of proximity I never used a baton. When I went to the orchestra, I simply didn't change. I find the hand is much more flexible than the baton. For opera it's the same. And I asked—especially at the beginning, now I don't ask anymore—"Does it disturb you if I conduct this way?" And they always told me, "No. We see your arm; that's much stronger than the baton." Singers told me that.

You don't ask anymore.

No [*laughs*]. Too late!

You're involved in the design of the new concert hall here. When will that be built?

I hope it will be finished for 2012. That's all I can say for the time being, because the legal processes are beginning now, and you have to watch the market, the contracts, the bids, and all that. I hope the economic situation, which has got worse, will not impede its construction.

How involved are you in its design and acoustics?

I'm not involved directly but spoke with the man in charge—a long time ago already—and we're constantly in touch. I advised them to look at the Berliner Philharmoniker, which is a very good hall, and inventive. They will not do the same thing, but they don't want a shoebox, either. They want a certain amount of flexibility, of mobility also.

Professional musicians say Paris really doesn't have a good hall.

No. You have theaters—Théâtre du Châtelet, or Théâtre des Champs-Elysées, which is not very good acoustically. You have Salle Pleyel, which was the only hall of this size. Pleyel is convenient and good enough, but not terribly good.

How about the opera houses, Bastille and Garnier?

Acoustically speaking, I find Garnier rather good, but too dry, if you compare it with La Scala, for instance. La Scala has much better acoustics than Garnier.

When you say "dry," what do you mean?

No resonance.

There were problems at Bastille when it opened.

They have been more or less solved. But the problem in Bastille, you remember, was all the turmoil when they sent [Daniel] Barenboim home. There was nothing but turbulence. I gave my resignation also at this point, because I didn't want to go along with people who treated Barenboim this way. So there was nobody, really—no musician, or group of musicians—to try out the acoustics when it opened. All they did was have a kind of performance which was essentially a fashion show in very poor acoustical conditions, and nobody was there to judge. It was a miscarriage.

I saw you at the premiere, last year, of Melancholia, a new opera by Georg Friedrich Haas. Do you try and make the rounds to see what new works are being performed?

I go as much as I can if I am in Paris. Because I'm curious to see if people have come up with something. In this case, I was not terribly impressed, I must say.

Is opera in good health today, generally?

Opera has not had its revolution, like theater has. Patrice Chéreau, or Peter Stein in Germany, and others have taken the spoken theater very far. In music, it's much more difficult, but you have always this: stage, pit, hall. There's always this kind of realism. Think about other traditions, like the Bunraku, with marionettes; or the Noh theater, also in Japan; or the shadow theater in the Philippines; opera has not done anything with any of that. Not a thing. And in opera now you have the possibility of having the sound everywhere, or of changing the sound, to organize its distribution in the hall or on the stage or in the pit, or exchanging it sometimes—nothing has been done, from this point of view. Nothing.

Is that the fault of stage directors or opera house directors?

It's also the fault of the people who write the operas. Who don't ask for something like that. Generally, their idea of theater is rather simplistic, I find.

Perhaps they think the public wouldn't accept anything more complicated?

No, the public has accepted this renovation in the spoken theater. They would accept renovation of the musical theater. The problem is that it is much more difficult acoustically. I've told this story many times, so stop me if you've heard it, but I remember once, when [Rolf] Liebermann [director of the Paris Opéra from 1973 to 1980] was here he wanted to stage *Boris Godunov*. He asked Joseph Losey to direct. And Losey didn't want the pit, because he thought the singers were too far away, and you have all this mass of sound in between, so they have to shout, and so on. So they covered the pit. They had monitors, of course, and the orchestra was way at the end of the stage, on a kind of podium, like a military band [*laughs*]. When Boris or Chouiski was in front, they could act more than if they had the pit in between. Then you heard the singers very well. But you heard the orchestra from quite far. You know that, in *Boris*, you have scenes with the chorus, which are not small scenes, but very important ones. Then you didn't hear the orchestra at all; you only heard the chorus. That's really the problem. Wagner, because he knew what he wanted, invented the covered pit. He wanted the illusion, so people don't see the musicians who are playing. It gives a sonority which is very different. He had what he wanted. Now we must think about the possibility of something more flexible, more interesting in the kind of relationship between audience, musicians, and stage.

Plácido Domingo says there are two schools in writing contemporary opera. Critics on one side want composers not to write much melody, while another wing thinks opera should go back and be more melodic. Domingo himself thinks we need a combination. "The voice needs to sing," he says. "It doesn't need to be saying notes. It needs a line. The voice needs expression." What's your feeling?

Well, that's a little simplistic, I find [*laughs*]. You cannot just think of opera as melody.

He said expression. You can't just sing notes.

Certainly, but look at *Wozzeck*. There are a lot of different ways of using the voice. I think it should be this way, and not only a kind of melodic line, like in an aria from an Italian opera. In Wagner you don't have only melodies. You have some scenes which are dialogues. And that's terribly important. So to reduce the kind of expression of an opera into a melodic line seems to me very drastic, let's say [*laughs*].

You were going to write an opera yourself.

Yes, with [Jean] Genet. I began with Genet and with Heiner Muller. Both died in the process. Not that I killed them [*laughs*], but if I ask for a third one maybe he will die also [*laughs*].

How far did you get?

With Genet, we did sketches of scenes. He wanted to amplify the *Wozzeck* plan—this was just his idea at the time. He was very impressed by the construction Berg made out of the Büchner play. He wanted to make something more complex, but where the formula aspect would have been very strong.

Is this something you still have in a drawer?

Yes, but it's not to be used. It's too primitive still.

I heard you say recently, "Music today is more and more an affair of specialists. That's fine for surgery, but not for music." Do you remember saying that?

Absolutely. I said that not only for contemporary music. You have people who play only baroque music, between 1700 and 1770 or 1780. There are people who begin with early Haydn and finish with early Beethoven. There are people specializing in late Beethoven and Bruckner and Mahler. That's really not culture at all. That's specialty. It's not good. You have restaurants in Paris which are very famous for making . . . what's the word . . . *canard* . . .

Duck.

Duck. And you know, you cannot cook ducks all your life! That's exactly the impression given to me by these people, who are cooking their ducks always the same. I find that the complete contrary of musical culture. And the way they look at the music of the past is a kind of dead look. You see they are always looking for authenticity, or a kind of authenticity. Authenticity for me is a kind of exoticism of history. You push the music of their time, *in* their time, so it's like putting a landscape in a kind of frame. Frozen, completely.

You added, "Musicians should be as good with Berg as with Mozart."

Absolutely.

You recently conducted Janáček's House of the Dead *in Amsterdam, with Patrice Chéreau directing, then said it would be the last opera you would ever record. Why?*

Because it takes too much time. I love working for the theater because my first job, when I was young, was with Jean-Louis Barrault for stage music. So I am very fond of theater today. And I like to work with people like Chéreau or Peter Stein. Stein and I did *Moses and Aron* in 1995 in Amsterdam, and again in 1996 in Salzburg. To be involved in a production, I want to be there from the very beginning. I am there for all the piano rehearsals. At that time, the director and I discuss, or don't discuss. That's how Chéreau and I worked in *House of the Dead*. And we understand each other perfectly because we work for three or four weeks, absolutely together. So after three or four weeks of rehearsal, the director and I are totally in phase. Then there is no discussion, or there is the beginning of a discussion that's solved immediately. I like this work, because I am totally involved. But when we produced *House of the Dead*, the preparation, the performances, and the recording took two full months—almost three months—of my time because it was rehearsed first in Vienna, for the Theater an der Wien, then we performed in Amsterdam, then we performed in Aix-en-Provence and recorded at Aix-en-Provence. I'm sorry, but I don't want to spend this time now.

You want to be there from the first piano rehearsals. Do you want your singers and everybody else to be there also?

Absolutely.

Otherwise?

Otherwise, no way. In opera houses, generally you have somebody who has never seen the production. Who comes there, one day before, and says, "Put this here, on the left." Or, "You go here," and so on. That's not good.

Can I ask what you like about opera? Why do you like to conduct it?

Because it's a kind of form which absorbs everything. Absorbs theater, absorbs music, absorbs singing—not melody, but singing, anyway [*laughs*]. I think that's very satisfying, because you are part of a bigger ensemble. When you give a concert you can have an imaginary theater, but the real one is always more exciting.

Is there anything about opera that you don't like?

I had the experience, I remember, in 1966, when I worked with Wieland Wagner on *Wozzeck*. I never knew, during the performance time, who were the musicians who played. There were some people who never rehearsed, or who maybe rehearsed one month before, one rehearsal, and who were there in very important positions. If you had oboe A and flute C in one performance, the next performance you had oboe C and flute B. You never knew who was there. And that's absolutely impossible, this kind of anonymity. You cannot accept that. You don't accept that in concerts. But you accept that in the theater most of the time. When we did *House of the Dead* we had the same orchestra, the same people, always. When I did *Moses und Aron* in Amsterdam we had the Concertgebouw Orchestra, and we always had the same people at the same place.

It's something you require.

Of course.

And if the opera house director says, "I'm sorry, we can't do it"?

I put that in the contract [*taps the table*].

Can you confess to anything in opera that has defeated you? Or something you've always wanted to do but never did? Or something you failed at?

Yes and no. My main defeat was the death of Wieland Wagner. He liked to work with me because he had always worked with people of the previous generation, especially with [Karl] Böhm, or [Hans] Knappertsbusch. So when I worked with him for the first time, he was with somebody not of his generation, but younger—I was nine or ten years younger than he was, though it was close, in generations. And he wanted to do much more with me. I was not tied to any orchestra at this time—it was 1966. We had plans to make two productions a year, in different houses. It never materialized, of course, because he died in 1966.

That's one thing you regret.

Well, that you cannot change [*laughs*].

Can we talk about an experience that marked you, that was instrumental in making you the musician that you became? Something that happened when you were a student, with a teacher, or as a performer, or as a spectator even?

No, it's everything. I cannot say that I had a vision suddenly, and it made me . . . [*thinks*] . . . no, it came progressively. Certainly there were some works which were more important for me than others.

For instance?

The Rite of Spring. It was one of the first works which was very impressive to me. I was very impressed the first time I heard *Pierrot lunaire,* the first time I heard the *Sonata for Two Pianos and Percussion,* Bartók. Things like that. I remember works very solidly: the *Three Excepts from Wozzeck,* which I heard for the first time before—long before, even—seeing the opera. That was very impressive for me.

For the premiere of Marteau sans maître, *I heard you had fifty rehearsals.*

Yes—that is, I suppose so, because I wasn't there. I came for the last week of rehearsals. I saw a couple of them but not all. Certainly there were a lot; I don't remember how many—forty or fifty.

Would you get that for a new opera today?

No, although . . . *Wozzeck* was presented for the first time in France, with Böhm and the Vienna Opera, in 1952. Then, eleven years later, in 1963, the Paris Opéra put it onstage with the French orchestra, and German singers, of course—you couldn't find French singers who could sing that. And I asked for fifteen rehearsals. Three for each act.

With full orchestra?

Yes. Orchestra, orchestra and singers, stage. It was very substantially done. The music was totally foreign to people, so it was necessary to have this, but it was well prepared, then.

Today we wouldn't see that?

Well, if I don't get them I wouldn't do it. It's as simple as that.

That's a budget question, I guess.

Yes, but they spend so much money for things which are not terribly interesting, they can concentrate on one project which is more absorbing than the others.

Is this something you see in opera houses around the world, or is it a European problem, or a North American problem?

I suppose—because I don't have any experience with American opera houses. I have very little experience here in Europe, even. But I know that at the Met, since [James] Levine has been music director, he asks for what he wants. He has great authority, he's been there more than thirty years, is well known and does very well. He has really put this orchestra at the top level. He has his own thing to share. I think that if you have a strong musical director you can really ask for something. Although you have to take the budget into consideration. But it's not only that.

You said you haven't done much opera in Europe.

Not too much, no. I did this *Wozzeck* in Frankfurt. Then I did the *Ring* in Bayreuth, which was very important, especially as it ran five years there. I did *Parsifal* also from 1966 to 1970 with Wieland Wagner as director, but he died in between. Then I did *Parsifal* again in Bayreuth, because Wolfgang [Wagner] asked me to do it as a kind of last production. Then I did *Moses und Aron* in Amsterdam and Salzburg. And *Pelléas* in Cardiff with Peter Stein. So that's all.

Is there a reason for that?

I did not want the routine of an opera house. I was baptized by the performance in 1966 of *Wozzeck*, especially when it was redone after the death of Wieland. It was a kind of homage to Wieland Wagner. And as a matter of fact, it was a disaster, because you had no rehearsal, you had people who were there for the first time, and so on. It was really dreadful.

You didn't mention Lulu. *You conducted the 1979 world premiere, here in Paris, of the completed third act by Friedrich Cerha. Patrice Chéreau directed.*

Lulu was very interesting. I knew Chéreau had done the Wedekind play, in the Teatro Piccolo in Milan. He had quite a lot of knowledge about the text. I explained to him how the music was, in relation to the text. We spent days like that. We did that for *House of the Dead* also. We establish a kind of common field, let's say, where we meet, about what we think about the piece.

Can you give a brief example of how you explained "how the music went with the text"?

That's difficult to answer. In *Lulu*, I explained to him, for instance, how Berg used the sonata form to organize the scene. Then how he used variations—for example, in the third act—to establish the various moments of the scene. Things like that. So he knows there is a frame of action, rather strict at the beginning—at the origin, at least, of the transcription—but also with freedom.

You don't do that with every director, I suppose?

No. I'm interested in discussing. I did that with Peter Stein for *Pelléas*, and for *Moses und Aron*. Because you know, the whole part of Moses is spoken, with rhythm and so on. With Stein, what was interesting is that he took the two protagonists, Aron and Moses, and had them say the text like an actor would have done. Then, when the singers came on to sing—or to tell, I should say, according to the rhythms by Schoenberg—there was a kind of acting way of looking at the text, which was very different.

He had explained that to you, maybe, in the way you explained the music?

He explained that to me, and I attended the rehearsals also, at the beginning. So I learned how to accept things with freedom with the text by

Schoenberg, because this freedom was justified by the acting. It was interesting.

With Chéreau you went from the Ring *in 1976 to* House of the Dead *in 2007. How has your working together changed over the years?*

We worked in Bayreuth until 1980, because we recorded the *Ring* in 1979 and 1980. Before *House of the Dead,* I had not worked with him since 1980 because he was essentially working in movies and in the theater. I followed his career, of course. But we didn't have any projects which interested me. He did this early Mozart opera . . . I don't remember the title . . . he wrote it for La Scala when he was nineteen or so . . . *Lucia Silla.* Something like that does not interest me. The conventions of the eighteenth century—you cannot do very much with that.

Any memories of the 1976 Bayreuth Ring? *Chéreau says it was a huge project, and a nightmare at first.*

He was working too hard. You know, putting on all four pieces of the *Ring* in three months is really quite a lot. Especially he changed; he asked the singers to think about their parts and to look at the text, which was a great, innovative push for everybody. I had problems with the orchestra. The problems were accumulating. And some parts of the audience were really dreadful. They wanted to interrupt.

What didn't they like?

The staging, everything [*laughs*]. You cannot imagine. Listen to the tape of the first performance of the cycle in 1976.

I've only heard the recordings.

The recordings were done in the studio. Certainly somebody has the tape of the first broadcast. You hear all kinds of catcalls during the performance.

Are they known for that at Bayreuth?

Generally, yes—but at the end of the performance. This was *during* the performance.

What did you do?

Nothing. I thought they would be only too happy for me to stop [*laughs*]. I just went on. I went through the fire, like Brünnhilde! [*Laughs*]

© Wilfried Hösl

Robert Carsen, or building the bridge between head and heart

Opera, says Robert Carsen, is a mix of head and heart. It could be a description of the man himself.

He's an interesting mix of mixes, really: New World candor and Old World correctness, for a start. He looks at you openly from behind his trendy, rectangular black glasses: casual, wide-eyed, you might even say innocent. That's the New World part (he was born in Toronto). But looks can mislead. Carsen also possesses a sizable measure of Old World reserve, picked up in his adopted England, where he emigrated when he was twenty.

Second mix: he is intellectual enough to have built a career on reinterpreting texts for the stage; this includes unearthing character motivation, and even Dr. Freud, in opera libretti, and is a trait formed during his acting days when he was taught to closely examine a written text. But Carsen also believes directors must listen to their intuition. "Successful ones accept that what takes place onstage doesn't always have to be logical, because music isn't always logical," he argues. Directing, for him, means serving both. And the fact that he can explain his approach to staging opera in intellectual terms yet avoid sounding dry about it—communicating instead an infectious passion—suggests that this balanced man of combinations is a fine fit for the lyric arts. His pared-down, audience-friendly productions, which always connect, confirm this point.

Despite a few strands of gray in his hair, he looks a young fifty-three. His small hands punctuate his words, which pour forth in a sort of border-less accent, another mix, of Canadian and U.K. English.

He doesn't consider himself an "opera director," despite having done more than fifty operas, five plays, and no films. "I got into opera because it came up," he admits. "I liked it, since I'd gone with my parents, but never thought I'd work in it. Then I just got more involved."

Today, Carsen is more than involved; you could call him the fair-haired boy of the European opera scene. Dozens of his productions are staged each year from Antwerp to Zurich. Two of them, which he discusses, recently kicked off the seasons in Paris (Capriccio) and Covent Garden (Iphéginie en Tauride). Nobody seems to remember the last time anyone could claim that distinction. He had four shows at the Opéra de Paris that year, a new production and three revivals. Something about his approach must be on target for him to occupy so much ground.

When we spoke, he was rehearsing for Covent Garden and Paris, shut-tling between the cities where he keeps his homes. He's an intense, quietly focused type, not impatient—we spoke for hours—but knows what he wants. The questions were designed to get him to explain how he works, and he gave himself to the subject with enthusiasm, as he clearly enjoys delving into character impulse and drive. But before the questions began, he asked one himself—the only interviewee who showed such initiative. "Just out of interest," he queried, "what work of mine have you seen?" Hearing the question, you know it's more than "just out of interest." For Carsen was preparing his answers, planning where the interview was going to go—directing it, in fact.

You didn't start out to be an opera director.

I trained as an actor. When I came to England, at age twenty, to study at the Bristol Old Vic Theater school, a teacher pointed out that I was con-structed like a director.

How is a director constructed?

I thought he was saying I was a really rotten actor. But he said I had a direc-tor's mind because I was interested in the whole picture, not just in my part.

I went to everyone's rehearsals, was watching everybody, and had suggestions for everything.

Had you done any directing?

Small things. I decided, well, maybe this is an interesting thing to do. I left the Old Vic School after two years and tried to get a job as an assistant director. I was twenty-one. It's not easy. I met Giancarlo Menotti, who told me I could be an observer at his Spoleto Festival, which was where my first job was. That's how I got into opera.

Through Menotti?

Yes, but what I mean is I was trying to find a job in theater *or* opera. And this job in opera came up.

What job was it?

The Queen of Spades, with Magda Olivero as the Countess. I had gone to opera with my parents, and liked it, but never thought I was going to work in it. Then, when I started to think of myself as a director, I just got more involved.

What do you like about it?

It's the most ambitious of the performing arts, because it combines all of them. In *Capriccio*, which I'm restaging for Paris, you've got orchestral playing, solo singing, ensemble singing, pure dance, you've even got speech. When it works, it's unique. It's created from an alchemical synthesis of the abstract and the concrete, the emotional and the intellectual. The words are the concrete, the intellectual; the music is the abstract and the emotional. The most satisfying thing is that it fulfills all your expectations—the numinous, the incomprehensible, the emotional—yet it can be extremely challenging intellectually. When it works, there's nothing that can touch it; and when it doesn't work, it's hell.

You're talking as a director?

I'm talking as an audience member. When you see something fabulous, it can fulfill you on all levels. It's vast forces: the orchestra, chorus, the technicians. Don't you find?

Is that something that appeals to you—the teamwork?

Yes. I like that.

You said in an interview that "opera is a mixture of head and heart."

I always say that. But I really believe it. And I can't exactly put into words why that is. The whole process of directing is serving the one while serving the other. A production that is emotionally cold and purely cerebral I don't think works; and a production that's only moving people around in terms of the music and not having any attempt to be challenging intellectually or offer some interpretation of the material is not satisfying, either. It's a question of finding the bridge, the balance.

How do you go about finding that bridge?

That's very intuitive. I don't know if I do find it. It's a complicated process, because on the one hand I want to serve the production and make the best performance I can for the particular audience in the place. But I'm also thinking about what it represents in terms of what that composer did, and why did he want to write that.

Give us an example.

Take *Iphigénie en Tauride*, which we're working on for Covent Garden. Gluck's rigor in leaving out anything extraneous is astonishing. Compared to music that preceded it, there's no ornamentation, no decoration, no purely orchestral passages or elaborate dance sequences or cadenzas or anything. It's all completely serving the drama. So you start with something which is there. Then look at this hideous story; you couldn't have a more emotional mess. A curse on the house of Atreus, the daughter supposedly killed by the father, the father killed by the mother, the mother killed by the brother; and with only two of them left, the girl's job is now to kill her brother. When I saw how Gluck explores that, I was not particularly interested in doing a production set in a specific time or place. It felt to me, in its psychological exploration, violently ahead of its time, pre-Freudian to a degree you can't believe—people dreaming about what's going to happen, a brother seeing his sister and thinking she's his mother. It's incredible. Not until Hugo von Hofmannsthal wrote *Die Frau ohne Schatten* do you get anything like that again in opera—the same psychosexual mix-up. So I thought it wouldn't be serving this work—although you can do it that way—by setting it in a war zone—though there is the background of the Trojan War. I don't think Gluck was interested in those events per se but wanted them to create a context. I thought if we set it in Iraq, for example, it would distract from the essence. So the choice we made was to make something out of time and place, like being inside someone's head. You have to figure out how you can do that. What you choose as a production team are your building blocks. But then you have to follow things through logically, based on those early choices.

When you say you didn't want to set it in Iraq, could that be a reaction against productions you'd seen?

I don't think so. I don't go to opera that much, and I don't like looking at videos of operas that I am preparing. Of course, if you hear about a production that's been done in a certain way, you want to avoid doing that. And if I know I'm going to direct a piece I tend to avoid going to see it.

Why?

If the production's very good it might make me think I'll never be able to do one as good. And if it's bad, it might put me off the opera, and I might think, Well, why am I doing this? I go more to theater and the movies and to dance. Of course one needs to see singers and be up to date. But I prefer to see other art forms than the one I'm working in. I find it useful and stimulating.

You directed another Gluck opera, Orfeo. *How did you approach that?*

With *Orfeo*, Gluck is dealing with archetypal things, the elemental parts of life we're all going to go through. You're dealing with something based on one of the great mysteries of life, which is death. We would all love to bring a loved one back from the dead. That's very moving, and only theater can do it: vicariously going through what someone else is going through helps you in what you're going to go through, or what you may have gone through already. Greek theater being a religious experience as well as a theatrical experience—catharsis—means enactment of these mysteries has a healing effect. You go through this, and you're cleansed and better equipped to deal with life. I do believe that. That's why I cannot direct Rossini. That's a surprise ending to that paragraph!

Yes, I was wondering where you were going.

You haven't asked me that question, but if there's anything I cannot direct, it's Rossini. It doesn't interest me at all. I have no sympathy with it. I recognize it's brilliant music. But it's brilliant music set to situations that don't mean anything to me.

Comic opera doesn't interest you? The Marriage of Figaro?

Yes, but *Figaro* is so moving. The marriage of these two young people is going to go wrong. I love comedy, although it's the hardest of all to direct, but there has to be something meaningful at stake, I suppose.

How about contemporary opera?

That's a challenge. I would like to do more. What's exciting is the collaboration with the librettist and composer. Being part of helping them achieve what they want. There's the excitement of working on a new piece that you don't have with classic opera. And I think that's a slight absurdity of our time. Mozart writes an opera called *Idomeneo* where the role of the King's son, Idamante, is originally written for a mezzo-soprano. For a revival they haven't got a mezzo-soprano but a tenor, so Mozart simply rewrites the part musically. Sometimes he writes an aria, and the singer doesn't like it, so he writes two others. We're about to do *Mithridate* and there are several versions of some of the arias, and Mozart composed it when he was only fourteen. There are some very practical people in the theater. Now, of course, you're not allowed to change a note, and it's all sacrosanct: there's the definitive version, and people get very upset if you try to alter anything.

You mentioned you like to work intuitively, then said opera is a team. Do you see any conflict there? Other members of the team have their intuitions as well.

Wait a minute. "Intuitive" was my answer when you asked, "How do you make the bridge between intellect and emotions, and make sure you're getting the right balance?" It's not a litmus test. It's an intuitive thing, in collaboration. It *feels* like you're doing the right thing. Having made a decision about what is this piece about and how can it speak to us. There are several things going on at the same time.

What are they?

One is what I've just said. The other is if you're doing a well-known piece—*La Traviata*, say—it's important to know what that work represented to the composer. Why did he bother to write it? I mention *La Traviata* because the story was close to Verdi's heart. It was something he was living through; this woman who was treated so appallingly, and the hypocrisy of his age. He was tired of writing about historical subjects and wanted to write a modern piece. In a famous letter, he said he wanted to write about "un sogeto dell'epoca." Which is why it's ironic that opera audiences sometimes forget, or are not aware of that fact when they complain about *La Traviata* being staged in modern dress. It's betraying that Verdi wanted to do anything else. He wanted to have the audience look at themselves on the stage. As Mozart did, with *The Marriage of Figaro*.

Do you think opera audiences or theater audiences are more likely to forget these things?

Opera audiences are different. The repertoire is much smaller. The same pieces tend to be done more than in the theater. Often there's a larger proportion of an opera audience that has seen the work before, so you want them not to be comparing what they've already seen. You want them to be right there in the moment, not running a movie in their head of the last time they saw the piece. Sometimes it's necessary to get into the production in a way where an audience won't have any grounds for comparison, where the drama will cause them to hear the music as if for the first time. It's another thing that's in my thinking. All these things happen at the same time.

Concretely, how does that translate into staging?

It has to do with how one chooses what's going to happen onstage, what the production is going to be like. They're not always conscious decisions. There isn't a simple answer to that, I'm afraid. I suppose the most important thing is deciding what the opera is about. I've often said the story of the opera is not necessarily what the opera is about. The plot is the train track on which the whole thing moves. Often what the piece is about is not the story itself, but in the subtext under the story.

Can you give an example?

On a banal level, you can say *La Bohème* is about a lovely young girl who gets sick and dies. But the opera is about life. It's about youth and that time in life when anything's possible. Of course, Mimi has to be ill, and she does die—but the piece is about living in the moment, in the most intense way possible, like kids eighteen or nineteen want to do.

How did you accomplish this?

I'd have to tell you the story of the whole production, and it would take too long! But we made it very young and crazy and about young people who don't follow the rules. We also decided to make it about young artists, about the thrill of young people discovering their creative energy. At that age, you feel life goes on forever. There's no sense of how much time you've got left, which is fantastic. I can give you another example with a more sophisticated opera like *Die Frau ohne Schatten*, which is often considered to be only an elaborate fairy tale. I started working on it for a production in Vienna. I looked at the time it was written and realized that it was contemporary with Freud. The woman without a shadow was rather like a Freudian case history. Then I started to look more carefully. And I saw that, how extraordinary, the Empress and the Emperor, who are supposed to have this fabulous relationship, are never in the same scene together. They don't have a real relationship. I realized that on one level, it was about a woman completely locked in her own world, a frigid woman, in fact, and there's confusion with her father. That led me to think, well, what is this fairy tale about? About a woman who has to get a shadow to get healed. And the shadow represents fertility. Fertility and frigidity; it's a Freudian study of a schizophrenic. So we did it that way. It was an exciting discovery, though it sounds very intellectual, which I hope managed to unlock the emotions of the piece. Because by treating it in this way you had a real problem you were dealing with, rather than something that merely remained a fairy tale that kept you from getting involved in this woman's struggle.

It sounds like you have great respect for authors and composers, while at the same time, you put yourself in the place of the audience.

That's what I'd like to think I'm doing, those three things.

How hard is that?

I had fantastic training in text study as an actor, where we examined scenes. I was fascinated by the things I hadn't noticed that were pointed out to me by a certain teacher, the same one who suggested I become a director. About how it's not just what the characters say, but what other characters say about them, and how carefully you have to study a text in order to find what's hidden in it.

Is the word for what you are doing, then, "directing," really accurate? It sounds like maybe you're doing something else.

Directing is not only about stopping people from bumping into the furniture, to paraphrase what Noël Coward said. It's a complicated thing. In addition to conceiving a production and developing it logically, intuitively, and emotionally with the designer, you have to bring everyone into your vision and hope they're going to enjoy it and agree with you and be stimulated by it. You have to also make that work with the conductor. But it's not enough to have ideas. You have to have a technical, practical side, to be able to take people and move them around and give them individual characters. There's so much going on, all the time. I'll give you another example. When I directed *Der Rosenkavalier* in Salzburg, I studied it, and it struck me as a rather unhealthy work. It's in the tradition of Viennese plays of the period—Nestroy, Schnitzler—where married people are constantly having affairs. The Marschallin is having an affair; her husband is off having another. She's got a young lover and is going to get another one. However, I was struck by two interesting details in the text which are completely unnecessary but which eventually colored our entire production. The two details, which are linked, were as follows: the Princess Marie-Therese von Werdenberg is married to the Feldmarschal. She's called the Feldmarschallin. The Feldmarschal is the head of the Austrian army. Nobody ever thinks about that, it seemed to me. The fact that this beautiful woman is married to the head of the Austrian army. We're only told one thing about Sophie's father, Herr von Faninal, apart from the fact that he's incredibly rich: he is an arms dealer and supplies the army which is stationed in Holland. "Er hat die Lieferung fur die Armee, die in den Niederlanden steht," says Baron Ochs to the Marschallin in act 1. And I thought, that's interesting. It's the Zeitgeist: the opera was composed two years before World War I, when Austria was arming itself. The opera would be exactly the same without those two details; if she were just Princess Marie-Therese van Werdenberg, and he were the Prince. But no, Hofmannsthal made her husband, this dark, threatening force who frightens everyone all the way through the opera, the head of the army. I thought, well, you can't ignore that.

How did you put that into your production?

I pushed it very far, and the Austrians got cross because I set the whole thing at the end of the Hapsburgs, just before World War I. And when Sophie and Octavian sing at the end, "Ist ein Traum, kann nicht wirklich sein." It's a dream, it can't really be, I showed, behind them, the Field Marshal leading the entire army into battle—so in fact the dream is about to end the next moment. But it all came from the text, and I thought was completely in line with the great tradition of these Austrian farces, which start at the highest level of society and end in the bordello. But I never know where that journey is going to take me, until I actually sit down and start to work on it. I don't think about a production in the abstract, like, "It would be nice to do this opera, and how would I do it?" I only start to think in the way I'm describing when I know I'm going to do a particular piece at a particular moment in a particular theater.

It sounds like you set about working months in advance.

Usually, for a big opera house or festival, you have to supply the production a year before. Theaters want you to hand in a model ten months or a year before, so they have time to study it, figure out how to do it, fit it into their repertoire, get it built and so on. One starts working up to a year before that.

If I were to ask you what are the three qualities someone needs to be able to do what you do, what would come to mind?

Hmm. To start with, you'd have to love the text and love music. Because everything you're going to do is going to come from the text and the music. You need to enjoy exploring that. Directors who don't like the music, or for whom the text has no interest, will not have a good time directing opera. Maybe the audience won't, either. That's an essential quality. And a lot of patience, in every respect. When people say that, one usually thinks it means patience with other people being difficult. I mean patience with the process. To allow it time. I think the most interesting directors are those who listen to their intuition and allow room for the fact that what's going to take place onstage doesn't always have to be logical. Because music isn't always logical.

Are you musical?

I can read a score, yes. I used to play the piano; I don't anymore.

Is that important for someone who directs opera?

Being musical is important. Being a musician I don't think is necessarily that important. It can save time. Directors who are really good musicians may have a more difficult time because the whole experience might become too concrete for them. The construction of the music. I like being musical and responding to the music.

We spoke about differences between opera and theater audiences. What differences do you see between staging operas and plays?

The major difference is, of course, that everybody's singing. An opera stage is bigger, and it's a larger-scale event—you don't tend to have choruses of sixty people wandering about in plays. But the actual process of creating the production is very similar. Beyond that, the entire dramatic span in opera is given to you by the composer. Everything has to happen within the time he has allowed. One conductor might do it faster or slower, but it's still within that framework. In a play you can say something very slowly, then pause two minutes, whatever you like. The rhythm and pacing of a play is shaped by the director and the actors, and therefore can often be radically different from one production to another. The composer is the dramatist in opera, in terms of timing and construction. A director needs to be sensitive to that, and then maybe ignore it. If you want Tosca to kill Scarpia in Sardou's play, you could take four minutes. In Puccini's opera you've got about twenty seconds where she says, "Questo e il bacio di Tosca," and that's it.

Does that help or hinder you?

There's a restriction but also a freedom because the timing has already been made for you.

Have we finished with the differences between opera and theater?

I don't know if I finished with the three most important things about doing my job.

Please; go ahead.

Above all, imagination. To be able to invent, to create a universe. Text study and lateral thinking. It's important you look at something and realize, well, this could be looked at another way. You have to have patience to hold it up to scrutiny—plus dealing with all the technical work and things always going wrong.

What advice would you give young directors?

Patience, imagination, intuition, text study and music! [*Laughs*] I was an assistant for nine years, and nearly gave up, because I couldn't get a job directing anything myself.

You said you like teamwork. A director has to work with everyone— conductors, singers, designers. Is there one who is more important than the others?

Unquestionably, for a director, the principal relationship is with the designer. That's where you create the whole universe—the intellectual and visual interpretation of the piece. The production you create with the designer is an attempt to capture some of the essence—you can't call it truth, because there is no truth in a piece of theater—of what is contained therein. Which in many cases, I think it's fair to say, is working on a subconscious level that perhaps neither the composer nor the librettist may have been aware was there.

Do you choose your designer?

Oh, yes. There are designers who do both sets and costumes; some do only sets and others only costumes. But that's the director's call.

How about working with conductors?

It should be fantastic, but that depends on what kind of conductor they are. Many work in opera because they love theater, relish being in an opera house with live performances and staging. They are what the Germans call *Theatermenschen*. Others wish all the singers were simply lined up at the front of the stage and that there wouldn't be any lighting or staging. I've worked with both. The conductors who are passionate about theater come to rehearsals, want to be part of that from the beginning and enjoy that collaboration. Others don't come to any of the staging, arrive only when the orchestra gets there, and suddenly discover this production which has been going on for five weeks, and don't always understand what it's about, and sometimes the effect can be very destructive. They say, "This isn't working," or "They're too far away—everyone come down here." Then you get into a *rapport des forces* [power play] situation where you have directors walking out, saying, "You can't ruin my show, I'm taking my name off this"—it's never happened to me—but it is very, very difficult. In an ideal world, it's also the job of the intendant to avoid this kind of situation by making sure the director and conductor come together early, talk, and share.

Have you found that most people are for this spirit of teamwork?

Everyone wants it to be like that, but not all theaters are concerned to make it happen. The other thing that's difficult is that it's like any marriage. You sometimes don't know what you're getting until you've got it. Some conductors just aren't that interested in the stage. Their field doesn't always lie in the visual or theatrical. Many have a passion for it—Jeffrey Tate, Seiji Ozawa, William Christie to name a few. Others—I won't name names—it's not condemning them, but it's more difficult because they don't have the reference point, they don't understand what you're trying to do.

It's not generational?

Not at all; it's completely individual. It's the same with directors. There are directors who don't understand music. It's just not part of their experience. Opera is collaborative. You have to do it together. That doesn't mean you have to agree. You have to respect the other person. When I've had a dis-agreement with a conductor, I've heard myself say, "I'm sorry you don't like this. But I feel passionate about it. So try to respect that this is what I want to do." Sometimes I find myself saying, "I don't necessarily understand all your tempi, but you're conducting and I respect that, so we have to work this out together. But working it out doesn't mean that only one of us has to change his thinking."

These situations come up during rehearsals, I suppose?

Yes. And the rehearsal room is a space where everyone is exposed. The singers have to try things out vocally and scenically. They might make fools of themselves or do something badly. You have to create an atmosphere where people don't feel they're being judged or exposed to ridicule. It's not a good atmosphere if everybody starts shouting at each other.

How do you work with singers?

I like singers very much. What they do is incredible. Singing is such an ex-traordinary thing to do and do well. Often they're singing in a language which isn't their own. They have to assimilate all the text, all the music. They have the physical side of a performance to deal with, too. That's an awful lot of juggling. The best ones come incredibly well prepared. And they have to hide the fact that there's any effort involved in doing any of that. For the audience to enjoy their performance, all the technical sides have to be invisible. The art which hides the art.

A lot of them aren't trained as actors. What do they look to you for?

I think they look for guidance. But the essential job, in terms of the actors or singers, is to help them create their character.

How do you do that?

You have to focus their thought lines. I say to a singer, "Now, when the other person is speaking to you, are you really listening? Or are you think-ing about your bank account? Are you connected to them, or are you thinking about something else? And if you're connected, why? And what do you want from that person?" That's the director helping people stay in character.

Motivation, is what you're saying.

Yes. Motivation, but on a very basic level.

Is that something singers tend to use?

Oh, yes. They sometimes may not have thought of it. But there's another thing which is important in the theater, and even more important for singers. Singers tend to learn the text *after* the music. That's exactly the opposite to how it was composed. So if you ask a singer in *La Traviata*, "Tell me: at the beginning of act 1, after Alfredo goes, what does Violetta say?" She'll say, [*sings*] "E strano, e strano." They won't *say*, "E strano, e strano." They won't *speak* the text. They'll only get the text by singing it. So I'll say, "No, no; *say* it to me." They very often cannot remember it without singing the notes. It's important to separate those things to rediscover their essence before putting them together again.

Your productions are often revived. What do you look for when you restage?

I'm re-creating the production we first created, but trying to improve it with each revival. This is often easier to do when the production is rented out than when it is revived in the original space because there is usually more time allowed when a production travels. Of course, with different singers one tends to alter some details and even some quite major things to do with interpretation, movement, or even costume, but not usually things which would alter the overall production design.

Can we talk about the bad things? What keeps you awake at night?

In my case, it's not things that keep me awake, it's things that wake me at four in the morning. I never have a problem going to sleep, but I sometimes wake up with things on my mind. When we're starting a new project, I constantly wonder whether I have done enough preparation. Sometimes you're not happy because you can't find a solution to a staging problem. You wake up early to think about it. Sometimes there are conflictual issues when things aren't going the way you'd like between people, and you worry. But yes, it is a profession that you take with you at all times, because there's so much going on. There's also the fact that directors, when they're staging something, are often preparing something which may be coming up just behind it, in a few months. You're rarely doing just one thing.

Something you learn to cope with.

I enjoy that. I enjoy going from *Iphigénie* to *Capriccio*. And I like to do things that aren't opera. I've done a couple of Andrew Lloyd Webber musicals, I directed a show for Disney. I've recently designed an exhibition for a museum. I like doing other projects, but you have to have the patience to hold it all up to doubt. Nothing ever works in the beginning. I always say the first rule of theater is: It never works the first time. And it would be wrong to expect that. You wouldn't expect an actor reading something the first time to get it right. It would be awful if he did: what would you do for the rest of the rehearsals? In the theater, like in life, it's about getting something right, not about being right. But there's a difference: life is not a rehearsal!

© Josep Ros Ribas

Patrice Chéreau, or truth, opera, and the director: In Wagner's footsteps

For a long time, opera did just fine without directors. Until Handel, who put directions in his scores, "staging" meant mainly "traffic control." The task of moving people fell to librettists who coordinated entrances and exits, scene shifts, extra parts, or chorus. Singers were on their own.

Even after the director arrived, some questioned his usefulness. For George Bernard Shaw, the best way to go to opera was to sit in the back of a box, put your feet up on a chair, and close your eyes. "If your own imagination can't do at least as well as any scene painter, you shouldn't go to opera," the Irishman admonished in 1922. Today, anyone can be content listening to CDs at home. So who needs directors?

The question is put to Patrice Chéreau, who is turning over Shaw's quip in his mind. We are in the spacious eighteenth-century flat in Paris's historic Marais district where the director has lived for thirty years. The house has high ceilings and wood floors, but bare walls. "They've just been repainted; I don't want any holes," is Chéreau's explanation, as he waves me to a chair. Around him, canvases, drawings, even marble friezes are stacked five-deep against the wainscot. The space that's left is monopolized by un-matched furniture that litters his library. The whole effect is of a décor-in-the-making, as if you've walked into a room on the first day of rehearsals.

It's an apt setting for him to explain the opera director's role, and, as expected, take a swipe at Shaw. For Chéreau, the director's raison d'être centers on one word: truth. Finding this "anchor in truth" is his job.

Now sixty-two, Chéreau has sought ways to unlock verity in drama for more than forty years in theater, movies, and, since 1969, opera, earning his place, not to mention many awards along the way, as one of Europe's top directors and certainly France's best-liked. He has produced more than thirty plays, his films have won at Cannes and the Berlin Film Festival, and he's staged thirteen operas, more now than his movie output of ten. In each genre, his goal is the same: telling a story with actors, illuminating the honesty of that story; translating what's on the page into posture, gesture, stillness.

For the tale an opera tells, he feels, isn't only in the music; it's in the placing of singers, too. It all began with Wagner, whom he calls history's first stage director.

The Frenchman's affinity for Wagner isn't hard to fathom: the German sparked a reform, putting actors first and singers second in their service to his works, which he called "music dramas," not operas. The bond with Bayreuth's founder was evident in the watershed Ring *cycle Chéreau mounted there in 1976 with Pierre Boulez. Since then he's staged Berg's* Wozzeck *and* Lulu; *and Mozart's* Lucio Silla, Don Giovanni, *and* Così fan tutte.

Ruggiero Raimondi sang in that Così, *mainly to work with Chéreau, whom he calls a "master." Says the basso, "He centers you on what connects you to each character and each situation. You learn as much about the others as about yourself."*

Though a Mozart lover, Chéreau finds modern operas easier going. Seamless dialogue, which has supplanted the recitativo-aria structure, makes the later repertoire more theater-like, simpler to reveal. When we spoke, he was absorbed by two projects: Janáček's final opera, the 1930 House of the Dead, *which opened in Vienna with Pierre Boulez conducting before moving to New York; and a return to Wagner with* Tristan und Isolde, *conducted by Daniel Barenboim and starring Waltraud Meier, for La Scala. He's on the phone with the Vienna Staatsoper now and checks his watch: he has a plane at five o'clock for yet another opera project. Hanging up, he confesses, "It's pretty frantic today."*

What's the stage director's role in opera?

My role is to find a way to transmit a work to the public. It's a role of mediator, if you like. That means I take a work written on paper and find actors to play it and decide what movements these actors will have in a certain space. You have to decide how to speak the text and how to reply to it. You have to do everything the actors don't know how to do when they're on their own without any direction. You have to watch them and orient them. A group of people who put on a play is by its nature a team, so you have an obligation to direct that team. You're also a coach, or trainer, for them. That means bringing them as far as they can go with themselves, ensuring they can be as strong as they can possibly be. At the same time, my role is to make you, the audience, see things; to have a conception of the work and to transmit it to the public. Along with that, I have to ensure that the public all look in the same direction and at the same thing on stage, and that they all understand the same thing.

That sounds like it's true for theater as well, not only opera.

It's true for theater, opera, and cinema. The technique differs, that's all.

The tradition, or convention of the theater director hasn't always been with us, has it?

It was imposed historically. Originally, I think, the authors themselves first began playing directors. Shakespeare wrote and played in his plays. He ran the theater. I'm sure he directed. I'm just as sure Molière directed his plays. He acted in them, but he certainly gave indications to his actors.

It's a relatively recent development, then.

For a long time opera directors didn't even exist. Mozart directed his operas. But the inventor of staging, the first director in all stage history—opera or theater—was Wagner. We have his scenic indications, his notes for the stage directions of his operas. They are very interesting. He spent time with the singers and resolved problems with the means at his disposal and using the conventions of his day. He also did and said many nonconventional things. That's why I say he directed.

What kind of indications do you give?

It begins with the really simple things. During rehearsals, the director is in the theater, where the spectators will be, so he or she sees things onstage that the actors don't. You need a director at some point; at one moment he will say, "No, I think you should come in on stage left, or back up, or stand on the right, or, let's play the scene here instead of there." That's how it starts. After, he can tell the actors that he can't hear them or doesn't understand what they're saying, or that what one actor is saying makes no sense. If there's no director, there will always be an actor who will come down into the seats offstage and watch the others in scenes when he isn't acting.

Do we really need a director for opera? I can go home, put on a CD, and be perfectly happy.

What I said applies to theater, but it's the same for opera. Operas were written to be performed onstage; they weren't written to be listened to merely for the music. You have symphonies for that. An opera is written to tell a story with people who sing on a stage. Opera is theater.

Bernard Shaw thought the best way to go to opera is to sit in the back of a box, put your feet up on a chair, close your eyes, and listen. "If your own imagination can't do at least as well as any scene painter, you shouldn't go to opera," he said.

Sure, but you can turn that around. You can say that if the director isn't capable of doing better than the imagination of the spectators, he's useless. Maybe that's just my personal pride, but that's how I see it. Sure, we can listen to an opera eyes closed. But that would make the stage meaningless; it would mean there would be no point in having a live orchestra and live singers. If we go to an opera, it means we want to see theater. We want to see this thing that exists nowhere else, the thing you can only find in the theater: people living on a stage who represent an action and who tell us a story with sentiments and emotion.

How closely do you work with the conductor?

You can't mount an opera if the director goes against the conductor, or if one doesn't listen to the other. Opera is a spectacle that's done by both. The conductor leads the musical part. This person has the advantage over the stage director, since he or she directs for real, and by that I mean live; he's there every night. Musically, everyone knows you can't sing an opera without a conductor. You need somebody who groups and directs the orchestra in the pit and the singers on stage at the same time. It's a technical problem; you need someone to beat time. But the story an opera tells isn't only in the music, it's in the placing of the singers. An opera needs someone to give these indications. That person is the director.

At what point in a production are you called in?

Usually the conductor and the singers are selected before I am. Sometimes we're chosen together, but not often. It's never happened that I've had an idea for a project, plus a singer who was interested, which I offered to an opera house. I've always been asked, "Would you like to do this or that opera?" For Wagner's *Ring* in 1976, Pierre Boulez called me. "Let's get together, I'm looking for someone to stage the *Ring*."

You have said that directing means "asking a question." What question is that?

Musicians have always asked the question of truth or credibility in the music they play. Singers never ask themselves this—when they haven't got a director. It's a problem. When Mozart or Wagner wrote music for singers, they were examining problems on psychological truth, in psychological situations. You have to follow this truth. Sometimes their ideas are really surprising. Since Wagner, we've understood that we can no longer simply settle for bringing singers to the front of the stage and have them sing their arias, like at concerts. When there's a scene with two singers, you can't have one person with nothing to do, behind the other who is singing in the foreground. It's a relationship between two people that you have to put in a space. That's where directing begins. I work with bodies, with people in a space.

Yet some say opera is not the world of reality and we must accept the untruth of it.

Yes, but people say all kinds of stupid things. The problem of truth or credibility always comes up; it's the clarity or limpidity of the story. A story is like a novel or a film; it's fiction, but fiction has a strong link with truth. If it's not firmly anchored in truth—or, put another way, if the spectator can't identify—it won't work. The whole thing would be pointless. My role is to make sure spectators can identify with the story that's unfolding onstage, including with a singer performing an aria—even if we don't sing in normal life.

Singers often lament that they are not taught acting and are therefore not actors. How do you deal with that?

Of course there's no training for them. But they aren't hired for that. They're not hired because they're great onstage; they're hired because they've got something rare, here [*taps his throat*]. There are two types of singers. One type thinks they are there to sing and nothing else. You see this kind less and less. The other is aware that they are on a stage and must construct a role. Singers conscious of this, whether they've learned how to act or not, can become very good actors. They can learn every day. So I'd say singers are really actors, but they are actors with special rules. You don't direct them in the same way as a theater actor. The main difference in opera is that you can see if a singer isn't an actor, or if an actor is no singer, but can become one.

Do you get enough rehearsal time to help them become good actors?

We have much less for opera than for plays. In the opera, there is no time for rehearsals. The big problem is we have to put it together in half the time we'd get for a play. Where I'd normally have eight weeks' rehearsal for a play, I get four for an opera. And then you have to work out time with the orchestra, which is another matter. There's never time because it's too costly.

How is directing theater or cinema different than opera?

Apart from things everyone sees and knows about, directing in opera, cinema, or the theater is the same. There's one main difference between film and theater however, in that with film you can't act like in the theater; in the theater your voice has to carry farther, you're up on a stage. These are huge differences. Another difference is that we frame one thing in cinema, while in the theater the eye can wander. In movies, we decide on everything that won't appear in the frame or in the shot. When we want to show something outside the frame, we move the camera or take another shot which is edited in after the earlier one. As I said, part of my job is making everyone see the same thing.

How do you do that exactly?

That's the director's technique. You have to focus people's attention on a particular thing, without necessarily placing it obviously in the center foreground. You have to find a simple way to make sure people see it.

But concretely, how do you do that?

By being a spectator myself. Once we've worked with the actors and organized a scene, you have to step back and look. You ask yourself: Is there something to see here? Is my intention centered on something, or is it on nothing? That's a job, too, being a good spectator, a good public, looking naively on what you've done yourself. It's something you have to learn. It's the same in the theater, and for the cinema when you're editing. I do that with the film editor. There comes a time when we look at everything. And it's happened that I say, "Well, I don't really understand what's going on here, what I'm being told here." Even if I'm the one who directed the scene. Because suddenly I'm a spectator, watching the film in a cinema.

At what point during an opera production do you become a spectator?

As early as possible. I do what we call a *filage* [run-through], sometimes with piano accompaniment. In 2006 for *Così* at Aix-en-Provence, I did the *filage* of one act after fifteen days. It wasn't very good, but it helped because we did it on a Saturday, which meant we had Sunday to dream up new ideas for Monday to help correct what didn't work.

Cinema is more fluid movement, while some opera—before Wagner, Mozart, say—is structured differently: recitativo and aria. How does this influence your approach?

It doesn't change the staging, where the goal is to break down a structure we no longer accept. Mozart tried to get beyond these constraints in *Così fan tutte*, with the quintet, for example. He wrote real staging whenever he wrote a quintet. There's one in *Don Giovanni* which stages the relationships among the five different people who are together onstage. All the ensembles in *Così* are incredibly interesting because they're written by a hand who knew stage direction. There are also smaller arias for Don Alfonso where he goes beyond the traditional *recitativo/aria* rather abruptly. And there is accompanied recitative [*accompagnato*], which is a fabulous way into the aria that follows. Composers in those days were already thinking about how to do away with the separation between *recitativi* and *arie*. The challenge of staging is to destroy it altogether or to use it to our advantage, but in any case to be flexible in our use of it.

Is this the lesson you've learned from Wagner? You seem quite influenced by him.

Wagner was the first to decide there would be no more arias. It was a radical thought. A few bits remain in his work, like the end of the first act of *Die*

Walküre, which is a classic love duet, and some *recitativi*. And in some of his earlier operas, like *Tannhäuser*, you can find big arias, but basically the old break between *recitativo* and *aria* has disappeared. Spectators applaud at the end of an act, not after an aria, which means the flow is unbroken. Wagner broke with the tradition completely. His operas all take place inside a new structure invented by him—a continuous, seamless structure which is very close to theater because no text is ever repeated. It's real dialogue. Before him, *Die Frieschütz* or *Fidelio* had started on a bit of a different track, but he marked a radical change to all that went before, including Mozart, due to the continuity of the music.

Is this type of seamless opera easier to stage?

A lot easier. Absolutely. It's constant dialogue.

Strauss, Berg, the same?

Pretty much. In some of these operas—*Lulu*, for example—you have singing and *sprechensagt*, the spoken-sung parts, and dialogue. Janáček's *House of the Dead* is yet another structure, though it resembles *Wozzeck* somewhat. These composers all worked within this structure and changed it each time. Their operas are all easier to do. The rest—costumes, lights—is like the theater and the cinema.

How is filming opera different than shooting it for a DVD?

In one way it's the same because we use different takes. The 2007 DVD of *Così* was shot by another director who has already filmed three or four of my shows. The one difficulty was that he had never done anything live, and going live always brings complications. You work better if it's not live; you get your material together, and you go calmly into the editing room and edit the footage. Live means you're already editing as you go. You move from one camera to another. This means you take your precautions; everything's a bit slower and longer; you don't take any risks to be sure to get everything. He shot the DVD over four days of rehearsal, using six cameras. Editing took two months, since it was a mix of those four different rehearsal days.

Is it normal to shoot four different days?

Nobody sees that it's four different shows.

You do.

We showed it on TV, and it was fine, a mix of four different shows.

Has working in opera changed your cinema style?

I'm more careful about a lot more things now. But it has changed my theater, also. I'm more careful about truth, let's say, or credibility; I try and direct with more exactitude. But the three genres are all mixed and all serve, bringing me different things. I've concentrated on three different ways of working in my career, but with one goal that's the same for all: telling a story with actors.

Are you a musician?

Not at all.

Does that help or hinder an opera stage director?

In my case, I think it's an advantage, not knowing music. Because it means I'm always surprised, I'm always forced to listen. It's a disadvantage knowing music because the singers think everything is written in the score. Now there's an enormous amount of information there. A written score is a phenomenal mass of information reduced to very few shorthand notes. There are technical indications, and you can decipher the composer's intentions when you hear the music or when a singer sings. I don't read the score because I'm incapable of it, so I listen more. I have to. Often, it's a big advantage being self-taught, because you learn more.

You've done practically as many operas as films today. Will this continue?

I'm not doing any theater for the moment, but I can't do everything. I accepted *Così* for Aix-en-Provence in 2005. That meant the summer of 2005 was *Così* at Aix, then in September it came to Paris's Palais Garnier. It went to Vienna in June 2006. It was reprised in Paris in October, then in Vienna in November. I began preparation of décor, costumes, and all that long before, and started rehearsals at the end of May; the final performance was on November thirtieth. You see how it takes up lots of space in one's calendar. In between, I did one film which came out, and I showed it at festivals in London, New York, and Madrid. But put it all together and you have a pretty full agenda. I did Janáček's *House of the Dead*, which opened in May

2007 in Vienna, then went to Amsterdam in June and Aix in July. But I was working on it for over a year before. The months go by.

Do you want to make more films?

Yes, I wanted to make one in 2007 and couldn't because of all that. But in the last few years, I was taken by two opera projects I didn't want to turn down. *House of the Dead,* because it was with Pierre Boulez, and I wanted to work with him again. We hadn't worked together in twenty-five years. And *Tristan* with Daniel Barenboim and Waltraud Meier, with whom I've already worked. That was for the December 2007 opening of La Scala.

The 1976 Bayreuth Ring with Boulez is considered by many as the first truly modern production, but it wasn't your first opera.

No, it was the third. I did Rossini's *Italiana in Algeri* in 1969. Then, in 1974, I did Offenbach's *Tales of Hoffmann* in Paris.

How do you remember the Ring? It's a big project.

Enormous. It was a nightmare. I did all four operas in two and half months. Eleven hours a day. I decided on the rehearsal time, not they, so I have only myself to blame.

All went well, though.

The first year I'd say it went only so-so. The second, yes. I reworked one-third of the staging for the second year. And the third year was very good.

You often say that actors' hands are important. Why?

Because they never know what to do with them! So you always have to find something for them. It's the same in life; hands are a problem. You enter someplace, and you don't know what to do with your hands.

In the pockets?

Never! That's the worst thing you can do.

What sort of things keep you awake at night when you're working on a production?

In the beginning, everything keeps me awake. When you start a project, opera or film, in the first days of rehearsal or shooting, you can't sleep at all.

You're questioning everything you're doing, and a sort of diffuse worry seeps in, and you can't stop your mind from working. You can't stop thinking about what you've done during the day. But after that things calm down, and you're all right.

© Virgin Classics/Sylvain Mignot

William Christie,
or going for baroque

Rehearsal has ended in the big hall in southern Paris. Surrounded by empty
chairs, scattered music stands and one harpsichord, William Christie sits
behind the raised platform where he recently reigned.

For openers, the smiling, bespectacled maestro stuns you by uttering
something few musicians will ever admit. "Great music," he intones,
"grows out of language."

The remark is unusual, since the typical polemic is "Prima la musica,
dopo la parole" (Music first, then the word—from Strauss's Capriccio).
Wagner, for example, believed music not only anteceded words, but lay
at their origin. But Christie's domain is baroque—often French—opera, a
universe of monodic forms in which text and music enjoy a special rela-
tionship. Though he is echoing Claudio Monteverdi ("Let the word be the
master, not the servant of the music"—1607), it's still an astonishing dis-
closure for a musician today.

As if his first avowal weren't enough, Christie delivers a declaration
even more uncommon: Conductors, he states, can actually learn from sing-
ers. It's something few omnipotent masters of orchestra and operatic divas
are inclined to reveal these days. But that comes later in the interview.

He has finished with his orchestra for the afternoon—Handel's L'Allegro,
il Penseroso ed il Moderato, *which will tour Europe—and looks relaxed*

in jeans, open shirt, and black tennis shoes. Perhaps his serenity reflects the end of a productive day. Perhaps he is reflecting on the pair of birthdays he fetes this year: his orchestra, Les Arts Florissants (from an opera of the same name by seventeenth-century French composer Marc-Antoine Charpentier), is thirty, and the conductor himself turns sixty-five.

American-born (Buffalo, N.Y.) and a French citizen since 1995, Christie is one of the principal prophets of the baroque opera tradition, now grown so wide. That movement is much the subject of his remarks.

Having made his career in Europe, he will make his Metropolitan Opera debut, at sixty-four, in 2010. Meanwhile, he and Les Arts Florissants conduct classes at the Juilliard School of Music next door. Aside from conducting and playing harpsichord, he has taught since 1982, working especially with vocal music, text, and language, in the talent farm in Normandy he founded and directs, Le Jardin des Voix, helping ensure that the baroque, now revived, stays alive.

When you get to a certain level as a conductor, as you have done, can you choose the works you want to do?

There are fashion victims in music. They are rarely conductors, though young ones sometimes get saddled with things they can't handle. Fashion victims in music are mainly young singers. They become victims because they are driven or obliged to sing repertory they're not technically or emotionally able to sing.

Is this their agent's fault?

Sometimes. Agents can be like Molière doctors, quacks that kill the patient. Conductors, if they want to get ahead, can do silly things. Some think they have to do everything, which is a different matter. Karajan was like that. It wouldn't be possible today, even if it were Karajan. I grew up with conductors who would conduct Verdi and Mozart, with a smattering of Britten or contemporary pieces. Their range ran essentially from the twentieth century down to Bach and Handel. But it all sounded pretty much the same. Now we have another phenomenon, which I like even less: the person who starts out conducting baroque music, then gets excited about conducting big orchestras, branching out into Beethoven, and from there climbing up to Bruckner. As if baroque music were some sort of trampoline.

Shouldn't a conductor be able to do everything, play all the repertoires?

It's rare that one says, "I can start with Bach and finish with Berio or Boulez." A few try. Some can do it, but they face the same situation as those fifty years ago who thought they could do everything with a modern orchestra. The problem is that many don't have sufficient conducting techniques to handle big orchestras. You can't conduct baroque music like nineteenth- or twentieth-century music. Anyone being trained today is essentially being trained for big, modern ensembles and twentieth-century music. Their technique doesn't work with a Lully opera. You need a technique with an enormous linguistic base to it. In these works, gesture exists to pull out words; it obliges singers and instrumentalists to play and sing text. You can't get that with modern technique.

Before moving on, we'd better define "baroque."

Baroque music fits into a tidy historical framework. It starts in 1600 and ends with the death of Rameau, in 1760. It's different for each country. The French want to stay apart, and until twenty-five years ago didn't even admit the term. They called it "musique française a l'époque baroque." You have two major baroque schools, the French and the Italian; then you have the grand offshoots of them: German, English and everything else. Bach is the greatest of all, nurtured by the two traditions.

You specialize in the baroque, but I've heard you say you don't want to be labeled an "authentic." What's the difference?

Specialization means essentially knowing what the ingredients are. It could be the score. It could be techniques appropriate to playing a baroque violin or a classical oboe. Knowing what the limits are in terms of taste and things, you have to add to the score. You can say [Alfred] Brendel is a specialist in interpreting late-eighteenth-century and early-nineteenth-century German music. The salient difference between what I do and what someone like Barenboim does is that I have a score I have to complete. We're not talking about Tchaikovsky, where everything is written down. Or Boulez. In my lecture at Juilliard the other day, I took a single page of the *Marteau sans maître*, and we counted something like seventy indications of dynamics or phrasing, articulation, tempo. It's a lot. Then we looked at one page of Lully. And there's nothing. Of course, you can't play *nothing*. You've got to add something.

When you're adding something, do you take into account local taste, depending on where you're performing?

By no means. You can't have a New York sound. I'm not going to do an olé-olé production for Madrid, or add castanets. You don't cater to the locals. That doesn't work.

You didn't answer me on "authentic"—how does it differ from being a specialist?

I'd say I'm a specialist because I've learned things that are appropriate to music. That doesn't mean I'm authentic. I would not like to be saddled with that description. "Authentic" means I'm going to produce this particular dish of rice in the Valencia style—*arroz a banda*—exactly the way it's done in Valencia. I'm sitting in Sydney, Australia. That's trying to be authentic. You get Spanish olive oil, Spanish rice, but then you have to fly in the Spanish fish. Can you do that musically? No. Can I say really I'm doing authentic Vivaldi? "Authentic" would mean it's exactly the way he wanted it. And how do you know? You read these idiotic reviews on record jackets, where they say, "This is being performed in an authentic way." What does that mean?

Does this create any problems when performing for the twenty-first century?

There is no problem putting seventeenth-century opera on in New York or Munich, but you have to look at how conventions have changed, if there have been improvements, how can you adapt. This can be a problem, but essentially all these things can be overcome. Some people think you have to have authentic dance, décor, and costumes. You can get into difficulties with this approach, because we simply don't know how people walked around the stage then. Those kind of indications are rare for opera.

You talked about conductors; how about orchestras? Can Europe's orchestras play baroque as well as modern music?

Europe's big orchestras, more than those in the U.S., are going through a music catharsis. You're meeting people who know much about many things. They play baroque oboe as well as modern oboe. They can play modern and baroque violin. Or baroque techniques with a modern bow. It's happening in Berlin and other places [*laughs*]. It's almost comic, because members of the Berliner Philharmonic string sections come in with baroque bows. It's crazy. I told them, "Look, we've got to iron all this out!" [*Laughs*] Viola or violin players belong to baroque ensembles, and there are early-instrument ensembles forming within the Berliner Philharmonic.

Why is this revival happening?

The baroque people have done a good job of getting this repertory out. It sounds different and has influenced the way modern people are looking at their instruments. It's happening all over. The Scintilla Orchestra in Zurich is formed of members of the Zurich Opera Orchestra. These people are playing *Salome*, Strauss on a Tuesday night, and Wednesday they've got their baroque fiddles and baroque celli, playing a Handel opera. To do that, you've got to be clever and supple, and especially, you've got to *love* this music. If you belong to the Scintilla, or to a baroque group in the Berlin Philharmonic, it's because you love this music and want to get closer to it. These groups have all made great progress. But I still get the impression that when baroque music is played by orchestras that play *everything,* it sounds like a foreign language.

Some say record companies, not musicians or conductors, are responsible for the baroque revival.

Sour grapes. It's false to say record companies are making the baroque happen.

You and Les Arts Florissants are now Artists in Residence at the Juilliard School. That's another development in the baroque renaissance.

There is going to be a permanent, and important, department of early music. The problem is providing a thing that the musical establishment thought was a passing fad—a milieu where if you couldn't make it as a modern player, you could make it there. Times have changed. At Juilliard, kids are saying, "I don't like this interpretation, I like what somebody else does on the cello more than you." It's also economic. Joseph Polisi, Juilliard's president, says we're preparing students for life's work as professionals, so we can't tell them, "We're going to teach you how to sing things from Mozart to the early part of the twentieth century, so don't worry about everything before Mozart." This is the way things were taught for years in almost every conservatory. There are still conservatories where they don't fool around: "You want to sing Handel? Sing it like Saint-Saëns." We're not preparing students for professional careers if we lop off this enormous part of the repertory. You want a student from Juilliard to be in the swim of things to get that audition in Munich for a Vivaldi or a Handel opera. And he or she sings like an absolute fool, and is not taken, because it doesn't sound convincing.

It must be gratifying being part of this movement.

I made my career in Europe because I thought it would be easier, and it was. Now I'm back, in the best music school in the world, and feel like an absolute king. Juilliard is a big part of our lives, because commitment was the most difficult thing. How can you provide regularity—the most important thing for students—if you're always overbooked? Being there, every Monday, is important. As Artists in Residence, we come in, spend a week, do a concert, prepare the kids in a program they sing on a Friday or Saturday night.

Do you need more rehearsal time for the baroque? Do you get enough?

Never—but I have more than many of my colleagues. As a guest conductor, I get the standard two days: four major rehearsals plus one dress rehearsal. That's fine if they're playing repertory they know or if the music doesn't require any stylistic competencies, like French bowing techniques or ornaments. In that case it takes longer.

How do you program your operas?

I've been lucky. Occasionally you get the opera house decision: we've chosen our repertory, we hope you like it, good luck. But that's rare now. Because you can do this in the standard repertoire, for *Rigoletto*, say. The opera house director will know who the good Gildas are. But it's rare to find anyone who knows anything about a Vivaldi or Handel opera. So we have our say, and that's good.

Do you see things evolving with opera house directors, in any way?

[*Much laughter*] This could be potentially very dangerous! It's a human problem, but also professional. Opera house directors—and often they're right—want a hands-on policy when casting. It's rare that a director, in Europe or the U.S., will say to a musical director, like me, "Bring whomever you want." These are complicated issues, because we're dealing with—you could almost call it ancestral ties with agencies. "You pat my back, I'll pat yours. You can have the star in four years, but you're going to take a bevy of people before that." Everybody works hard to get what they want: impresarios, concert agencies, singers. There's also the question of pride. A director of an opera house wants to say, "I cast that person, and their success is thanks to me." This works sometimes very well. Some directors are more skilled than others in putting together a cast. They've got better musical sense, a sense of the market, a sense about discovering—taking a young voice that isn't well known. Sometimes you win, and sometimes you lose. It's all very human, and I'm philosophical about it. But there are problems. It is easier to cast a Gilda or a Turandot. Someone falls ill in a production of *Frau ohne Schatten*, you can find somebody. You get on the horn, and the agencies will help you. If I'm doing *Les Indes galantes*, and my Zima falls into a hole the day before opening night, that's where you start to have problems.

Are you getting more of a say in casting?

The best houses realize they've got to enlarge repertory. If you decide that you've got to provide Handel, Rameau, Vivaldi, and Charpentier—the pre-Mozart repertory—you've got to start thinking about how to go about it. So there's a dialogue. "Let's get together, do some auditions. Tell me what you think might work. We'd like to have a few big names, could you work with them? Maybe we could have a work session." In the best houses, you listen to auditions with the musical director, the musical advisor, the opera house director. So to reply to your question [*laughs*], we have problems with casting. Sometimes I've had to bite the bullet and accept a cast I would not have chosen.

How often does that happen?

It's rare. This repertory—Handel, Rameau—doesn't correspond to known voice types. It's not sung by a lot of opera singers. Which means they need help. And that's been good, because for big houses like the Paris Opéra, or even Glyndebourne, we've been able to introduce new talent. But there are situations whereby I'm stuck with somebody who just doesn't fit the bill. It's like dominoes. The title role is chosen by the director, and everything then has to fit into place. Sometimes it's damned hard. You would have taken a different voice type—a tenor, not a high baritone.

Is it only a question of the voice?

There are so many ingredients to old music. We don't play all the time at 440 [vibrations, or cycles per second, the U.S. pitch for A] or 442. We're not a modern orchestra. And we've learned that back then, pitch was a wildly different affair. You could play Monteverdi a whole tone higher than modern pitch. And you should! You can't really sing correctly French late-seventeenth-century music if you're stuck in A 440 or 442. It's killing for the singers, especially tenors. We know that the diapason in late-seventeenth-century France was a whole tone *lower* than now. That's something conductors and singers should consider when programming Gluck opera. Sometimes the theater director is thinking about Mr. Star and not about things like that.

He's thinking about marketing.

Yeah, and I bow to that. I've got to sell myself, and I like being sold well by somebody else. In the best situations, you can sell but maintain your integrity. Peter Gelb, for instance, is selling to a new media audience; he's selling new talent and new repertory. He's doing things his predecessor would never have dreamed of. I'm working at the Met soon, and Peter has been marvelous, because you can discuss everybody and everything openly.

It will be your first time at the Met?

Yes, my debut. At my age. Wonderful.

Daniel Barenboim made his debut last year.

That's right! [*Laughs*] The oldies are coming. Our debut is with *Così* in 2010. The year after, we're going to do a wild baroque pasticcio, taking the best of baroque opera repertory and giving it to people who love to sing that stuff. And it's an all-star cast. But with new lyrics, a new libretto, in English.

Is anything specific on your mind when preparing for your debut? Are you thinking particularly of the New York audience, for example?

Obviously, it's to give them my musical vision of the piece. Showing people that you have ideas, that you're capable of seducing the orchestra, the singers, and the audience with your ideas. Convincing them. I'm very excited about working with an orchestra which is one of the best in the world. I'm scared shitless as well, obviously, because that orchestra is formidable.

You recently made another debut, at Madrid's Teatro Real. How did you find those audiences?

Amazing—audiences all over Spain are amazing. One wonders how things evolved so quickly. First of all, their halls. We're suffering still in Paris, where we don't have a good hall for symphonic music. Spain is like Japan. Every town in Japan got a new hall in the last ten, fifteen years. In Spain, you've got La Coruña, Bilbao, Santander, Saint Sebastian, Zaragoza, Valencia, and there's going to be a new hall in Madrid. Though I must say that even if the halls are wonderful in Japan, they don't think in the long term about audiences or programming. In Spain, the musical venues seem to be used more intelligently. I can cite a program we did recently that you'd think might be difficult for a Spanish audience: Sophie Von Otter singing seventeenth-century French music. That's not everybody's cup of tea. There's something very alive and energetic about Spain.

You've talked about having your say with opera house directors. How about with stage directors?

It's a give-and-take with the stage director, who has something to say as well. But I've got something to say, too, about where the singer is going to stand. I don't like that awful bit where she's hanging off the edge of the stage.

Why do the classic operas need constant updates from directors? Do they need to be retold for each generation?

It's a good question. Can you imagine a Wagner revival with the costumes and scenery of the 1870s and '80s? You've seen the photos. Can you imagine the Rhinemaidens today as they were originally? We can do that, but it would be pretty horrible. Actualizing opera is a good thing, especially when you marry aesthetics and styles which can work together. I like working with art directors whose visual sense has a rapport with the way I make music. It's like mixing styles of furniture or interior decorating. You combine things that make sense.

Developing a sense of family is vital if a production is to work. How hard is this when singers jet in for one performance, then jet out again?

Most people don't behave that way. When you work with people who are committed to what they are doing, they don't pull those kind of stunts. Sometimes they might have a problem with dates at the beginning. But most are conscientious and wouldn't accept to do an opera if they didn't have sufficient time. There are certain schools or areas in the world where they seem to encourage youngsters to become grand divas, pulling temper tantrums, behaving with a studied lack of discipline, and not wanting to become part of a team. English and U.S. singers by and large have a reputation for being committed and serious. They learn their scores and show up on time.

A last question on singers: Can conductors learn from them?

Sure. Certain conductors don't breathe. A nice thing about my orchestra is they breathe like singers. Baroque music begins with the voice. You cannot imagine any instrumentalist trying to cope with Bach or Handel or Vivaldi if they don't understand the supremacy of the voice. It's the best instrument and can teach all the others. It's what man began with. Before he started to beat on something or blow on something, he was organizing sounds for himself.

What do you like about opera? Why did you want to do it?

[*Thinks, then in a whisper*] Because it's a complete show. I like being in a dramatic, theatrical situation. I like communication, I suppose, in all art. I like music that wants to move and touch its listener. I don't like music that's standoffish and difficult, which requires the listener to make an effort. I don't like easy music, either. Let's face it, you've got to have done your homework to appreciate a lot of good music. You've got to be educated. But once that happens, I like music that wants to give something to its listeners. I would say I'm more at home with this kind of communication than with other kinds of music. I'm going out on a limb, because someone's going to say, "That means you don't like *The Art of Fugue,* and you prefer a big, blowsy Handel opera." Well, I suppose, when the chips are down, yes. But I listen to *The Art of Fugue,* and I listen to Frescobaldi and love to play fugues, love to intellectually appreciate my music.

What's "standoffish music"?

I'm sorry, but I have to include a lot of contemporary music—essentially for the voice, but all kinds. Music that requires an initiation process which becomes extremely difficult and tiresome. I'll be very rude: in the American panoply there are composers who essentially require . . . [*pauses*] . . . an effort that's too great for me, to penetrate into what this music wants to say to me.

Are you placing yourself in the mind of a spectator when you say that?

I'm placing myself as a participant and a listener. I like Elliot Carter more intellectually than viscerally. I played an early chamber work of his for harpsichord and instruments. But there are pieces by Carter that, frankly, bring more difficulty than pleasure, both for the performer and the listener. I feel the same way about a lot of contemporary vocal music, American and European, written in the last thirty or forty years. I'm not at all in love with a lot of what went on in France in the '20s and '30s, which I find dry and dated—Milhaud or Honneger—although I love Ravel.

Are there works in the post-Ravel repertory that you like?

I love Harrison Birtwhistle. He's done some extraordinary things. John Adams. I can just name a few of the people I've listened to recently. But there's older music as well, which I find extremely difficult.

Can you recall an experience in your life that has marked you, either as a student or as a professional, that has been fundamental to the musician you have become?

[*Thinks*] Those moments of truth where suddenly things that have been difficult or complicated or difficult to understand suddenly become easy and clear. That's happened three or four times in my life—not playing, but *listening* to music, and to somebody else play.

In the audience?

Yes. I suddenly realized, "Of course, this is what it's all about!" It happened when I was at university.

Can you talk about it?

I had been fascinated by music ever since I was a kid. I loved the sounds of instruments, musical forms—I loved oratorio and cantatas and I loved harpsichord music. I went to Sander's Theater in Cambridge [Massachusetts] and heard [Ralph] Kirkpatrick play two books of the *Well-Tempered Clavier*, by memory, on two successive days. And I remember walking out of the second night, saying, "This is what I want to do. I want to be like him. I want to be able to play these pieces. I want to be a musician." I was on a tightrope. I wasn't sure, at all. What that meant was writing a letter of appreciation to someone I didn't know. And getting a reply back, which thrilled me, obviously. I thought, "My God, he's actually read my letter, and taken the time to reply." And then an invitation to go down to Yale and play for him. Because of course I mentioned in my letter that I was a pianist, that I'd been fooling around with the harpsichord.

How old were you?

Nineteen.

Does that happen now, in the other direction? A young hopeful writes, and you remember Kirkpatrick and respond similarly?

I remember there's a way you have to treat people who write you, yes. There's a way of responding. It's very moving. I had a student in my class at the conservatory who spent three years with me. And *years* after she left, she told me, "You know how it all started? It was at the very beginning of Les Arts Florissants, and I was a teenager. The group sang some Monteverdi." And she said, "I literally passed out, because it was so breathtaking and so beautiful. I was with my parents, and they realized something extraordinary had happened." That was *her* epiphany.

Any other experiences you'd like to share?

There was another, at about the same time. I was ripe for this kind of thing. I suppose I could have turned out to be a religious nut or something. I was discovering something which was essential. Again, this was at Harvard, but later—1966. One of my classmates came into my sitting room and said, "You've got to listen to this." He put on a recording, which had just come out—Janet Baker singing Phaedra in the *Hippolyte and Aricie* recording of Anthony Lewis. I had never heard a Rameau opera. She was singing the fourth scene of the fourth act. And it was one of those moments where time just stops. I don't write letters that often, but I wrote her. And sent it off to the record company. She and I are now friends, have been for a long time. When we met for the first time, years later, she said, "You're one of the people who have said to me, 'If I am here, doing what I'm doing now, it's thanks to that moment.'"

Can you confess to anything about opera that you don't like?

[*Thinks*] Bad actors. Bad musicians. Bad orchestras. Bad costume designers. Bad scenery. Wicked, and evil sometimes, stage directors. They can make the experience simply appalling. I saw one of the slimiest productions of Monteverdi's *Orfeo* a couple of years ago. A willful stage director who destroyed things. This is a caricature evening, but I remember in Odessa many years ago there was a *Don Carlo*, in four languages, at least. They were singing Russian, Ukrainian, Italian, German. And the impression I had was that they were all too old and all immensely fat and past their prime. And the scenery and costumes were at the same level. You had to close your eyes—not because they were too old and too fat, but because of the costumes. You still find this.

"Wicked and evil"—that bad?

Someone who thinks he is more important, who thinks he has a better idea, or more talent, than the composer or the librettist. When someone says, "This libretto's crap. We're going to change it, rewrite a few scenes." That's happened to me.

How often does an opera fall into the hands of an "evil director"?

More often than one wants to admit. The whole *regietheater;* I mean, there are some things that are simply appallingly bad. There are things that can be quite good. But when someone says, "We have to do something with these pieces, because they have to be appropriate to a modern age, they've got to say something to us," well, you can go off the deep end when you do that kind of stuff. Respect for music, respect for the singer, respect for the libretto, seem to me fundamental. I love mixing modern and old. I love Wagner in modern dress, as I love Lully or Rameau in modern dress. A production can be wild, it can offend people, but I like it to be immensely respectful of what the work is musically.

The word "respectful" brings this to mind: At performances I've seen what appears to be a scowl on your face, flashed at audiences when they cough or make noise. Am I correct? If so, can you please comment?

It's very simple. There's a good cougher and a bad cougher. You would think the Spanish are a bad audience. But in Madrid they're much better than in Paris. A New York audience for opera at the BAM [Brooklyn Academy of Music] is wonderful. The New York Sunday-afternoon audience at Carnegie Hall can be disgusting. There's a wonderful story told by a friend of mine who went to a chamber-music recital at Carnegie, and he taps the old bag in front of him, who has been coughing her lungs out, and asks her, "Couldn't you be a little bit quieter?" and she says, "Young man, I've been coughing here for forty years."

So when I see you scowl, you're remembering the old bag?

I've said it to the person behind me: "Have you noticed that my orchestra— and there are sixty of them—don't cough? Why do you cough? We try to make an effort." Coughing is disruptive. It just happened again last night. But as I said, there's a good cough and a bad cough. You can sense the good cough immediately.

One singer told me that during lieder concerts, the audience coughed when he finished a song because they had been so concentrated they'd forgotten to breathe or swallow.

Of course! And that's fine. When I stop playing music and hear this chorus of coughing, you realize people have been making an effort. You don't scowl at those people. But the inveterate, nicotine-weary person, just coughing their lungs out, no. It's like cell phones. I read that my friend, Simon Rattle, stopped a concert, walked offstage, came back, and said, "If that happens again, I'll do it again." There's no excuse for this.

Let's end with teaching. You do a lot of it. What's important to keep in mind when teaching music? Particularly baroque music or vocal music?

[*Thinks*]

What do you try and impart to your students?

Give them what you know, what you want to transmit, and get them out as quick as possible. That's very important.

The practical aspect.

Yeah. Give off what you need to know, then let them go. I love teaching. It's wonderful, seeing them come into the studio and working with them, doing what they want to do, then letting them go. Or using them professionally. On the other hand, I have an absolute, gut-level distrust of a teacher who wants to rebuild his students in own image. Or the guru who says, "Without me, you'll never be any good."

Do they really work like that?

Of course they do.

You don't try and judge if someone needs help understanding the context of a work? That's not your role?

Of course, you point out things that need to be done. But it has to do with the practical aspects of teaching. If someone has a rotten French pronunciation, you say, "You'd better work on your French. Find yourself a good Francophone coach. If you sing this music, the linguistic aspect is terribly important." Or, "You're oversinging. This is not Verdi, it's Monteverdi. You're using a technique and style which aren't appropriate." Those are the kind of things you work on.

Is your approach at Le Jardin des Voix different than other singing schools?

Wonderful things happen all over the world in teaching voice. What might set us apart is that we're not trying to rebuild someone in our image. It is not the grand diva's master class, telling them this is not the way it should be done. And we can't do anything on a long-term basis. It's not like school because we can't keep them. We take them for a month. I'm not really interested in any other result than in turning out a concert. That's what it's all about. And I'm not really interested in taking people who are still in studies. We're looking to help young, beginning professionals. Someone who's just left the nest. This is the hardest moment in their careers—to get going. They're out of conservatory, their parents are no longer paying for anything; they're on their own. There are lots of young singers in Europe and the U.S., and it's hard to get that career started. That's the young singer we want to help.

Do you enjoy being at the beginning of their careers?

It's stimulating to participate in that. It's exciting to guide young talent. We audition all around Europe and choose people we like. One of the selection criteria is they must have voices we like and voices that work. They also need charisma. Out of two hundred applications, we took seven this year. We sell a series of concerts to top halls where they perform—this year it's London, Paris, Lisbon, Madrid, Geneva, Berlin, and New York—and they get paid professional fees. The top critics, agents, and impresarios all come and look them over.

Do you select instrumentalists for Les Arts Florissants from across Europe as well?

Les Arts Florissants has fourteen nationalities. This is the superb reality of my daily life! My life today consists in gathering members of a young Europe, who work in a big capital—Paris—and play their favorite music, which is European from the seventeenth and eighteenth centuries. It's hard to be more cosmopolitan. But musicians have always been nomads who travel constantly. And music has always played a role tying people together. It has solidified Europe. One thing about music: it doesn't like borders.

© Mark Lyons

James Conlon,
or surrendering your soul

You easily imagine James Conlon as your dinner guest. He's warm, he's sweet, he's open, he's almost cuddly. You can envision him comfortably seated on your couch in smiling and relaxed postprandial chat about movies or music. He listens to you, looks at you intently, and seems to care about what you say. You like him. His affable manner has made him a hit with Paris Opéra personnel, too.

He has returned this spring, where he spent nine years (1995 to 2004) as principal conductor of the Paris Opéra, for performances of Simon Boccanegra. In his small dressing room (one of two), we sit close and crowded amid three chairs and a piano.

We talk, and he continues to hang on the questions. But there comes a point when it seems that the guard has gone up behind the smile. He's still listening carefully, fixing his dark blue eyes on you, but now you wonder: Is it because he's wary of those questions or uncomfortable in interviews? His brow furrows, almost as if he's hearing the questions for the first time. They aren't always answered, as you'll see. Sometimes he'll shepherd the conversation along his own route. This makes you feel that he's confident in what he knows, or has prepared, but less so outside this realm, so he stays away. You wonder at his answers: Are they improvised, and how good will they sound? You be the judge. Avoiding what one doesn't know is not only a safe communication technique, but, in this case, adds spice to the atmosphere. You like him better for it, because it makes for a livelier interview.

And no one could put it any better than his first-rate response to "People are afraid of opera?" which sums up the subject using movies as comparison.

At times, he speaks slowly, choosing words with care. At others, his voice will rise—when talking about the United States, for instance, or his other crusade: artists whose work was suppressed by the Nazis.

He's not tall, but he's dapper, dressed neatly in black shoes, black trousers, and a black turtleneck under a powder-blue V-neck sweater. The uniform would pass in Southern California, where he operates part of the year as director of the L.A. Opera. His brown hair, neatly combed, suggests a no-nonsense, let's-get-the-job-done conductor. Watching him work, there seems to be no visible interference from emotional swings. He's cool on the podium.

He was born in Manhattan and makes his home there, but he spent more than two decades as music director across Europe: first with the Rotterdam Philharmonic (1983–1991), and in Cologne (1989–2002), and finally chief conductor in Paris.

Why did you go back to the U.S.?

I've been traveling to Europe for thirty-five years, and I started conducting here in 1975. I love it. But I had such a great time that I realized I was ignoring my own country. I felt I hadn't done enough to give back to the cultural environment that had nurtured me. I also have two daughters, and we had to start thinking about college.

Do you make an effort to spend equal time in Europe and the U.S.?

Any conductor on the international circuit is going to spend a certain amount of time in Europe and a certain amount in the U.S. I've always tried to divide my activities equally; though you can't balance every year, you can balance it over long periods. In my case it's 46 percent symphony, 46 percent opera, and about 8 percent choral music, because I have a choral festival in America as well.

What jobs lured you back?

I took two positions. The first is the Ravinia festival, the summer home of the Chicago Symphony, which, frankly, is one of the world's greatest orchestras. That's a long association I have as guest conductor—it goes back to 1977. That's a very concentrated four or five weeks: three programs a week, very intense.

And the second job?

I started as music director of the Los Angeles Opera. That was at the invitation of Plácido Domingo, a friend for thirty years. He called me here in Paris years ago, before I left, and said, "It would be great if you came here!" I said, "Plácido, I've just got two enormous jobs off my shoulders. I've been in Paris nine years, and Germany was backbreaking. I'm looking forward to goofing off—maybe working eight months a year, instead of eleven and a half." But Plácido is a very persuasive guy. We had a lot of talks, and at the end I laughed and told him, "All right, you talked me into it." I'm very glad he did.

How did you find the L.A. Opera?

It's only twenty years old and has grown enormously and very fast. By standards of an institution, twenty years is overnight. It's part of what interests me about L.A. In the next twenty years, it's going to explode.

You say you were looking to work eight months a year. Is that a place you're aiming to be eventually, once you reach a certain age?

I thought that age was now, but it isn't! [*Laughs*] There are other things you want to do in life, but not right now. This is my lifetime passion. It's what I love to do. Passions are passions. You can't say no.

Why did you want to conduct opera?

I'm not an opera conductor. I must emphasize that. I detest the distinction between opera and symphony. It's fairly modern that people "specialize" in one or the other. Go back one hundred years to Mahler, Toscanini, Klemperer, Walter, even into the modern age of Karajan or, today, Riccardo Muti, Claudio Abbado, James Levine. Not a single one would have renounced one or the other. In the great tradition, it was seen as two aspects of a single art. And that's the way I see it.

How so?

On two bases. One is you cannot detach these things. The culture is the same and all related. It's like a puzzle, and that puzzle is our classical music tradition. It's Mozart and Haydn and Brahms and Beethoven and Wagner and Verdi and Debussy and Stravinsky and Bartók. With some exceptions, it all fits together. If you love that culture, you can't possibly split yourself up and say, "I only like opera," or "I only like symphonies."

The other reason?

The second is more of a recommendation to others. When students ask, I say, "What you learn on the podium of a symphonic concert, and your knowledge and commitment to the orchestra as an instrument, will serve you immeasurably when you're conducting opera. And conversely: constant contact with the human voice, with drama, theater, language, poetry—all that comes with the opera—and most of all, that sixth sense of the spontaneous and what happens in theater, which is different because it must always be live at that moment—all that is something you'll take back to your symphonic life. The two will be complementary." Every artist—every human being—has to do what his nature tells him. If somebody said to me, "I don't like opera, I'm not going to conduct it," I would say, "Don't." And vice versa: if you like conducting opera and don't like conducting symphony, I'd say, then do that. I would be untrue to my nature if I split them, but the fact is I can't do without either one. It extends to choral music as well.

Let me repeat the question: What do you like about conducting opera?

Well, first of all, by happenstance, my first contact with classical music was opera. It's what opened the door. For me, it's a natural, it's obvious.

What opera was it?

It happened to be *La Traviata* but could have been anything.

How old were you?

Eleven. Within months, my life took on a new picture. I wanted to play the piano, got violin lessons. I started full blast. It was overnight basically. I went to three or four operas, then started going to concerts. Obviously it was meant to be; it was there genetically, or whatever it is. But it took place at a certain time. By the time I was thirteen, I knew I wanted to conduct. And there was never a question again from that time.

Did Maria Callas really give you your start?

In a sense. I was a conducting student in Juilliard, and it was my last year. There was a production in the school of *La Bohème,* and a famous conductor was supposed to conduct but canceled ten days before.

Who?

Thomas Schippers. They had to find somebody in a hurry. They wanted a professional, and there wasn't one. So I rehearsed the Juilliard orchestra while they looked for a conductor. This was the year Callas was giving her master classes—1971, '72. It happened in February 1972. The school president had heard I was good but didn't really know, so asked her. Callas watched me rehearse for about fifteen minutes, walked out and told him, "There's your man; he's got a great future." I was just happy doing the rehearsals. But it turned out to be my first success. I was lucky because I started young. I got to work, during the first ten years of my career, with people I had adored from a distance—Tito Gobbi, Boris Christoff, Callas, Rostropovich.

Would you call yourself an emotional person? How do you express yourself in music? Do you choose music—operas—with that in mind?

There are about five questions in there. I'll try and pick them apart.

Start with emotions.

Do you know any human being who is not emotional? I don't. The kind of music making I'm committed to is a music that's a representative admixture of heart, soul, brain, a sense of aesthetics and beauty, a sense of architecture, a commitment to passing on the spirit of whatever particular piece of music you're conducting. No aspect of your humanity can be pushed out of that mix without, in my opinion, detriment to the music. We've all seen overly cerebral persons, overly emotional persons who don't think, we all know people who are lopsided. I don't like lopsided music. I want music that's complete.

What's lopsided music?

When one of those elements we've identified is too big or crowds out the other.

So it's a question of balance.

You don't sit there and say, "Well, how am I going to balance my personality?" At least I don't. Everything I do and my whole artistic credo is based on something very different from what you're asking. It's irrelevant to me, when I make music, who I am.

Should that be the case?

I hope you'll be patient with me, because now that you've opened the box, I'm going to give it to you straight. In my days at Juilliard, we had great discussions. It was late at night; you've finished practicing, your fingers won't work any more, your brains are dead and the great philosophizing goes on—and should go on. For us, it was objectivism versus subjectivism. How do you find your own voice? Should you find your own voice? The fashion at the time was that everybody was seeking his own interpretation, his own feeling about the music, looking for his own identity. I had an instinctive allergy to the whole viewpoint. I was more interested in the Other. In other words, I look at the piece of music and want to know what it is. I have no interest in who I am or what my voice is. I want to know what the composer wrote. I want to see if I can intuit what the piece makes us feel, what it makes us think. I want to know *it.* I know who *I* am. The paradox is, the more you're constantly seeking the Other, the more you find yourself.

How does that happen?

For me the first step, after you've developed your tools as a musician, is to surrender your soul. Make yourself empty for the piece of music to come in. If you can empty your soul, then your job is to let it pass right through you, through your instrument—violin, voice, piano, baton.

But don't conductors choose tempi and loudness and such things?

Sure. But that's your musical art. Your ear, your sense of balance, sense of color, phrasing, your sense of drama if it's opera. If you open your soul, you're open to all those phenomena. You hear a piece of music, study it, play it. The music starts to speak to you. The beauty of subjectivism is that each of us sees it differently. You'll see it a certain way, I'll see it another way. And I'll see it a different way five years from now.

Is there something you've learned about yourself conducting Verdi, say, or something else you've learned through another composer—Wagner, for instance?

I adore both and can't live without either. They're a part of every year. Do you learn? Yes. Can you extract that and say, "I've learned this lesson or that lesson?" The answer is no. These are works that speak to deep emotions, and I think that in the course of a lifetime your constant contact with all this classical music forms your personality. And it's not just true for us musicians. It would be true for a greater part of society, if all people were open to those things. Because it activates what I think are very important values. I believe in spiritual values, humanistic values. I think art has one corner of the universe where it reveals those things to all of us, and that's very important.

Is this the message you want to bring to an audience?

My first message is speaking to people who are not musicians or experts. It's a message to which I'm absolutely devoted, especially in America. One of the reasons I went back is that I got a lot from America, and I want to give something back. The biggest thing I could give is to use my personality to help stop the hemorrhage in young people hearing classical music. The arts fell out of U.S. schools in the 1980s; all the music is gone. Now we have a generation of adults who make money, accomplish what they think is the fulfillment of life, but they've never had any contact with classical arts— neither music nor literature. For me that's a national disgrace. And a tragedy, and dangerous. Because when you have a population that does not have contact with the roots of our own civilization, you have a population that's capable of making terrible mistakes. I don't think I need say more. Sorry to run on.

No problem. You work very closely with certain orchestras. Is there a drawback in being too close?

What does that mean?

You get too close spiritually. You lose objectivity, freshness.

I don't agree at all. Not just a little bit. I don't agree, period.

Some say it's better to be a visiting conductor. For freshness' sake.

They are two different dynamics. I've done both. Even in the years when I had my own orchestra, I was a guest conductor, and I still am.

How do you motivate these orchestras? Do you inspire the players?

You hope you do. Either you are, or you're boring them to death. One of the most important things is establishing a direct relationship to music making and engaging the soul and talent and intelligence of any orchestra. That's important, because if it's a good orchestra, you're with one hundred people, all of whom have talent or they wouldn't be there. There is music which is imposed, and you can get discipline or order from that. But that interests me less than music you inspire, when you bring out of them what they already have within themselves. Imposing an approach isn't as good as eliciting a fully committed spiritual activity from a group. But that doesn't mean it's a democracy. When you're conducting, you take over. You set a tempo, you decide when you want to deviate from that, you decide when you want to stretch it, when you want to voice a chord from the wind instruments this way, or when you want the phrase that way. You do all that, and it's imposed. But there's a difference between imposing because it's a question of authority or eliciting what's already there. When you conduct, you're basically bringing coherence into any given moment.

That's what most people would like to know. How do you manage to do that?

If you could put it in a bottle, you'd have schools producing thousands of conductors. It's the only activity in classical music that no one has ever been able to bottle. There's no formula. It's always been said that conductors are born. It's true, to some degree. You can't make somebody a conductor who doesn't have the nature. You can train it and develop it, but you can't create it—just like you can't create an operatic voice. To some degree, it's personality. There are born leaders and people who aren't. Artists are sensitive people. They have to be nurtured or channeled or tolerated, or you let them have their fits. A conductor is someone whose job is to bind an enormous variety of personalities into a coherent whole.

Are there things you find yourself doing repeatedly with orchestras, to inspire them? I don't want to say "tricks," but approaches that seem to work?

Yes and no. Yes in the sense that my basic tenet is that complete and serious devotion to music making is always the strongest card you can play. You're not up there to do anything but that. You're not up there to show off. You're there because you're privileged to be making great music. The first tenet is 100 percent devotion toward the musical products.

Do you expect that of the instrumentalists?

I expect that, and they expect it of me.

Do you always get it?

Of course not. If you ask me am I satisfied, I'd answer that I'm happy doing what I love, which is conducting, and I'm never satisfied. I don't believe in such a state. You may have momentary satisfaction, you may be happy with a performance, and think it went well, but you wake up the next morning and have to start from zero.

I cut you off; you were talking about the ways you inspire an orchestra.

I was speaking generally. On the other hand, every day is different, and every place is different. Every country is different, and every orchestra is different. And it's different from the way it was two years ago when you saw them last. So you're living in the moment, in that respect. You have to be flexible and inventive as to what this orchestra needs today to get a little better. What can we do to go from yesterday's rehearsal to tomorrow's rehearsal? There's no rule.

What are the qualities a conductor needs most? You mention flexibility and inventiveness.

Very difficult to answer that question. But I would say there are any number of qualities. There might be ten, twelve, or twenty-five that are desirable to have as a conductor. Nobody's got them all, or even half. The job is too immense for any one person to have it all. If you ask how come there are conductors who only have half the qualities necessary, or ten out of twenty-five, the answer is because it's so intangible and defies total mastery. So even if you have seven or eight of them, you've already got a lot more than most people. And you use those seven or eight or whatever they are.

Which ones do you use?

I have no idea.

Flexibility, inventiveness?

Impossible to say. You're asking me questions when I operate from the other direction.

Is that why you wanted to be a conductor? Because it was such a big challenge?

I did it because I couldn't *not* do it. Without any reason to believe that I would be able to conduct some day, I made that decision when I was thirteen years old. I made it because of an inability to do otherwise. It's a passion. The nature of passion is that it's all-consuming. It's a gift. It can be a burden. You can choose to walk away from a passion. But if you say yes to it, you live it. I'm fortunate in that I found that passion very young and discovered one important thing about it: it never is finished. However long I live, I'm sure that on my last day, I will love music the way I have all my life. And you have renewable strengths, renewable energy, every day when you are motivated through a passion.

Is there an explanation for that?

Maybe, I don't know. Literature and art, psychology and religion have been grappling with what passion is and what it means. That's what's going on with me. It started when I was thirteen, and that was over forty years ago. It's still there and hasn't diminished. What I'm doing is always guided from a point of view of what's coming from within.

You travel a lot. Do you see any differences between orchestras?

There used to be characteristic sounds, certain schools of playing that were more available. There are fewer today than a generation ago, certainly fewer than fifty years ago. There's a tendency now for that to become more uniform. This uniformity is decried by some and welcomed by others. There are many viewpoints, and I myself am pretty mixed on the subject. But it's partially inevitable.

What differences do you see?

The big differences are cultural. How does a group of one hundred people function? In that respect, it's a microcosm of their societies. Just as there's a flavor and a sense of what is French, there's a flavor of what's Italian and German. The actual work relationship is formed by those differences. This has many applications. The concept of rhythm, of discipline, the concept of beauty versus accuracy; these are areas that when you penetrate them, you see each of these countries has a profile and *vive la différence*. A pianist might go on tour and play piano, then go out to dinner. But as a conductor, you are obligated to interrelate with one hundred or two hundred people who are from that particular country, or immigrants or travelers like you. So you're getting contact with all of that. I love that and find it's enriched my life.

Have you seen any trends, say in American orchestras that you don't see in Europe, or vice versa?

I've seen what I identify as the American paradox. It's one of my two missions. The other is rediscovering music suppressed by the Nazis.

We'll talk about that in a minute. What's the American paradox?

At this moment, we are probably the country that is producing more great orchestras and more young musicians than any other. And we have every reason to be proud of that. There are more great orchestras, at the moment, in America than probably in any country.

It's a big country.

It's a big country, but we've produced them.

It's a rich country.

It's not just the money. You can have all the money in the world, but you need people who can play. We've got them. Nowadays, when there's an opening in the viola section in the Chicago Symphony, there are 250 applicants, the worst of whom is probably twice as good as somebody from a generation or two ago. We've got so many people coming out of schools and conservatories. Where it was traditional to talk about the big five orchestras, now there are at least fifteen or twenty, every one of which is good. When I was born, there were two major opera companies in America: the Metropolitan Opera and the San Francisco Opera. The Chicago Lyric was not yet born, the L.A. Opera did not exist. But now there are regional opera companies all over that didn't exist when I was born in the 1950s. You've got more symphonies, more opera companies, more resident string quartets in universities than ever before. You've got music schools all over producing a phenomenal level of young musicians. You're producing all that on a very high level—probably higher than any other time in our history, or in history, period. So what's the paradox? The paradox is I don't know a single arts institution that is not battling to keep its public. That's serious. What does that mean?

It goes back to what you said before, about education, the arts vanishing from schools.

We've lost contact, as a nation, with high culture. By high culture I don't mean snobbism. But that's part of what's gone wrong, because elements in the political environment have allowed that vision of art to affect political decisions. That it's for the elite or snobs or highbrows. This is a tragic stupidity. Because classical art is for everybody.

Do you think an American Ministry of Culture would help?

No, I think we need a multilayered recommitment to classical art: painting, music, and literature. I feel strongly about it because it's my passion in life. But objectively, when a society turns its back on its classical roots, it does so at its peril. It has to be reinvented in the schools, both public and private. It should be reinvented by the government. I don't mean government should take over. But it should be spending more money. I have to defend America in one respect: indirectly, the government does support the arts because it allows tax deductions for major sponsors. That's a form of support. And it's a form of decentralization of support. I'm not sure that putting it back in government hands is a good idea. I'm simply saying the government should do more to promote it and make it attractive to society as a whole.

Is the situation better in Europe?

This wasn't always a problem. But I speak with friends now, in every country, and everybody's concerned—in France, in England. They're very concerned about it in Germany, because Germany seemed a place where this would never be a question. And they say it's starting. I remember going to Moscow when it was still the Soviet Union, and you couldn't find a place in the house—sold out, every night. People were dying to get in. I remember playing every encore we had, audiences screaming—unbelievable.

And now?

Now, it's capitalism. People have to afford it. Not everybody can.

Do you see differences in audiences among the different nations where you play?

Again, it's cultural. They have different natures. Some are vociferous. Some sit on their hands. Some are very emotional. Some are warm, some very opinionated. Some are very open. Americans are generally very open. I've noticed a change in Japan. Twenty years ago, everybody was very serious, listening very attentively. Polite applause—I don't think because the music wasn't appreciated, I think because it was considered vulgar or common to make too much noise. Now it's completely changed; I think partially because many Japanese have traveled to Europe and seen screaming opera houses. European operatic audiences tend to be more demonstrative. It goes with the sense of grandeur of the emotions associated with opera. I must say that I find the quality of listening in Germany to be extremely satisfying. There's a profound love of classical music. Germans listen in a special way—almost metaphysically. They hear a piece of music with their emotions. They ask themselves, "What do these emotions mean, what's behind them, how did that piece make me feel?" The public in Germany is especially good. And, I must say, eastern Europe, too. My experiences there—Poland, what is now Slovakia, Russia—they're fantastic.

What would you tell an audience—someone from outside—that they don't know about how opera is put together, that would enrich their experience next time they go?

I've never seen a person who, when I've invited them to watch a rehearsal, does not come back completely fascinated. Yesterday, a woman told me, "When I see what you do I'm completely floored. At a performance, we see the conductor come out, bow, then start the music. And everything just comes—it's like magic. But when I see what you do every day, the investment of time, coaching, the psychological side, I'm amazed."

Are you saying it would be a good idea to open rehearsals to the public?

We do it in L.A. I regularly invite people and tell them to sit in the front rows so they can see what's going on. I think it's a great idea. Last night, I spoke to a group of university students during intermission. They were seeing a rehearsal, most of them for the first time, seeing how something gets put together. This week a young Italian conductor asked to come and watch. I told him it was a little boring right now, no orchestra, we're doing stage rehearsals. "No, I want to come," he said. And he said he spent the most informative week of his life.

Don't singers or players prefer that the public doesn't see what goes on during rehearsals? They don't want them hearing the director or conductor saying, "That doesn't work, try something else" and the like?

Sure. You can't do it all the time. As a rule, you don't do it with the public. As soon as it's with a public, it's like a performance.

Anything else you think would lure new audiences to opera?

Start right at the beginning. Start before they're four. Bring them for half an hour. Just get them into an opera house. There are many people in our society who have never been inside a concert hall. They see this big building, and it looks like a fortress to them. They see people going in with tuxedos, they see these cars driving up. How am I supposed to feel if I'm a kid from a poor neighborhood? It's like enemy territory. The fear has to be taken out first. Inhibition is the biggest problem in America.

People are afraid of opera?

I'll give you an example. When somebody tells me they went to my concert, and I ask them how they liked it, before they even answer, they say,

"Well, I'm not a musician" or "I never studied music" or "I don't know anything about classical music." Right there is your first problem. Because music is meant to be listened to, experienced; it flows through you and—boom—off you go. Now if you went to a movie, and I asked you how you liked it, you'd say you loved it or hated it or thought it was stupid, or you can't stand thrillers, or you cried or laughed. People know exactly how they feel, because they're not inhibited. Why? Because movies are the cultural products of our society. People grow up with them in a natural relationship. What's the relationship in schools and in early life with opera? Unfortunately, for a lot of people, there's none at all. It's doesn't even exist, it's not on the planet.

How about the family environment?

Everybody's got to do it. Schools, families, art institutions, everybody.

Your other mission, as you call it, is supporting music by composers that was suppressed by the Nazis.

An enormous volume of music has been lost from the period of 1933 to 1945. Not just music written in that period, but all the composers—most of them Jewish, but not all—who were banned retroactively. You've got music written anywhere from 1890 to 1945, and composers who were banned and emigrated but whose public personas were destroyed. So even in the 1940s and '50s, they might have been teaching, they were existing, but there was no forum for their music to be heard. It's a very large umbrella and an enormous cultural loss.

Some people say there are no lost masterpieces.

I attack those clichés. Since there have been civilizations and wars, there have been lost masterpieces. We all watched a modern version of that when those [Bamiyan] Buddhas were blown up in Afghanistan [by the Taliban in 2001]. The peculiar factor in Nazi Germany—and to some degree Stalinist Russia, though we know less about it—is that this short period, twelve years, represents the biggest rupture in one of the greatest traditions in Western civilization, which was the Germanic classical-music tradition. The core talent was taken out, suppressed, killed, forced to emigrate, go underground. But the most important thing is the environment which had nurtured the type of cross-fertilization—polemics, schools of thought, collegiality, the whole thing which had functioned for centuries—was ruined. And for various reasons after the war, nobody was able to pick this up. Most of this music has remained known by experts, but the public has been ignorant. I include myself. I'm a practicing musician and have given my life to music but was forty years old before it hit me what was there.

How many works are you talking about here?

Hundreds of operas, thousands of symphonic and piano works, chamber music and songs. This will outlast my lifetime. This is not conceived as a remembrance to victims or anything like that. I'm doing it because our history has been written with the omission of this extraordinary amount of music, and it's our job to put it back on the map. What I've done, both in Ravinia and Los Angeles, is set up situations where there will be not tokenism, not an occasional tipping of the hat, but a systematic effort to start to reverse the situation.

You've made a couple of opera movies, Madame Butterfly *for Frédéric Mitterrand and Ken Branagh's* Magic Flute. *What differences do you see in that genre?*

There's no difference, and then there's a small difference. First of all, I don't go for the shooting, so I'm not recording out of sequence, like they film it. You record the way you would a normal audio CD. Then they film to that CD. My activity is always in the first stage. The first stages are conception, planning, auditioning, seeing the screenplay, and trying to understand which direction the director is going. When it comes to recording, in one sense it's like any other. But you make it on multiple tracks, because they have to be able to make voices approach or go away, depending if they're in close-up or wide shot, for all that stuff on the screen. So you record under circumstances which are very challenging, and you have to be good at it. That means technically you've got people singing in different rooms, or you have your own mike. Sometimes we bring everybody in and do a take of a scene normally, with everyone in the room with the orchestra. Then we do the same thing with everybody isolated, so that if they need to, subsequently, in the mixing, they can bring one voice in and another voice back.

How much of that is you, and how much is the studio technicians?

If the orchestra is together and sounds good, that's you. You work with the cast the way you work with any other. What's peculiar to opera films is the demand to have young people. It's almost a contradiction in terms: you want an eighteen- or nineteen-year-old because that's what you need to be convincing on the screen, and frankly, at eighteen or nineteen you can't sing these things. So it all starts with a compromise. Sometimes it works, and sometimes it doesn't.

Are you happy with the films you've done?

I love doing it; it's very satisfying. Sometimes you like the result, and sometimes you don't. After all, I let go of it after the sound track is done. I believe opera movies are a legitimate transposition of an art form from one medium to another; it's out of a theater and onto a screen. As long as the musical values and the substance of the work are respected, I'm all for experimenting. Some of the experiments work, some don't. But I do believe that some great movie of an opera, someday, is going to really pop the cork on this. Because it's a way you can speak to a lot of people who won't go to an opera but might go see a movie that turns out to be an opera. I think that will make a difference. But it's still in its infancy; it's not as if there's a formula and everyone's following it. It's very, very hard. I make one condition, and I made it to Ken Branagh for *The Magic Flute,* and he didn't have a problem with it. I said, "There's one non-negotiable position before we start. Not one note can be cut, and there can't be one note that isn't Mozart."

But you wouldn't know about any long or short versions, geared for different international audiences.

I haven't seen it in a theater. I've only got my CD at home. One of the problems is that you give birth to these things, and it comes out. Fair enough. But the point is that I believe in the concept and hope the future will see a big breakthrough that begins to make a difference.

Final question: In the older opera houses, are you ever conscious of the spirits of your illustrious predecessors?

It sounds nice but doesn't correspond to anything I can relate to. When I saw where Verdi was born, it brought tears to my eyes. Something like that, sure. Theaters; La Scala. It meant a lot to me the thirty years I conducted at the Metropolitan Opera because I grew up there. Those kind of things have some meaning to me. But living humanity is the most meaningful thing. It's the people I meet, with whom I work.

You don't have a favorite or lucky pair of tails, either, I suppose?

No. To me, it's a natural activity. I do it every day. If you have too many fetishes you'd get in your own way. I believe the moment you're on that podium you're a conductor and an artist, and it's 100 percent. And the minute you walk off that podium, you're a human being, like anybody else. I think that should be your answer.

Simon Fowler/Virgin Classics

Natalie Dessay, or healing the sick voice

Once upon a time, a talented French singer studied hard, got the breaks, and saw her career take off. The year was 1991. A decade later, she had reached stellar heights in light soprano and coloratura parts across Europe and North America.

Then, one day, Natalie Dessay was told she had "something" on her vocal cords. The doctor didn't know what; it was impossible to say more without operating. The fairy-tale movie went into freeze-frame.

By far, any singer's worst nightmare. It beats boos, stage fright—even being stuck in traffic at curtain time.

Singing became suffering. "My voice wasn't responding," she recalls. After a performance of Bellini's La Sonnambula in Vienna, she didn't want to go on. "I thought, I'd rather kill myself than spend the rest of my life this way." She was not yet forty.

Cancellations followed—Paris, then New York—while she contemplated the unthinkable: a career change.

Over the next three years, she underwent a pair of vocal-cord "face-lifts," as she calls them. In the first, doctors removed a pseudocyst on one, believing a bump on the other would disappear. It didn't. Two and one half more nightmarish years followed before she endured a second surgery. More missed bookings, disappointment, and soul-searching.

The sort of anguish one can only imagine is behind her now, and the soprano discusses the matter openly on this day, with distance in her voice that is time's gift of healing. But from our booth in an empty East Paris bistro, the voice rings with emotion, too, because Natalie Dessay—who prefers the English to the French spelling of "Nathalie" in a personal homage to actress Natalie Wood—is peppery and quick to ignite. You sense turbulence beneath the waters. Determined, argumentative, and swift to speak, her green eyes burn as she leans forward making a point, elbows planted on the table, and you get the impression you are speaking to, or sitting dangerously near, a fifty-kilogram powder keg. Her father was an explosives engineer, she says. Perhaps that explains it.

The main point she is determined to make just now is that since her surgery she has been on a mission. It is her duty, she says, to rid vocal-cord malady of its stigma as a taboo subject among singers. "Many singers have problems but never talk about it because it means you have a poor technique." It's an undeclared attitude of blame you sense everywhere, she believes.

In reality, such disorders can spring from a dozen origins, including the psychological. This, Dessay states, was her case, which she discusses frankly.

She made a DVD of her hospitalization and treatment, which has been seen by colleagues and has altered more than a few mind-sets. Many admit to her that they've had problems, too, but kept mum.

It took a year and a half for the diva to recover, physically and psychologically. The corporal abilities returned first, confidence last. Today, that self-assurance is back fully, as anyone who has seen her perform can testify. For those who haven't, the fact that she named her three cats Polyp, Nodule, and Cyst certainly proves it.

Why did you see the doctor in the first place?

I felt something, it was like a grain of sand. And not only while singing—I felt it all the time, even when speaking. I could *feel* my voice, which is unnatural—I had never felt my voice before. When you talk, you don't feel it speak. It's uncomfortable, especially if you're a singer. If I hadn't been a singer, it would have given me a smoky sort of voice, sexier maybe. But a singer needs a clear voice, not choked.

How bad was it?

It wasn't that bad, but it was a small discomfort all the time.

How was it affecting your singing?

I couldn't reach the highest notes anymore. Or pianissimo notes, which require the mucus to be extremely elastic. So I began to worry. It was September 11, 2001. I was in tears, utterly desperate! I got in a taxi, and that's when I learned what had happened in New York. I stopped crying immediately and listened to the radio. I told myself there was worse in the world, you're not going to die from this, we can operate. Next to the Twin Towers, my problem was nothing. I told myself I could change professions. Sad— but not the end of the world! In any case, if I had no choice, what other attitude could I have?

Did you stop singing?

No, I continued for nearly a year, accepting engagements that were more spread out, more irregular. But the anxiety was always there. I told myself, maybe the operation won't succeed, maybe they're going to find something more serious. One never knows what they'll find.

It's said that singing bel canto—Rossini, Bellini, Donizetti—is itself good for the voice. Did you try that?

Didn't work. I waited a bit, to see if things would improve with time and with rest. Or with rehabilitation or treatment. Often when you have the beginnings of a nodule, some kinds of treatment or exercises will make it disappear without surgery. But then I sang *La Sonnambula* in Vienna. And I thought, "I'd rather kill myself than spend the rest of my life this way!" Singing was such suffering! Normally, it should be an immense pleasure. I didn't see how I could go on. I could sing, but it cost me a horrible effort to do it.

Can you describe it?

I never knew what was going to come out of my throat. I had to force the voice and push on it. I couldn't sing softly.

Did you have to cancel any engagements?

Since we sign contracts years in advance, I had to cancel with some opera houses. What's extraordinary is that of all my employers, nobody tore up any contracts. "We'll wait for you," they said. That was incredible! I appreciate this show of confidence. That's also why I've tried to speak out about it, to be as straight as possible about it. In this profession, you don't have the right to get sick. You're not allowed any failing—especially concerning your vocal cords. It's a real taboo; singers never talk about any problems they have because it could mean, in the collective unconscious anyway, that you have a poor technique. Now you see all the time that athletes, dancers, anybody who uses their bodies—I'll say almost past the limits—can have problems or get hurt. Football players have bad knees, tennis players get tendonitis; everybody thinks it's normal, and it is normal. Using or overusing parts of your body to the extreme means you risk getting hurt.

Why do you suppose it's accepted for athletes but not for singers?

I don't know. All I know is that opera unleashes passions, myths, false ideas. When a singer fails, he or she has a bad evening, the audience is upset and disappointed because their dream is shattered. That is why they boo and even insult a singer on stage. This probably never happens in a theater play or ballet.

What do you think was the origin of your problem?

Vocal-cord problems can come from dozens of reasons, including the psychological. I won't say I have the best technique in the world, but mine's no worse than anybody else's. What happened to me happened for a number of reasons, including the fact I had children and hadn't anticipated what life was going to be once they were there. I was unable to organize things with the children and with my husband [baritone Laurent Naouri]. I was lost in the middle of all these things, unable to manage. It was just too much. I guess life decided I needed a crisis to shut down and think.

Were you working too hard?

I never sang more than thirty-five engagements a year, maybe forty—operas, concerts, everything. That's not a lot. But it was probably still too much for my personal rhythm. I blamed the profession a little bit—it's a difficult one. I'm used to saying now that I fabricated these things to have the time to think. It was quite a violent thing. It's not necessarily useful to do this sort of thing to oneself, but it is common knowledge that most illnesses are self-induced; that's a secret for nobody. I fabricated something inside myself: a pseudocyst on one side and a polyp on the other. That's something that normally doesn't exist. You get one or the other, not both. But that's me—I never do things halfway.

How did the pseudocyst form?

Nobody really knows what it is, how it gets there, why it appears there and not somewhere else. Why not on the ovaries? I had another cyst on my hand; maybe I'm somebody who just gets them. It appeared on my vocal cords because that's where it had to appear—I have no answer to why it showed up there. But it did let me take some time to reflect on things; about my life, what I wanted to do with it, and how I wanted to work in this profession from now on.

You seem to be saying quite openly that both exterior and interior reasons were responsible.

Life at one point simply decided that some emergency was necessary for me to call a halt. It was like a midlife crisis. I was nearing forty. That's the way I see it. Some people go through something like this and get a divorce; I got vocal-cord problems.

Tell us what a throat examination is like.

A camera can be inserted in the nose or the mouth. Some doctors say they see better with one or the other, while patients differ as to which is more comfortable. I prefer the mouth, although sometimes having the camera in your throat makes you feel like you're going to throw up. I practiced a lot with my doctor—I'm a perfect guinea pig! I learned a lot, too.

What's it like, seeing your own vocal cords?

It's great the first time, very impressive. It doesn't have this effect on me anymore, though. I've been looking at mine for so long—since I was twenty. But you realize these tiny things are your vocal cords. They don't fit your idea of what you think they're going to look like at all. They're really small— two tiny membranes that move—and you see them quite well. When every-thing's okay, they are all white and smooth. What impressed me, on the other hand, was seeing the operation on the DVD.

We'll talk about that DVD in a moment, but first, you went from examina-tion to operation. What did the surgeon do?

He cut out the pseudocyst in the first operation. Normally, if you have a pseudocyst on one side, it's not unusual to have something on the other. And normally, this other thing disappears once you've removed the pseu-docyst. Mine had nothing to do with the pseudocyst; it was a polyp. After two and a half years, however, it was still there. I had to come back and have a second operation. There's no way of knowing it's unrelated when you start, apparently. I was a surgical first.

And it all went on that DVD. Whose idea was it to film your operation?

I hadn't planned to be operated on and filmed. We don't have a say in what's real, you know. Reality happens, and we live it, that's all. Reality hit me, and we—the director and I—decided to film my vocal-cord operation, as it was part of a larger work we're doing on the life of a singer. The first film we did was called *Une rencontre* [A Meeting], about our meeting in Santa Fe and a concert I did in Orange, France. It was a portrait of a singer. The director has since become a friend, and we've decided to make more than one film on a singer's life. We show what a singer does, how she does it, and present opera to the audience in a way that takes them by the hand. We've filmed interviews, TV appearances, how I work at home, rehearsals, lots of things.

Is this something you like doing?

It's interesting since I've learned a lot about production, editing, the audio-visual world. We're making these films together. She's the eye and shows what she wants; she has total freedom. It's a way to present opera, taking it down off its pedestal, trying to show people that beauty isn't reserved for an elite. That the sublime works of Mozart, Verdi and Donizetti are also for them. And especially for them. We're not making these films for people already familiar with opera. We're making them for those who haven't had the chance to experience the immense emotion you can feel when in the face of such beauty. It'll be great if this message gets across.

Are you particularly concerned with this message of getting new people into the opera house?

Yes, and a good way is telling them these works are for them. I'm not forcing anyone; lots of people prefer the Rolling Stones. There are things for every taste. I'd simply like to bury the notion that opera is elitist, because it's completely false. "Elitist and too expensive" is what they usually say. It's untrue, because at the Bastille you can have a great seat for fifty euros. How much do people pay for a football match or a Madonna concert?

What do you say to people who have never seen an opera, to lure them?

Don't go to the opera telling yourself how much you're going to miss or not understand. Don't feel bad if you don't know the story or libretto. Don't worry about that. I'd like to stop people who don't understand the plot from feeling guilty about it. Go with as open a mind and senses as possible. Even if you don't understand the plot, you're going to be on the receiving end of many things. You should go feeling ready to receive.

Isn't it a question of education?

Before education, they need a first shock. Everyone I bring to the opera—family, neighbors, friends—are novices who have all told me, without exception, "I never would have believed opera was like that!" They'd never been and came out stunned. In the positive sense. People first need a chance to see opera live, to experiment and feel the impact of the human voice unamplified, live. Then, little by little, they get interested; they read the stories, find the libretti, then their taste can start to form. But first, they need that initial physical encounter. It doesn't always click with everyone, but everyone deserves the chance to feel it, once in their lives.

What do you like about opera?

Opera for me is total spectacle. It can totally miss the mark—as a matter of fact, it does most of the time; it's far too complicated to get everything right. But when it works, it's the most beautiful thing that exists in this world. More beautiful than dance alone, than concerts alone, than the circus—more beautiful than anything, when it works. It's got everything.

Going back to your surgery: How long did rehabilitation take?

Rehabilitation usually lasts between eight months and a year before you can sing again. That's not enormous in a career.

You made a total recovery.

Yes. It took a year and a half to find complete elasticity and especially confidence. Physically, you heal rapidly. Nearly a week after the operation you can sing—physically, you can. It's in your head where you can't. You've lost confidence. I sang in public after eight months. Maybe it was too soon, but it was the last stage of my rehabilitation. I continued doing my exercises and massages, two or three times a week. Exercises didn't include real singing; you make little sounds instead.

How has this entire episode changed you?

I now know the value of what I have. Before, I thought it was normal to sing. Now I realize it's a great bit of luck. I appreciate more having that chance to sing. I chose this profession because I wanted people to hear me, and now I take advantage of every instant when I sing. Of course I reworked some things in my technique. But fundamentally I didn't change my way of singing. On the other hand, I've changed the way I *think* about singing and about my profession as a singer. My career now is influenced by the way my voice changes, which it does naturally, over time anyway.

You mean it would have changed, without the vocal-cord problems?

Yes, and I'll never really know how much that evolution was affected by the problems and how much would have occurred naturally. I'm around forty; it's a time in life when the voice changes, especially a light one like mine. I always felt a big contrast between the light, airy voice I had and the fiery temperament I was born with. Both seem to have blended now. I have a deeper, more lyrical voice, which goes much better with the temperament— which hasn't changed! I've managed to unite the two. Before, I was sort of schizophrenic. Now I'm together, and it's made me much calmer.

What has been the reaction of other singers when you speak about your operations?

People who know that I had this problem talk to me about their own suffering. They've admitted that they've gone through similar things, and nobody knows it. They've thanked me for speaking out. I'm talking about well-known singers, great singers! Many colleagues, some from my own generation, even young ones. Some who were operated on before their careers began who have gone on to great careers. One woman told me she didn't say anything about it at the time because she didn't want to run the risk of never working again. "I preferred saying I had a personal crisis," she said.

Have both men and women told you this?

I've mainly spoken to women, but I know it happens to men, too.

You seem quite content to have spoken out.

I hope I've contributed to changing things and toward helping remove this guilt from the minds of singers who have got hurt. Not only can you no longer do your job, but you feel like a loser, a failure, when it happens to you. Unconsciously, you're made to feel guilty. People's attitudes are "Well, it's no surprise you've got vocal-cord problems, the way you sing!" Or "It's your teacher's fault—she pushed you too hard," or dumb ideas like that. But you don't have to hear people talk to understand; you sense this attitude right away. That's the way it is in this business. Others, friends, say, "You shouldn't talk about it! Aren't you afraid?" But I'm not scared to talk, and I don't really care what others think. It's liberating for me, and I hope to help free others from guilt.

Where would you say your career is headed now, since the incident?

I don't know. *Traviata* is a big achievement for me. I want to continue to sing bel canto, French opera, and baroque music. For the rest, we will see what will happen.

Do you work less now than before?

No, I don't work less, I work differently. The most important thing is not what you do, but with whom. I try to choose the people with whom I want to work and with whom I know we'll do something interesting together. I try to be more selective in my choices and involved in the conception of the projects. I reserve the right to say no to a project. What I often refuse are traditional stagings where I'm not directed and where nothing happens. You're dead in that sort of thing, even if it sells tickets. I'm there to please myself, too.

What about pleasing the public?

I'm not there to please them. I am there to try and surprise them.

How about critics? Do you read them?

Not anymore. I used to read them a lot and was quite affected by what they wrote. So I decided to never read them again, and that was a big change for me. Each time I'm on stage I give the best I have. I can't do any better at that particular moment. If they aren't satisfied, I can't give them any more because I've already given my all.

Lots of singers are not good actors, or say they aren't. Are you?

Acting is my favorite subject! I did theater when I was young. I'm interested in it, read a lot about it, go to plays, talk to actors, and try to learn more each time. I say I try to put myself in the service of the director, since most of the time they come from theater. I like to think they'll help me in my acting, help me give more. Because singers aren't taught how to act or move at all. It's crazy, because an opera singer *is* an actor. You have to use your body. There remains this huge lack in our training. I learned how act in theater, not during my singing career. All singers follow different paths. I took private lessons, very few conservatory or institutional classes, but I took enough to realize they don't teach enough acting. Anyway, I think the young generation is much more involved in acting than in the past. It is a very good thing.

You said once, "Singing is not enough. It's not only technique; I want to discover a soul."

If singing were everything, I'd only give concerts. Acting in opera is a total experience, and I like that.

Two last questions before we return to the surgery: Do you ever feel the spirits of your illustrious predecessors in your dressing rooms at venerable opera houses in Europe or around the world?

There are theaters which are inhabited by spirits, sure. And often bad spirits. But I don't bother with that. If you start worrying about that sort of thing, you'll never do anything at all. I don't think of my illustrious predecessors who have sung Lucia before me. There are so many, and they've all done so well.

How hard is it to get back into real life after three hours on stage—as Lucia, say?

People imagine it's hard to get out of a role like that, but actually, not at all. I'm not the one who suffers onstage. It doesn't really work that way. It takes me time to leave my dressing room, but as soon as the curtain falls, I go out of my role. But I still need a long time before and after the performance just to enjoy the moment. It is also a matter of energy. Before you need to gather it; after, you need to let it die down. But it is important to go back quickly to real life.

Actors all have different ways of approaching this, don't they?

Yes, and the result depends on each actor. There are some who act with themselves. I think that's dangerous. An actress friend of mine says she takes people along with her on a journey. That expresses it best for me. You leave a place for the person watching you, and their imagination, so they can travel along. Acting is a technique that you develop with time and with directors you meet. It involves a lot of research, and everybody has a different approach. You can use your own experience and imagination, and it takes a long time to use your emotion in a proper way. That means without hurting yourself, with the necessary distance between you and your character, but at the same time leaving the door open to the real and deep emotions. Young actors can only look within themselves for their emotions to give something. But in time, when your technique develops, it becomes much more interesting.

I'd like to close with some final questions on your vocal-cord problems. If I were to come to you and say I've got the same trouble, what would be your advice?

Go see a voice specialist—see mine if you prefer, though there are others. Get checked several times over several weeks. If the situation doesn't change over that time, you'll have to decide to operate. My advice would depend on each person. Some prefer to suffer in silence; others want the entire world to know. But things just don't happen by themselves. I'd also suggest looking into the interior, or psychological, factors that might be responsible. It might necessitate an entire rethinking of your lifestyle. I'd impose nothing on anyone. Each person must do what he or she feels is right.

Every case is unique.

Sure. My doctor told me she and her colleagues see things and can't even say what they are. For example, my husband consulted her, and on one cord was a big obstruction. Two days later, it was gone. Nobody could say what it was! Something swelled up, and then went down again! These things happen, and nobody can say why. Each individual produces things in his or her body which are totally mysterious. Surrounding the vocal cords are an infinity of things that remain unknown. Science can't tell you what they are. We're not only bodies, you know; there's more to it than that. But at the same time we are very much bodies. You can't forget that you have one.

So you'd advise people with voice problems to begin by looking inside themselves?

Confronting your possible psychological problems that might contribute to a bodily malfunction is a first step. But there are many steps to climb afterward, toward healing. And there are many ways to heal. I had two operations on each vocal cord. I guess the good news is I don't have more than two vocal cords!

Dr. Elisabeth Fresnel

Dr. Elisabeth Fresnel is the Paris specialist who discovered the pseudo-cyst and polyp on Natalie Dessay, her patient for ten years. Fresnel is a phoniatrician—her specialty is phoniatrics, which covers communications (voice, words, language, hearing), though she works mainly on the voice. She has treated all kinds of singers, from opera to jazz. She is not a surgeon, but she works with the one who operated on Natalie Dessay. She saw the singer intensively before the first operation, then before, during, and, especially, after the second operation.

What happened exactly? She told you she "felt something"?

She couldn't sing right. When I saw her, she was having real vocal difficulties. She was singing a lot—her agenda was absolutely crazy.

Was she singing too much, or singing the wrong roles, or poorly managing her time?

I don't think it was a technical problem. The two operations showed benign lesions on the vocal cords, the sort of thing that can happen to anyone anytime—even to someone with perfectly good technique. I think the fact she sang a lot, all the time, wasn't really wise. She did too much and accepted too many things. But she's conscious of this and now takes on less work. She still sings a lot, but more reasonably.

Certainly you've seen other artists who sing every day.

Yes, but she was singing a *huge* amount. That's not unique to Natalie Dessay. It's a complicated business. The period of rehearsals before an opera premiere gets shorter all the time. People at her level travel enormously, they take airplanes constantly. That means dry air onboard and jet lag. They arrive at their destinations and begin four or five rehearsals right away. Roles are chosen with their voice in mind, so usually mistakes aren't made of this type. But they have to manage their family lives, too. They are caught up in a whirlwind and don't always have time to stop, rest, or readjust. They have to always be the best. I often say of opera singers that they aren't CDs you put in a machine, make them sing the same aria forty-five times, night and day, and expect them to always do it perfectly. They have the right to be tired, to have slept badly, to have a cold or a sick child. They are human beings, after all.

What happened to Natalie Dessay isn't that out of the ordinary, then?

No, it's something that occurs. What's out of the ordinary is she was the first to talk about it. She said openly that she had vocal-cord problems and was operated on. Vocal-cord cysts on singers isn't a pathology I see every day, fortunately, but it's not all that rare. It has absolutely nothing to do with any technical flaw. But when it happens, vocalists' professional demands are such that they will continue to sing with that pathology. So everything gets worse, of course. And it will start to affect the other vocal cord.

How did you examine her?

There are different ways to scan the larynx. Ear-nose-and-throat specialists usually use a nasal fibroscopy which descends through the nose down into the throat over the larynx. It must be very small, since you can't slip anything big through the nose, which means you don't get a really good image of the vocal cords. Phoniatricians generally use more rigid optical devices. I have many of them, and they are all connected to an exterior camera and light source. There are several angles; I prefer ninety degrees, above the tongue. It doesn't touch the throat and doesn't descend any farther. The patient must keep the mouth open and the tongue out. So obviously you can't examine anyone who is singing. You can while they are doing vocalises, but that's about all. This gives the best view of the vocal cords. It lets you see how they vibrate, open, and close. You can see if anything's wrong.

She spoke of a "pseudocyst" and a polyp.

The first time we examined her we saw a pathology on her vocal cords which plainly was something for surgery. It was amplified by the fact she continued singing a lot with it. After a certain time the body has to compensate. It starts putting into practice mechanisms which are not the right ones but which are compensatory. These mechanisms didn't create the lesion in the first place, but the lesion is such that if you continue working, you aggravate it. That's why there's always some rehabilitation with opera singers. You have to stop the mechanisms they've put in place. Often they've been in this situation for some time when you first see them, and it starts to become settled. But Natalie also used her speaking voice very badly.

How do you mean, "She used her speaking voice badly"?

She didn't stand or hold herself right. She didn't use her speaking voice properly. It wasn't of good quality. When you sing you must have an absolutely flawless technique: breath, posture, articulation, all must be perfect. The spoken voice is less demanding, but that's still no reason to do just anything with it. Natalie's all right now; she's made a lot of progress.

How big a problem is this?

It's relatively common among singers. Their breathing isn't good, the voice is veiled or not at the right height—it can manifest itself in different ways. They have a technically magnificent singing voice but a speaking voice that isn't right. They have to work on their speaking voices, too, because even if you're a great singer, at the end of the day you talk more than you sing.

It seems amazing that someone who spends years training the voice to sing would overlook this.

It's strange, but quite frequent. We rehabilitate many professional singers' speaking voices.

Natalie talked of psychological problems that might have caused her cyst and polyp.

She believes that, yes.

You don't?

I think it's hard to really say. I don't think her problem was psychosomatic, but organic. There might have been factors that helped. One develops an illness more easily when one is not right for other reasons, that's for sure. But it's not completely psychosomatic in the sense that one can't objectively find something.

She says openly that she was having a hard time managing her family life.

I know. I don't totally agree with her [*laughs*].

You believe her body created something abnormal?

No, there was a real vocal pathology. One that wasn't dysfunctional, as we say in the jargon. That wasn't Natalie's case. She had a real organic pathology, not a dysfunctional one.

What's a nodule?

A nodule is a lesion the body creates because you force the cords. Nodules on the vocal cords is a frequent pathology. You use the voice so badly that the cords bang together violently instead of gently. Each time you do this it causes them to thicken. It can come from singing and speaking. A man's voice, on average, has a median of one hundred hertz. This means a man opens and closes his vocal cords one hundred times a second. For a woman, it's two hundred. Women have higher voices than men. If one hundred or two hundred times a second you clash the cords together, there comes a moment when automatically they start to thicken.

It's something the body produces itself?

Yes, because you don't know how to use your cords properly. That's what we call a dysfunctional pathology. It's something we see in children very often. Kids cry at school, on the playground. A nodule is always due to poor use of the voice, and this creates a lesion. In principle, you don't even operate; you simply rehabilitate the person with a good technique so they start using their voice correctly, and it disappears—unless it's very old. But rehabilitation normally cures it: good habits, good technique.

And polyps?

Polyps are bigger, and form on one side only. Of course, if not treated, in time you'll produce something on the opposite vocal cord: it'll be a nodule, but a reaction to the polyp. One produces the other.

And a cyst?

Cysts and pseudocysts are organic lesions. They are all benign, but you're simply unlucky. They can happen to anyone anytime.

Why "pseudocyst"?

Because it's not a real one. The real cyst is in the thickness of the vocal cord itself. A pseudocyst appears between the mucosa and the ligament. It swells up the mucosa and develops more often on the edge of the vocal cord. Again, all these are benign lesions.

Natalie Dessay had something on both vocal cords.

We thought one was a reaction to the other, which is why we operated only on one, assuming the other would disappear once the first was removed. But the second was another lesion. It was just bad luck. She continued to feel something funny. Natalie is very demanding and asks a lot from herself. She was very upset. So we removed the second thing.

Why so long between operations?

It's something we do all the time. Operating on both cords of a top singer like Natalie is a long process. You have a lengthy recovery period, you have to find, then retrain your singing voice. We were convinced that one was a reaction to the other. And it shrank a bit at first, but afterward kept growing. She sang very well but was still a bit bothered. Her profession and vocal demands made it plain she couldn't continue with it.

How did you plan her postoperative phase?

There's a total program that accompanies surgery. Surgery alone is not enough. We decide what we're going to do, when to do it, and what engagements the singer must cancel. Remember, singers are often booked something like five years in advance. You have to work on all aspects of the voice. It takes time.

How much time?

In our procedure, patients work for two months with a team, then start singing again. But they have to rework their entire vocal technique, because they were working in bad conditions before, which led to an operation. But by then, they've had a long rest. When operating on singers, it's wise to tell them they'll have to wait from four to six months before going onstage again. That's the physical side. There's also the psychological.

Natalie told me that in a month she was physically cured and ready to sing, but psychologically it took longer.

She couldn't sing for *two* months. When we operate, we give patients a sheet of paper with orders on it. We explain that for six days, they must not speak at all. Total silence for the vocal cords. We tell them to write everything down on a slate. For six days, nothing.

What if I have to cough?

Better not to. Coughing is very traumatizing, with its huge pressure of air on the cords.

Sneezing?

No. If coughing persists, I'll prescribe a treatment, which I don't usually, but we must stop it, otherwise the scarring won't be right. Six days of total silence. This is why it's never emergency surgery. We explain to patients that they must organize everything, particularly if they have children, so they can be comfortable in a situation where they don't have to talk. After a week, the surgeon and I examine the patient again, and then you can speak normally—but not for too long. Because of Natalie, we added another rule: no whistling.

Why was that?

She whistled the day of the operation! I explained everything to her, but didn't think she would whistle! She drove home after the operation, and a few hours later I had the person who accompanied her on the phone—not Natalie, because she couldn't talk—and I heard whistling! I said, "Who's whistling? Is that Natalie? Tell her to stop right now!" So we added this rule.

Why no whistling?

It also creates pressure and movement in the larynx.

Would I be allowed to talk on the telephone?

No, except for very short periods. The telephone forces the voice, especially mobile phones and, in particular, mobile phones in the street or where there's lots of noise. For the first six days, nothing; between six days and one month, no singing, no projecting the voice—no speaking loudly or call-ing anybody—and the telephone as little as possible.

How about eating, swallowing?

No problem. When you swallow, it takes another path. That's why people who say honey is good for the vocal cords don't know what they're talking about. What you swallow goes nowhere near the vocal cords.

So I can start using my voice properly after one month?

After the first month you can *project* your voice and telephone. Between one and two months after the operation, you can't sing. This is complicated with singers, since they want to test their voices to see what they're capable of. Natalie was obedient for the most part. When I saw her after two months, she had tested her voice, of course. She told me, proudly, "I found my high F!" I roared back, "What!?" And she said, "Well, I just sang three seconds." But they're all like that! They can't stop themselves from making sure it's still there.

Is it important to know music to treat opera singers?

You have to know what singing is. You have to understand what their lives are like. You need a minimum of musical education to understand the pro-fessional demands involved in order to help them. I studied piano, singing, and acting to learn how to work with these people. These aspects all come into play, which is why I have a team of voice coaches and psychologists. The voice is a precise mechanism, but it's also the reflection of the person's psychological state. The voice says things that words don't. Sometimes words say the opposite. You can hear fatigue, one's state of nutrition, hydration—any number of things. You have to know how to manage all that. It's not easy working with demanding artists. Natalie is wonderful. Once she under-stood, she was fine.

© Leonardo Vordoni

Joyce DiDonato,
or the wider connection

The young Yankee diva is standing outside a dressing room with, strangely, "Pierre Boulez" marked on the door. Joyce DiDonato has big blue-gray eyes, and bright red lipstick is shining out of a layer of makeup. Dressed all in gray with high black boots and hair pulled back in a ponytail, she ushers you inside the dressing room, which stands empty except for her yellow purse and pale blue scarf. In their company, we spend a dazzling seventy minutes.

DiDonato is energetic, dynamic, very human and open about herself, and a good talker—she wanted to be a teacher and would no doubt have been a good one. Articulate on opera, singing, and many other things. Eloquent on voice and on emotions. She will discuss the power of music, and the greater, perhaps cosmic, connection it suggests. You get the feeling she is a happy person. And she is a dramatic communicator, though we're offstage. Her voice drops to a whisper to make a point, and you lean forward. Note how she jumps through the third question to go directly to the story she wants to tell. Her face lights up like the moon when asked about bel canto singing. At one instant, seated on the couch opposite, she lifts both legs and crosses them under her, lotus-style. Coincidentally, it was at this moment that she spoke about the ultimate "bigger" or cosmic connection music has.

She's also a good listener. During the interview and after, you feel there has been an exchange, that she has played along but given of herself. She answers the questions and is informative. You come away thinking you've learned something. The teacher again.

She has had three interviews this day at Paris's Opéra Bastille. In town for a run of I Capuleti e I Montecchi *(Bellini), the mezzo-soprano began by saying she was born in a suburb of Kansas City, Kansas, "in your typical ranch house, middle-class, a block away from my Catholic Church and school where I went from kindergarten through eighth grade. Right up the street from the shopping mall. I mean, this is Americana! I went to college in Wichita, in the middle of nowhere. Same as Sam Ramey."*

Did you start singing in church?

[*Nods yes*] My dad was the choir director up the road [*laughs*]. A real choral, liturgical man: Byrd, Palestrina, Bach. That was my training.

Getting into the Young Artist program at the Houston Opera Studio was an early break. How old were you?

I went in when I was twenty-six and left when I was twenty-eight. That's ten years ago.

Is that late—twenty-six?

Yeah. And in my first voice lesson, the teacher said, "You're smart, you're musical, you have talent, but there's no future in the way you're singing." I was mortified, but also just old enough to trust he was right. I wasn't telling anybody, but I'd go up for the high notes, cross my fingers, and say, "Oh, God, please work!" He said, "You've got about five years left. You're singing on youth and muscle. That's only going to last so long."

Was he right?

I *knew* he was. So it took two years of me tearing my hair out, crying, "Why won't they cast me in anything?" Thank God they didn't. Because it gave me time to cocoon away and figure out what I was doing. I took a year to strip away everything. I was like iron [*raps the metal table, which resounds, loud but tinny*] here [*touches her throat*]. Then it took a year to start building the technique. Then a third year of starting to *trust* the work we had done—and that was the hardest part.

You say you were singing on "youth and muscle." What does that mean?

I had a tremendous amount of tongue and jaw tension. He would stick his thumb up into the middle of my jaw, here [*pokes her thumb under her chin*], and it was not malleable at all. Like iron. I was using my tongue and jaw muscles to squeeze the sound out.

What should you have been doing?

The jaw and tongue should have been totally relaxed, with everything coming from the breath. We are a wind instrument, basically. It's like a clarinetist trying to squeeze the sound through the reed with only their lips, rather than moving the breath through it. You can get away with that for a while because when you're young, your muscles withstand a lot of tension. It's like an athlete who never quite gets the fundamentals but can sprint fast for a short time because they're young. So I learned to use the breath flow, rather than squeezing out the sound.

How did you get on the wrong path?

Trying to sound like an opera singer, I think.

Nobody told you?

People were convinced by the sound I was making. You can create a lot of good sound by going "aaahhh!"—really forcing it out. Plus, I was musical, and I acted okay. So they saw the final product without actually analyzing what was happening. I got by with it for a while.

And you didn't confess to anyone?

You don't dare tell anybody, "I'm not sure what I'm doing"—you act like you know! There's also a physiological phenomenon for singers, which takes a while to figure out: what you're hearing is not what the public hears. You hear yourself on tape, and the sound is different from the resonance you hear in your head. So, early on, it's a natural tendency to sing so that you sound good *to yourself*. Using this kind of "squeezing" technique, I sounded big, there was a lot of *ping* in my sound—meaning it's going to travel across an orchestra to generate a lot of buzzy sound. But it wasn't always pretty! [*Laughs*]

You put yourself on this wrong road, based on ideas you had?

Absolutely. You want it so badly, and you see other people winning competitions or getting cast, and you think, "I've got to work harder." So you do, but in the wrong way. It's good enough that people buy it, for a while. But finally I had somebody say, "You're getting away with it now, but in five years you're going to be done." He really had the ears for it. Most people were saying, "Sounds good! It's loud! Your voice has a lot of resonance."

Who was saying that? Obviously not good judges.

Well, you do a competition and come in third place, and that's encouraging!

But that means people who judge competitions aren't always qualified.

That's a complicated issue, because what exactly are they judging in a competition? Are they judging what they hear in that moment? Are they judging potential? Are they saying, "There are problems, but she was the best one *that day*"? To have all your ducks lined up, in this business, at twenty-three or twenty-four is rare. The phenomenon today is that there are a lot of people who can produce something really exciting on youth and muscle alone. But does that mean they know what they're doing? What we're trying to do requires a lot of different elements merging together. I don't think it happens at twenty-six. It happens with age. The body has to mature. We have to master languages. We have to master artistry. There's a lot required of other professions; I'm not trying to single us out. But the top female singers today—Renée Fleming, Natalie Dessay—have built careers slowly and organically.

Everyone says singers get pushed too fast.

It's rare that there will be a long-term career if they are. It's *imperative* that we be in a culture that nurtures taking your time and building a career. Because to sing these characters that require so much emotion and maturity and *profound* comprehension of music and soul and heart, I want somebody that's older and has lived a life and knows what they're talking about, to give that to me when I pay three hundred dollars for a ticket. I want an ease of singing, and maturity: an artist onstage who knows who they are—who's not trying to impress the audience: "I'm good, right?" like some people do. We need to take our time. We need to figure out who we are.

Haven't singers always been pushed?

It's more obvious now, because we've got YouTube, glossy spreads in *Vogue*, things like that. It's more in-your-face. But you can't tell me the age of the diva was born ten years ago! We didn't invent this because there's high-definition TV. There's always been a hunger for glamour from the diva. But there's also been hunger for being moved and touched. We're in a society where there's instant gratification, demand for sexy teeth, tits, and ass. We should never underestimate the power of what we're doing. And the need—

especially in today's technological world, where everybody's separated—to never get away from the soul that's in this music and the power to reach people.

Can you, when you're listening to a young singer, hear what that person heard when you were twenty-six?

Yes, because I take on the physicality of that singer. If I'm watching a singer doing this [*tilts her head to one side*], I start to go [*tilts her head again*] myself. I feel it. And think, "Oh, no! That hurts!" I'm empathetic because I've been through it. I'm not a voice teacher; I don't have the skill to identify physiologically what's happening, the larynx is "this" or "that." But I can tell when a sound is free and when it's not. And more often than not, the sound falls into the second category! [*Laughs*]

Is there any way I could tell? Something you could tell me to listen for? "That was a true sound." Or must I have gone through it myself?

I'm not sure, but I do think the lay person responds. I love athletics. When I watch golf, I don't have to be an expert to see the difference between Tiger Woods and somebody who's ninety-ninth on the Pro Tour. Being ninety-ninth is great. You have a high level of skill. But there's that ease and effortlessness with Tiger. I wouldn't know how to say Tiger Woods is effortless because "his chip shot is blah-blah-blah"—but I sense it. I get that, as a lay person simply because it looks so *sweet* when he swings. So I think people in the audience get it when a singer is at ease physically. They may not know tonally what's happening, but they get the sense, like "Wow."

That's what you want.

Yeah. I think it puts the watcher at ease. If you see somebody doing something tense, you take it on. I think the audience responds when it's right.

In the performance of I Capuleti *I saw, one of the principals was ill. Does that create any problems for you?*

It depends on who's coming in. I didn't get much rehearsal time with Patrizia [Ciofi, who replaced a pregnant Anna Netrebko, singing Giulietta to DiDonato's Romeo], but we've sung together a couple times onstage and done recordings. I know her. She's a committed actress. She comes on, and she's responding to me. The general public has no idea—and it's probably good they don't know—how courageous and frightening it is to come into a production like that. You're replacing a superstar, you've had no time on the stage, you've had no time with the orchestra, no time in the costume. You're feeling your way, just trying to remember what comes next. And you're trying to remember your words. And where am I supposed to go? And, oh, wait, I'm not in the light, so where do you find the light? And, oh, at the same time, let me try and be a credible fifteen-year-old who's singing gloriously. It's a lot of balls in the air you're trying to juggle. But Patrizia is a wonderful artist. She was committed to telling the story. So that was easy—and exciting, because I didn't know what she was going to do next. It's not like we're doing [*in a robot voice*], "And here's where you go, like this. And this is where I go, like that." There was nothing canned; it was very spontaneous. I think that's something the audience responds to, because they feel [*sharp intake of breath*], "He's going to kill himself! Oh, no!" And maybe they stop taking for granted that they know the story for a minute, and get caught up in it. If you're with a singer, however, who's not generous and good [*laughs*] and doesn't respond, it would be a nightmare.

Is it a big issue, singing when you're lying down, as you did at the end of act 2? Does that make it harder?

It can. You have to have a strong technique. There is a standard position, and singers get made fun of for it: you go to the front of the stage, and plant yourself. They call it "park and bark" in the industry [*laughs*]. There's a very physical component to what we do, so there's something organic and wonderful about planting yourself firmly into the ground and going for it. A voice teacher would say, "Imagine your legs are tree trunks, and the roots are going ten feet into the ground." That way, you feel connected to your body, which means hopefully connected to the breath. Because the breath is the only thing that puts your sound, and your words, out three thousand seats, to the back of the theater. Without breath, you're done. So sometimes singers feel if you're lying down, you miss that physical connection. I don't think it's necessary, but there's something comforting about feeling like I'm rooted in my body 100 percent.

How about singing in other positions?

If I'm hanging upside-down, that's bad. Suspended in the air it's hard to feel like you've got your feet under you. I've done it flying on a platform above the stage, and that's hard. But lying down? No, because I can still connect.

Do you enjoy singing bel canto?

[*Her face absolutely lights up*] Yeah! [*Laughs*]

I'm going to have to put "her face lights up" here.

[*Laughs*] It's a selfish thing, but with these composers, it was all about the voice. They loved their singers. It's a *gift* to do this. I love singing Strauss. I did my first *Rosenkavalier* a year ago. But in a four-hour evening you get about fifteen minutes of that. The rest is interjectory, "ba-da-da-da-dum," more acting; you become part of the texture of the orchestra, which is a central character all to itself. So when you finally get to the trio at the end, it's a big reward that you get to stand there and sing these arching lines. Romeo is like two and one-half hours of that kind of singing. It's all legato and long lines, and you get to just hang up there. Actually, it's all about the emotion. But the emotion is transmitted through the voice. As a singer, it's incredibly gratifying to know that the composer trusted the voice to give the emotion. And, yes, I love it! [*Laughs*]

Can you describe your voice?

No, because I don't hear what you hear. I could say I love stretching my voice, love asking a lot of it, love taking it to the extremes, and love to use it to convey emotion, text, and the story of these things. But is it caramel, gold, or silver? I don't know.

Is that why you like to sing opera? To convey emotion, text, and stories?

I may be particular in this, but I'm not a singer who loves to go to opera. It's too often work for me. But I love to be *in it*, to project it from the inside out. That's what attracted me. I didn't hear an opera and say, "I can't wait to do that some day!" I thought, "Eh, I don't know . . . They're going waou, waou, waou!" It's when I got onstage and actually did it that I was hooked. Because it's such a challenge. I mean, you have to be—well, there are exceptions—but you have to be a strong intellect. To dissect musically what's happening. And textually. You have to have languages; you have to have musical skill.

Most people, including yourself, note how important emotions are, and many see opera as an emotional experience, but now you're talking about the intellectual skills you need.

To get to that emotion, you have to do a lot of groundwork. It's a thrilling sensation, physically and physiologically, to sing. Going back to the tree roots and tree trunk, I feel like there's this force that goes through me: it's the breath. To be able to sail over an orchestra and have three thousand people hear you—unfiltered—that's viscerally an exciting thing. Then intellectually, it requires so much. I'm always stimulated. I pull out a French piece, then a German piece, then Handel, Bellini. It's exciting to figure out what Handel was intending, and then trying to go into a dense score like Strauss. It takes a lot of work to musically make sense of what Strauss wanted. Then you get it and think, "Of course!"

How hard is it to sing different composers, one after the other? You sometimes do several new roles in a single year.

For me, it's all music. Each composer has a slightly different language. You have to know the style and what's expected. But these composers knew what they were doing. They gave you a great blueprint on the page. So I go to the blueprint, and that tells me I don't have to put *my interpretation* on top of it so much. It's not so complicated. I play the piano. So I sit at the piano and go through the score, reading that blueprint.

On your own?

Yeah, that's how I feel I can come to ownership of the role, if I try and figure it out first. Then I'll work with the conductor. It requires everything musical in me to do this. But I also think there's a spiritual element to what we're doing, too.

Let's talk about that.

I don't think you can hear the vocal lines, of *I Capuleti*, for example, and think it's just random. That it's not . . . [*pauses*] . . . hinting at something bigger than ourselves. I'm not sure what any of that means, though.

You talked about breath coming up from somewhere, connecting to something, moving through you.

[*Whispers*] Yeah. Absolutely. To think that one human being put this all down on paper? Just scribbled down some little black notes? And then, here we are, decades, *centuries* later: an orchestra of eighty, a cast of five, chorus of I don't know how many, one conductor. And it takes all of us to breathe life into those little black notes that this one guy wrote down. Yeah, some of it he recycled, and some of it, was it inspired or not? He was trying to put food on the table, he was trying to be a star. Who cares? Somehow, in those three hours, we all gather our forces and put this out there. Then it hits one little old lady in the back, and she goes [*draws a finger down her cheek to indicate tears*]. I don't know what it is. I don't profess to know. But I do know that it's bigger than myself, bigger than all of us.

Have you ever come close to losing control over your emotions onstage?

Oh, yeah! [*Laughs*] This is why I'm convinced it's bigger than myself. I was very close to my father. He passed away eighteen months ago, after a rough battle in the hospital. He was the first person I was close to that I lost, that I saw die. And the next thing I had to do was come here to Paris and sing *Idomeneo*. I sang the son, Idamante, and he has a big aria, which says, "I've just lost my father." And I thought, "Are you kidding me? This is my first role back?" Then, six months later, I lost my mom. And the role I had to do was Octavian, whose grief isn't obvious, like *Idomeneo*, but is all about time, and things changing and moving on. I never, *ever* would have agreed to do those two shows if I had known what I was going to go through personally. But I couldn't have asked for better therapeutic experiences. All the "stuff" that moves through you when you sing . . . [*thinks*] . . . you can't help but go there. It was one of the most cleansing things I could have asked for. I was lucky to be forced to, literally, regurgitate these emotions. So I had to calculate what I was doing, had to step back a little. I knew I couldn't *really* go there in performance, so I let myself do that in rehearsal, crying if I had to.

And everyone said, "Get a grip."

No, not at all.

They knew your story?

I walked into rehearsal, and everybody gave me a hug. I came late; they knew why. I work with the best people in the world that are immensely supportive. We all know how hard what we do is, this singer's life. In particular, Ramon Vargas—the father, Idomeneo—he lost a son, years ago, when he was quite young, I think. So here we are, I've just lost *my* father. There's a complicity, so there's security; you know what I'm going through, so it's okay if I don't make it. It's okay if I break, because you've got my back.

Do you think this connection had something to do with that particular composer—Mozart, in this case? Do you feel it in some music more than others?

[*Whispers*] Oh, yeah. There's a purity about Mozart, and Bach. There's something—do you call it "divine"? I hesitate to confine it by putting a word on it. There's a purity there that's cleansing. Doing *Idomeneo* after my dad

was a gift. Hardest thing I've ever done. If you told me the day of his funeral, or while he was in the hospital, that I was going to have to do that, I
would have said, "Impossible. I can't." I think any other composer . . . if I
had to do Rossini, or something, well . . . [*whispers*] *but it was Mozart*. I do
think there's some connection there. I don't have this all worked out and
don't think I need to, but I do think music connects to something.

How do you feel about audiences?

I'd like them to get involved. You know, it's just opera. You don't have to be
afraid to clap in the wrong spot. We want people to get swept away; I wish
the barrier would break down more.

How does one do that?

We're doing our job by trying to make it as believable as possible. I want
people to not have to work too hard to suspend their belief. The less work
they have to do to experience the emotions and the story, the better.

That's while you're onstage?

Yeah.

And it's not pandering?

No. Pandering and dumbing-down is the *worst* thing we can do. I trust the
genius of this work. I trust that it has to be done in the best way. And I trust
that it won't be for everybody. And that's okay. I don't think we have to sell
it to everybody. It's never been an art form for everyone, so it's okay if you
don't get it, but I think you should give it a shot.

*What does "trying to make it as believable as possible" translate into on-
stage? Big, telegraphed movements?*

No, sometimes less movement is stronger. When I say, "don't dumb it
down" I mean don't take away the complexity of these stories. Yes, sometimes the plots are stupid—*Sonnambula, Puritani*—but the emotions, the
psychological journey of these characters, is not. Don't dumb that down.
These stories have been around three hundred years. Look at *Poppea*. That
struggle and thirst for power—are you telling me that's not applicable
today? It's more applicable than any reality television show. These are things
that make you think. Please don't take away how complex it is. Maybe some
people don't want to be challenged. They come to an opera on Thursday

night, they've had a long week at work, okay. On the other hand, if you really engage them, like great theater, they're going to go, "Ah! [*Exhales slowly*] This is great." That's what I want. I want people to go, "Ah! Wow!" [*Exhales slowly again*] I don't know how you'd write that! [*Laughs*]

What else would break down the barrier?

Getting people when they're young. Before these preconceptions and prejudices form. "Opera's boring." Really? There's incest, there's rape, there's torture, there's killing. Boring? Really? I can't *tell* some of these stories to my nieces and nephews, because they're not old enough! One of the biggest favors people can do, before they come to the opera, is a bit of study. "Oh, who has time?" Well, it's an investment. If you make the investment, the payoff is big. Come, and have read the story or the synopsis, so at least you're not trying to decipher too much, because there's a lot to process when you sit in the theater. Do a bit of work. Do you have to listen to it ahead of time? Maybe. Maybe it's better to experience it spontaneously.

Here are some things I saw on your Web site: "Anyone who doubts that trust is no longer bankable today need only look at a musical rehearsal of strangers: it's ALL about trust. And that's only us players on the stage—it's not even considering the audience, which functions on a different level of trust and surrender! The stage teaches." What does that mean?

That ties in with *Idomeneo*. To be effective as a performer, you have to make yourself vulnerable. If you're defensive, you can get away with it for a while on the opera stage, because there's a grandness to it. But to really touch people, you have to open yourself. That means knocking down the wall, not allowing yourself to stay behind a façade even though you're in character. It makes the voice more appealing and makes your performance more honest. At least those are the kind of performances I respond to. But to do that, you have to be willing to take a risk. You have a chance to look stupid; you might crack on a high note. You might run out of breath or forget the words. You might try something that looks really goofy the first time. But if you're working with a cast where they say, "That's okay, let's try it, see what happens," it involves trust. You have to trust the orchestra to play the right notes. Most of the time, they do. I'm trusting the conductor's going to be there; if I'm in trouble, he's going to get me out of it. It's laying yourself open. You trust the audience that, even if I make a mistake, you're going to be with me. It's a cool sensation when it happens.

Can you give an example of if you're in trouble, how the conductor can get you out of it?

Maybe one night your breath isn't underneath you, or you start to run out of breath or need the phrase to move a bit faster. Or it's a particularly good night, and you hold this one note a little bit longer, and he's going to wait. He's listening.

This also from the Web site: you're talking about recording. "Sadly I do not have a pair of 'ears' out in the theater that knows my voice, knows my limits. It's up to me and my ears, and if I can filter out EVERYTHING I hear that is BAD (which on first listen is EVERY SINGLE NOTE), I'll make rational choices and, hopefully, improvements!" What are you saying?

That says a lot, too, about how you can't trust what you hear when you're singing because it's not the final product. As I'm singing, I'm the only one that hears this sound. What everyone else hears is different. Also, on a recording you're thinking about a lot of other things, and may not notice that you're out of tune, or trying to go for a certain effect, and think you're doing it enough, but they go, "Actually, it sounded sort of halfway." Or you say, "I like this effect, I'm going to go for it." And they say, "It's too much, too exaggerated." Performing via a microphone onto a tape is different than what a live theater is going to get. It's a different venue, a different medium. You need somebody out there to tell you what the actual result is. My husband [Leonardo Vordoni] is a conductor and quite good about telling me if I need more or less, if something's good or bad.

How do you manage recordings, then?

I record a take and listen immediately. Of course, I want it to be perfect. Most singers are perfectionists. It's very annoying. Because the only thing that jumps out at me is, "I missed that." So you have to be good to yourself, and say, "Wait. Don't overreact. What's actually happening?" It's difficult to judge your own work, because a lot of different dialogues happen in your mind. You hear yourself with a lot of history [*laughs*]. I could be hearing this, but I'm really hearing my "squeezed" voice from fifteen years ago.

Is there an experience which has marked you, which you remember as being fundamental to the musician you became?

Two things. First of all, my father. I was a music-education major in Wichita and did my student teaching, for a semester, mornings at a high school and afternoons at a grade school.

You wanted to teach music?

Yeah, to be a choral music teacher, until I was about twenty-two. My student teaching was in low-income schools. One day, a first-grader was acting out, really disturbing the class as I was trying to teach "Row, Row, Row Your Boat" or something. I was about to yell at her, and the teacher grabbed my arm and said, "Let it go." Well, this little girl, seven years old, it turns out, was being sexually abused. Her mother was a prostitute and a crack addict. Just so disturbing. And I was sitting there naively thinking, "Music can change the world." I was torn, because I was performing operas at school and loved it and was thinking I really wanted to be an opera singer. But here, during the day, I thought, "I have to do this. These kids need real guidance. Their mothers are prostitutes and crack addicts." And I told my dad, "I don't know what to do. It seems selfish to be an opera singer when the world needs teachers." And my dad, bless him, said, "Joyce, don't think there's only one way to teach. That there's only one way to touch people, educate them, and reach out to them." And that was the key. That was the license I needed to give myself permission to do this without guilt. I don't have any doubt now that I'm where I'm supposed to be. And it's not an arbitrary, indulgent career I'm doing. I feel it's important. My dad's voice freed me.

What was the other experience?

That was driven home after 9/11. I thought, "How can I be an opera singer when the world is crumbling?" But people turn to music to understand, to grieve. I believe more than ever in the power of music, in the necessity of it. Is it necessary, like searching for a cause for cancer? No, but I think in our human condition we need it. That's one reason I write on my Web site. I know young singers go there, and they're looking to learn. So I feel there's a purpose, beyond just singing pretty, to what I do.

You're singing Romeo, a pants part, or travesti role, in I Capuleti. *Anything special in your approach there?*

I don't think about it so much anymore and don't remember, when I first started doing my Cherubinos, if I analyzed physically what I was doing. For me, maybe the one thing I'm aware of, especially in these more virile, heroic pants roles, is that the movements are more brusque.

That's you, or the director?

It's how I think about it. They're more angular, move more quickly, as opposed to a softer, more curved performance as a girl. But it kind of comes naturally. Again, it goes back to the text. If you're a man singing, "I hate you and I'm going to kill you" the gesture follows organically. Also, I have to say my husband is a very romantic man. If I have to think about how I'm holding a girl, I just reverse roles with them. He's a good teacher in that regard.

How much interpretation is there in singing opera? How free are you to sing the notes the way you want?

Often it's a matter of opinion. I'll sing one phrase, and there will be five people: two experts, two lay persons, and an opera singer. They'll have five different opinions about what I did was right or wrong, or in taste, or too much "this" or not enough "that." One is basing it on how Callas did it forty years ago. One is just saying, "I like this." Another says, "No; in the letter we have from Rossini to Bellini, he writes . . ." Everybody has a different opinion. People say there are things a composer wrote in when he intended something specific to happen. Others say he knew the singer would do that anyway, so didn't write it, because it was *understood*. It's a wide topic.

It depends on what the work is?

Sure. Strauss, Massenet, Puccini wrote everything into their scores. Every portamento. There's a little retard over these two notes, and the third is in tempo. In Massenet, there's essentially no interpretation to make at all, because every little thing is written in. Bellini, much less so. This conductor [Evelino Pido] is quite good with Bellini. It's rare that any measure is exactly one, two, three, four. It goes one, two, threeee, four-ONE, twoooo, three-FOUR. However, he's not one to let you have too much indulgence in holding high notes. You want to do a big one, he says no. At the end of my first big scene, a lot of conductors, and a lot of the public, want to hear ba-dee-baaaaa-DA! He doesn't want that. Because it's not written *fermata*, he wants the music to go ba-de-ba-da. So you do that. That's his decision. It's certainly valid. But people in the audience go, "Why didn't you hold that last note?"

Is he doing what he should? Shouldn't he negotiate more?

What I want from a conductor is, first, to be inspired. But he's the final interpreter. He's the one who has to coordinate all the forces. The best conductors take the strengths of the singers, highlight what's good, camouflage what doesn't work, then hopefully you have a dialogue and find a convincing interpretation. Evelino has strong ideas, which I'm not opposed to, but at the same time, I have my ideas. In the duet with Giulietta, he wanted me to sing slowly. But I said, "I think he's very passionate. I think he really wants to drive home his point. Can we sing straight through?" He said, "Okay, let's do that." We discuss it, and you find a compromise, something that's hopefully cohesive.

Can you confess to anything about opera that you don't like?

I can't stand singers that make it all about high notes, that are indulgent and selfish performers. Everybody knows who those stereotypes are. Was that discreet? No! [*Laughs*] It's so unappealing, and opera can be so much more. I don't like opera when it's done poorly. Honestly, there's nothing more ridiculous. It gives every person in the world every reason in the world not to go. And it gives every foundation every reason to not fund it. I have such high expectations for myself, for my colleagues, and for the art form that I don't think it should ever be done less than excellently. It's possible to do it well a lot of the time. I don't think it's possible for it always to be magical. That's an element that's out of our control.

Is there anything about opera that has defeated you?

I . . . [*thinks*] . . . hmm . . . don't think so. I've certainly given better performances in my life than others, and there have been a few performances I didn't like. These have been very few, but it's been a chemistry onstage where there's been an element of "every man for himself." I don't know how to deal with that as a performer. I'm singing, and the other person is looking straight through me—no connection. I realize they don't care what I'm doing, they're waiting for their moment to sing. Then they step in front of me, and they're singing and could care less.

How often does this happen?

Not often, thankfully, but those are the times I feel defeated. Because there's nothing I can do. I feel like the only person onstage in this weird story, and like, "Hello!" To survive, you join the game, and do the same thing. On the other hand, one of the coolest compliments I ever got was Tuesday night. Anna [Netrebko] is six months pregnant [a reason she canceled certain performances in this run]. It makes my Romeo feel very virile! We did the death scene, and I'm holding her hand, and we finish, and the curtain comes down. We hugged each other. She says [*in a Russian accent*], "Joyce, I forgot to tell you. Don't look my stomach when you sing." I said, "God, I'm sorry!" I thought I was making her feel self-conscious. She said, "No, not for that. Baby kick crazy when you sing! I don't want you look my stomach, you start to laugh" [*laughs*].

Plácido Domingo,
or Olympics for the voice

In the hushed, half-lit theater, a young baritone has just finished a passion-ate Verdi piece and has dominated the stage with convincing acting. When the music fades, he is not greeted by any applause or encouragement. Si-lence surrounds him. The singer waits. The pianist shuffles his pages. Sec-onds pass before Plácido Domingo, seated ten rows back, in muted lighting and flanked by the jury members he has selected, thanks him politely. No one in the audience utters a word. The jury people study papers by dim theater lamps. Domingo alone speaks, and his voice, unamplified by a microphone, lends an intimate, even pious atmosphere to the proceedings. The maestro inquires if the singer has prepared a second number, a zarzu-ela aria. The exchange is minimal. The singer stands on a bare stage. Floor, backdrop, and piano are all black. It looks like a tough place to audition, and today twenty young hopefuls have to go through it. Clearly, what these candidates need, besides a good voice, is guts.

It's the semifinals of Operalia—the singing competition Domingo founded in 1983 to unearth international talent and help promising vocalists up one of life's most difficult career ladders.

All day, for four days, the maestro and his elite group watch as young singers file onto the stage, stand alone but for a pianist, and in formal con-certizing regalia, give their best effort. Twenty have already been weeded out. The survivors are in Day 3. In the balcony, video cameras held by family members, friends of the judges, other contestants, and guests record the event.

Operalia is in Valencia this year, and will apportion $175,000 to rising stars from Spain, France, Latvia, Mexico, and the United States. Its gala awards ceremony, featuring the competing finalists accompanied by an orchestra conducted by Domingo, will tomorrow open the maiden season of the new Palau de Les Arts Reina Sofia, part of the seaside town's futuristic City of Arts and Sciences. The whalelike opera house, with its white concrete curves designed by local architect Santiago Calatrava, stands with other shrines in the park—an aquarium, planetarium, iMax theater, and science museum—each standing in its own separate pool of clear water that reflects the blinding Mediterranean light.

Through Operalia, the Madrid-born tenor provides not only generous prize money but—more important—follow-up work and sometimes even contracts on the world's foremost stages. Operalia likewise gives the maestro—who cut his teeth in his parents' zarzuela (Spanish operetta) troupe before debuting in La Traviata in 1961 and who honors their memory by offering a zarzuela award—his chance to pass on his legacy as he contemplates life after five decades of singing.

Operalia is close to Domingo's heart, and this is what we're here to talk about. We begin with the contest but move on to other matters, just as personal.

Rehearsing, for instance. You'll hear him say he likes to create a "happy atmosphere" when working. It's the same for interviewing. He has a broad smile when we meet, and he is polite and very accessible—a gentleman. And everyone—I mean everyone—in the business says the same about him.

He's dressed in a blue jacket, open blue striped shirt, and blue trousers, and he is sporting a trimmed gray beard. He's a plain man in some ways who doesn't strike you as particularly intellectual or scholarly. He speaks slowly, his soft, sweet-sounding speaking voice uttering short phrases, one after the other, lovingly, each like an offer of rare flowers.

You have many wonderful singers at Operalia, every year. How do you choose who wins?

It's difficult to come to terms with how many you pick for the finals. This year was phenomenal. There are perhaps four people who are *right there.* But there are about fourteen others where the difference is one point between them. Three or four singers have the same amount of points. It's why we decided to go with twelve rather than ten finalists, and I think that's right.

You decide who votes, but don't vote yourself.

I pick the jury. The most important thing is to have theater directors.

Why is that important?

Because that guarantees they get immediately excited by the voices and start to contract them. Many of these judges have done a lot for the singers, right from the first time they heard them. Even without the final, many are already thinking of contracts—there are a few everybody wants to sign. This is a beautiful way of window-shopping for them. There are at least seven theaters represented among the jury, which means the singers have the chance to go to them. It's good to have jury members who are ex-singers, but ex-singers can't help me as much.

Why did you start Operalia?

Many contestants are people who have grown up with me, and I'm immensely proud of that. This is the whole idea of Operalia—to continue this chain of things. The year after they win, they are singing in Aix-en-Provence, Covent Garden, Bordeaux, all the theaters, because it's a guarantee.

They win a lot of prize money, too.

Most will have substantial prizes for support. The money is very important. This competition is like the Olympics for the voice. Because the singers come from different parts of the world. And unlike many contests, they don't have to worry about anything. Everything is arranged: we pay their trips, their hotels, everything. They arrive, and the only thing they have to do is sing. They have a memorable time, whether they win or not.

What do you look for during the competition?

The best thing, basically, is the quality of the voices. That's what we look for.

And how does that manifest itself?

One of the candidates might touch you more; simply the voice moves you more.

It sounds like rating them is a subjective, individual matter.

Yeah, but generally, everybody on the jury almost always reacts the same way. You see it by the points they give. If not unanimous, they are very close. I don't necessarily think exactly like all the jury, though I mostly do.

Is there ever any discrepancy among jury members?

I was wondering what was going to happen today, because it was close. We see how well they do in the semifinals, then put the points together, adding from the quarter-finals, then we decide. And it comes so close, it's amazing. Nobody suffers. We realize that either giving points for today or giving points for both days will come out exactly the same.

What else do you look for in contestants?

Another element that's important is charisma. Every day you hear important voices, but how many of them are going to make a career? It's the quality of the voice, but we also see if they have the *equipment* to do a career. Important also is their personality. It's important that they are believable. The way they express themselves. The way they appear in front of the public and in front of a jury. I have great admiration for them because I never sang in any competition in my life. I admire everybody who comes and takes a chance.

You did an apprenticeship. Do you think singers today have the opportunity to do that, or do they get pushed?

Singers today get pushed very quickly sometimes.

By impresarios or managers?

No, the fact is it's just the needs of the art. There are many more theaters, more companies today than there used to be. So more singers are needed. Many make it earlier; it's easier for them to arrive in the big theaters than it was for us in our time. But also they are exposed very early because the media coverage is so big. It's an advantage, but if something goes wrong, everybody knows it right away. Before, you would work in a theater, and maybe two thousand people knew what happened in that performance. Today, if something goes wrong, you are going to see it on the Internet in the next hour. This situation makes them very big immediately; the record companies start to work with them and for them, which is logical. But if it's easier today to arrive, the important thing, as always, is to maintain, to stay there. One has to drive them well. You have to be careful.

How do you do that? During the competition your relationship with them is quite short.

Yes, but I provide follow-up to the competition. I have a Young Artists Program both in Washington and in Los Angeles, where I'm the opera director, and I have just opened another in Valencia. Sometimes you want some of these singers in the Young Artists Program. I can invite them to cover or sing performances in these cities.

So you're not only looking for singers who are ready to have big contracts?

I look for singers who aren't ready, too. It could be an exceptional voice that is not quite ready; the person is so young, you say, "Let's have him or her." I like to bring them to my school. But I never like to take a person I see who is not enthusiastic about it [*grimaces*]. Or somebody who is not disciplined. Or somebody who is not punctual. Because there are so many other people that can take their places.

Are you talking about the winners, or do you include the losers?

The losers, too. I talk to everybody; I like to encourage them. One of the finalists this year is twenty-one. Another is twenty-two. We have a tenor who's twenty-five. They are absolutely ready, some of them. Others, you have to give them more work. But they can certainly do an aria as well as any professional—even better.

How much time would you say you spend on Operalia during the year?

I think, generally speaking, it's constant, because I'm always listening to voices, thinking about which ones might come. There's not a day in the year when I'm not working, thinking about Operalia. But of course you have to divide the time. I also have to think about Washington and Los Angeles.

Yes, you're pretty busy—singing, conducting, directing two theaters, not to mention recording. How often do you actually get to see them while they're in the Young Artists Program?

I have a lot of exchange time with them. When rehearsing, I listen to what's going on, I sit at the piano and correct. When I'm in Washington, for instance, if I'm rehearsing in one room, and hear a singer in the next room, I just go in. I stay fifteen or twenty minutes with them. I hear a rehearsal and say, "This one, this one, and that one—I want to see them tomorrow." I'm constantly working that way. At the moment, between singing, conducting, and being director of the theater, these duties don't give me all the time I want to be involved with them. But certainly I will, more and more. When I won't be singing, I'll be able to spend more time with them.

Do you think a major voice will come up, even without a competition?

Absolutely.

What major voices have you seen emerge through Operalia?

Even the first year, the winners were amazing. Nina Stemme, Kwangchul Youn. Then José Cura, Elizabeth Futral, Rolando Villazón, Giuseppe Filianoti, Joyce DiDonato. Recently we had two Russian sopranos who are going to be a sensation; they are already singing in Aix-en-Provence: Olga Peretyatko and Ekaterina Lekhina. Aquiles Machado, another tenor from Venezuela. Of the French singers, I have Stéphane Degout, a wonderful baritone, and Ludovic Tézier. Every year there are more. Two or three Chinese sopranos have been doing a phenomenal career. After Villazón, I had another two Mexican winners who are fabulous: Arturo Chacón and David Lomeli. So many extraordinary voices from Mexico and South America are coming.

Do you see any reason for that?

I don't know. It comes with time. We're also having singers from Russia, and all the east European countries, the ex-Soviet Union.

Is that because they couldn't get out to the West before?

Probably. Now they are coming out and blooming and flourishing.

How have you seen Operalia evolve over its decade and one-half of existence?

What is fascinating is seeing the advance programs in any opera magazine, and all the people that have been winners, or finalists, in Operalia. It's probably close to 80 percent. That evolution is wonderful. And it's growing. If anything, people have realized the importance of competition.

You have a French tenor as finalist this year, and mentioned two others from previous years. Are you finding more French singers these days?

That's an important point. French singers don't turn up so often. We have a good representation of them, and I'm always looking for them.

What else is different about this competition, compared with others?

There's a Public Prize. Different competitions have started using it, but I did it for the first time. The public can vote. They pick a winner, and the prize is ten thousand dollars. Sometimes the prize goes to someone who is not the overall winner, but because of the personality and the sympathy of the artist, the public likes him or her and they select them. Also, Operalia always takes place in a different part of the world. Every year, we change our venue.

The level seems to remain high, year after year.

Every year, it gets higher. Sometimes you have a year when things go down, but rarely.

Is this because contestants have become more professional or more savvy?

I'll tell you one thing: every year, they come more prepared. But it's one thing to be prepared and another to be in with the people. Singing is unlike any other career. You can study to be a great doctor or lawyer. The grades, testimonials, and tests will say you can make a great career. You can't say that with singing. You can have all the recognition; they can give you the awards and you can make all the lists, but the public is the one that gives or takes away. The public makes the personalities and the popular singers. Everybody wants to be popular, but it's the public who decides.

A question about repertoire. I wasn't here yesterday, but you had a heavy focus on Italian today. Is that deliberate?

It was a coincidence. We had some German repertoire yesterday. You see, today we were listening to only one aria per person. Or two, if they were competing in the zarzuela. We rule this way: They pick four arias. They say, "These are my arias." So they have the choice. For the first aria, they decide what they want to sing. The second aria, we ask them. And today, for the semifinals, it cannot be either of the arias they sang before. It must be a third, and we pick it. For the finals, from the time they enter the competition, they have told me what they want to sing. And unless we have a problem, we keep to that.

Do rating zarzuela and opera demand different skills from a judge?

I'll tell you what's happened. We have seven candidates and passed all seven today. Because it was a matter of passing four or passing six. Now Valencia is a city that that loves zarzuela. So we wanted to give at least six. But they were seven competing, so we kept them all, with one additional aria. For the finals, we'll either award two prizes or three or four.

Let's turn to a past winner, Roland Villazón, who took three Operalia prizes in 1999 (second place in the men's competition, plus the zarzuela and the public prizes). He has said some very nice things about you.

And so do I about him.

He calls you "maestro" but says you have never given him lessons or told him what to do with his voice.

He's right. I have never given him vocal advice. When we did a recording together [*Gitano*, zarzuela arias; Villazón sang, Domingo conducted], we talked. But I never like to give advice. Rolando is such a gifted artist, and he's just like a sponge. He takes, just like I used to do. I was learning from everything around me. This is the important thing—to be able to learn. You don't have to study the whole time. But you see things, you see the artists, you see what you have to do, you see what you don't have to do, which is also important. I give advice to people in my Young Artists Group because it's part of my obligation towards them. But not to Rolando.

He says in Spanish he still uses the polite usted *form with you, not the familiar* tu *form.*

Yeah. He still calls me *usted* [*smiles*] because it's kind of a respect thing, let's say, nothing else. It's because of the difference in our ages. But I consider him my artistic son. We do many things in a parallel way. The enthusiasm for the career, the love, the passion, the dedication we have is very similar.

And he says he admires your character, how you manage to stay cool all the time.

I agree, I really never get upset. With hardly anything. I enjoy my work. When I arrive in a theater I give the best I can. I not only try to give the best artistically, but when I'm out of my character I like to create an atmosphere that is a happy one, a comfortable one, for everybody. That's the way I like things, because it's something so positive. You realize you live so much of your life in the theater, so I like to make it a happy time. It makes things easier. You have to be serious and concentrated, but at the same time, light. The real moment comes at the time of the performance. Then there is a difference. You have to be believable in the character you play. People who don't know me see me being so normal in rehearsals, then when the moment of the performance comes, they say, "Wow, what's the matter? That's a different guy than we saw in rehearsals." Because I change: I'm the character. But when we're rehearsing, I'm available to everybody.

I'd like to talk about some moments in your career. In 1983, you had to sing Otello *in San Francisco with very little notice.*

Theater is such an anachronism. You go really to another century. The change has to be [*claps his hands*]—boom. That day, I was somebody who had arrived from Madrid the day before. I was starting rehearsals of *Lohengrin* at the Met. And they called me. "Plácido, the tenor for opening night in San Francisco tonight cannot sing. Can you do it?" I said, "Let me go to the piano." I vocalized, and said, "Yes, it'll work." I asked permission from the director of the Met. I took a private plane. There was going to be a big opening-night dinner after the opera. But they did the dinner before, because they had to delay the beginning of the opera. During the dinner they said, "Plácido now is flying over Chicago, now he's flying over Denver, now he's landed in San Francisco, now he's coming in a car." It was sensational. I hadn't done *Otello* for more than a year, so was reading my score on the flight. And I arrived, and I was *Otello*.

How hard was that, to go from Wagner to Verdi?

It was fine. At the Met once I sang exactly that—*Lohengrin* and *Otello*—and was conducting some *Bohèmes*, in the space of three weeks. My voice has had that flexibility. As long as I have my time to rest between performances, I feel fine.

You've sung Otello more than two hundred times.

I sang 225 performances. This includes three performances of Cassio.

How can you remember that?

[*Laughs*] I write them down.

You write them down?

[*Smiles*] I write down every performance I've done.

You're the only one who does that.

Probably. Many people count but like to say, "I've done this thousands of times." But to say "thousands of times" is a bit much. Certain baritones will sing Scarpia five hundred times. But maybe because I have so much repertoire, the operas I've done more are Cavaradossi in *Tosca*—I did 224 performances, but that includes two performances of Spoletta. And *Otello*, which I did 225 performances.

Is it as exciting every time you sing it?

This is the only way to do it. I don't know any other way.

Can I ask about Tosca? Think back to the live performance, in the real settings—Saint' Angelo, Palazzo Farnese—that you did for TV in 1992. In the first act, you came down the stairs, slipped, and fell. Forgive the question, but I'm just wondering. What happened? Was there a story there?

I just fell. I fell on my knees. The live performance was aired that way. But because you have to be protected in something like that, we recorded that *Tosca* a week before, at the same hours, the same things. So we had another one. We did two complete runnings: one day, then resting three days, then the real one. If you see the tape now, you don't see my fall. You were able to see it only in the live performance. We have to have that, because what happens, especially in Castel Saint' Angelo, if it rains? We keep the live feeling, but for the document, if there were little things like this, you repair it.

Do you listen to critics?

I have a lot of respect for critics when they have something constructive, something intelligent, to say. I don't like critics when they try to follow predecessors, the Bernard Shaw types, in being cruel, trying to be phony-smart. Yes, you can say things are not good; I don't mind. I might agree with them. That's one thing. But when they start to use cruelty—and I'm not talking about me, I'm talking generally—I have read a lot of them where they are enjoying themselves when they write. Sometimes also what you have is a review of eight columns, and seven columns—if it's an opera by Verdi—they are talking to you about Verdi, about Verdi's time, telling you about all the knowledge they have. Then, in the last column, they talk about the performance. And that's their review. If you're a writer, fine; write a book. But if you're a reviewer, concentrate on what you have to write. Even if it's negative.

I'm interested in the aspect of being a crossover: a singer-conductor. How many years have you been conducting?

Almost thirty years. Before, I used to do it very seldom, and now I do it very often.

What have you learned from being a singer onstage that you apply as a conductor to other singers onstage?

I think the conductor learns from the singer and the singer learns from the conductor. All my life I've been a musician and have studied my scores—since I was very young—from the orchestra scores. I will really know the colors of all the instruments, the weight of the orchestra. I take from one and think one gives to the other. So my experiences as a singer I certainly apply as a conductor. And my experiences as a conductor I take for the singers.

Can you give an example of something you learned as a singer that you apply as a conductor? Things you remember when you were onstage that you wished a conductor would have done, or things the conductor did that you now use when you're on the podium?

I've been very lucky, I'd say for 90 percent of my career, to work with great conductors. Karajan, Kleiber, Muti, Mehta, Barenboim, Solti, Böhm, Sinopoli, Levine, Kubelik, Abbado, Chailly. All the really great ones.

What did you learn from them?

I observed them. First of all, besides the technique, I was able to see what they saw in the scores that nobody else was able to see before. The thing is to see what is there. And I think, "I have known this work for so many years. And yet, there's something new there." In the shape of the phrasing. In the dynamic, on the extension of the phrase. On certain instruments, which all of a sudden comes like you've never heard it before. That was the most important thing. The second thing is I like to see how they appreciate, the *way* they appreciate the composers. And the way they blend with the singers. Who was just conducting and who was really making music, very deep. I started to analyze, and said, "If I were conducting, I wish I could accomplish what he's doing."

Some people say the problem with conductors today is that there is no shortage of talent, but, unlike the ones you mention, they haven't risen through the ranks, learned all the instruments, and can sing all the parts with the singers. Do you agree?

Yeah, that's coming more and more. Before, it used to be the tradition that most of the big symphonic conductors came from the opera theaters, so they knew opera. Karajan started in Ulm as a chorus *repetiteur*. Others are so gifted now that they are coming from the symphonic world.

Do you ever conduct by heart?

Very little. I can—I certainly know the repertoire. But I refuse, because every time I find something new in a score. And the singers have to have a reliable conductor. Because if you don't have the score, and you make a mistake—that's not fair. So you have to be careful. But there are people who are very gifted at that.

What's the most important thing to know about conducting?

I think the most important thing about conducting opera is to really feel the text, with the music and the mood of the moment, in the drama. You have to put those three things together in order to select the tempi. Because it depends what you are saying, in which moment, with the text, and with the music. You have to read it. Then you also have to see, as a conductor, what you have *under* that phrase. Where you can emphasize. How much more beautiful, for instance, is "Celeste Aida" when you have the reprise of the aria with the celli under you. You are singing, in both cases, legato. But the blending! One of my favorite instruments is the cello. So when I re-peat the phrase with the celli, I know that's the maximum legato I can offer. And I'm giving a lot more strength to the phrase than the first time I did it.

When you speak to the singers, and, as conductor, suggest, "Let's do it this way," do you think they listen to you more because you've been a singer?

Definitely. In the generation of singers today that I am conducting, a big percentage have grown with my music. They have grown with my record-ings. They have grown with my performances. And they trust what I tell them. In any case, I understand the problems of singers. The most fun in conducting is to anticipate when a singer might have problems. You see by the speed he takes a phrase that he might be going to rush, or he's going to be slower. And to be able to help him. "Okay, this isn't what we had established, but in this moment, you feel it differently, so you have to do it differently." Because sometimes singing isn't a matter of being capricious. Sometimes it's a matter of having to change gears at the right moment. Because we have an instrument that doesn't work by keys [*wiggles fingers as if playing a trumpet*] or doesn't go by . . . [*holds up an imaginary flute and blows into it*].

Breath.

No, it goes by breath, but that's your own instrument.

It's not mechanical, is what you're saying.

That's right. And the most beautiful thing, and the most interesting thing, is when you know you have to help a singer, and you are able to do it.

You also are director of the opera in Washington, D.C., and in Los Angeles. What difficulties have you had in that role?

I tell you—the single, most difficult day in the life of an opera theater director, is the day they present you a production. Because on that day, you see the mockup, you see the design, and you have to decide if it's good or bad. You have to decide, "Well, I'll take it or I won't." From there, everything happens.

How do you decide?

Someone like Robert Wilson has a certain style, a reputation. You know more or less that everything is going to be like something else he has done. It's a kind of security. His prestige is big, and his taste is impeccable: the harmony, the aesthetics, the lighting. I don't think you can get it wrong. Robert Carsen has done many interesting things. There are many new people, who come from the theater most of the time. Maybe they feel a little lost when the music is there, or when the ensemble is there. And then they want to scandalize.

Are you saying you're against nontraditional staging?

No, I'm very open; I don't mind an opera changing from one century to another, if it has a reason. As far as I'm concerned, you can play *La Bohème* anyplace in the world, at any time. But I would recommend that if you are changing the time and the city, do it in the local language. You are talking about Luigi Filippo, a king from Italy. And you are in the middle of Broadway, doing it today, so you can't say "Luigi Filippo." Change the name, do it in English. That's all right. You keep the music, you keep the spirit, you keep the feeling of it.

You were recently involved in a modern opera (Howard Shore's The Fly, *a coproduction with Los Angeles Opera which premiered in Paris). How do you see opera creations? Is opera in good health?*

Every day, we get more and more creations, new premieres. I think it's necessary. Opera is an art form that has so many works that even if one more opera wasn't written, we have already all the masterpieces. But that's not fair. We should give new composers the possibility to write things and the possibility to do them. Today, critics are on one side demanding that opera composers not write too much melody—that's one wing. But there is another wing that's thinking, "Opera should go back and be more melodic."

Which wing do you support?

I think we should have a combination of both. You can still have melody, but harmonically you make it work. Because the voice needs to sing. It doesn't need to be saying notes. It needs a *line*. If you can connect that line and then harmonically make it modern, very contemporary, that's fine. But the voice needs expression.

Have you found that sort of contemporary opera, to your satisfaction, as a singer?

Two of the most satisfactory composers today with reputations, because they've done many operas, are William Bolcom and Tobias Picker. They find the combination. They have a lot of experience. In the case of Howard Shore, *The Fly* was his first opera. He was a little concerned not to do what he has been doing in the cinema, but to be more in opera. I think he has written a score that in many moments has a lot of poetry. But of course the subject itself, the fly, has to be music that disintegrates, in a way. When the character is disintegrating, he feels harmonically and melodically—especially in his last phrases—the character is really deteriorating. I think he wrote the right music for this story, and I think between him and [director David] Cronenberg they created an event the public loves. I know the reviews have been mixed. Not terrible, but mixed. But the public enjoyed it. They were tremendously enthusiastic.

Can you think of anything about opera that you don't like?

I don't like a bad performance. There is nothing more glorious, more complete, than a really great performance of opera. But there is nothing more boring than a bad performance of opera, that's for sure. Another thing I don't like is when a director doesn't have a determined idea and wants to be difficult just to be difficult, and wants to be different just to be different. Or scandalize. Some directors, especially in Germany, have made careers because they made a big scandal, a big shock. They are people who obviously are good, but they come from the theater. Then they go to opera and make a big scandal. And because they have this name, they can do it a second or a third time. You know there is talent there, but if there's not a reason behind a production, I can't take it.

Do you feel that having a successful career in opera has meant making big sacrifices?

The big sacrifice is that you cannot have a normal family life. Then the years pass by. I'm lucky, because I have a family who are as enthusiastic for music as I am. My wife and my boys all understand about my career. If anything, my wife probably likes it even more than I do. She was an opera singer, now she's a stage director. That's the only thing you regret sometimes, not to have all the time in this world. For instance, if I want to go see a Formula One race or a tennis match or football final. Sometimes I'm lucky and can program my things, but it's not so easy. I'm less of a reader than Rolando Villazón. He takes time to read a lot. Because of my career—I have 130 roles in my repertoire—almost everything I read has been related to my characters. Which is a lot of history. But I would like, one day, to dig more into my reading, which I used to do, in my early years.

You mention your family, but how important is your relationship with the public in your continuing to perform? I've heard you say that you felt it was your duty to keep singing while people still want to hear you.

Absolutely. I tell myself, "I don't want to sing one day more than I should." But I also don't want to sing one day less than I can. One day less than I can please the public.

Do you think you'll know when it's time?

I think so, yes.

For the moment you still work a lot. When you were in Madrid for Handel's Tamerlano *recently, it was the first time you didn't take an airplane in, what—one month?*

I was *five weeks* without taking a plane. That hasn't happened to me in I don't know how long! I'll have to research it and see. I was working hard, rehearsing and performing, so I just never left [*laughs*].

© Andrew Eccles/JBG Photo

Renée Fleming,
or balancing on the high wire

The suitcase is still rocking in the hall. Her plane landed late; she has rushed from the airport and hastens into the Paris flat, where journalists wait. Despite the jet from Oslo, and being midway into a seventeen-day, ten-city European tour, Renée Fleming looks rested, even regal, as she drops into a chair and begins to take questions. Unfussy yet stately, friendly but poised, Fleming is three parts easygoing American, one part operatic splendor. The mix works.

It should—it has taken years to get right.

The soprano is noteworthy in that she talks, more than others and more matter-of-factly, about herself and the misadventures that attended her slow but steady rise. She surveys her career candidly, as though reviewing an absent friend's. Adverting occasionally to her 2004 memoir (The Inner Voice), which chronicled how she found her voice, it is clear the Strauss specialist remains acutely conscious that the same hidden forces that bestowed it on her can one day snatch it back. Both finding and keeping such a treasure require what amounts to a lifelong balancing act. This is the mix that took so long to blend to completion. Seemingly, there's more to it than Maria Callas's "I just bark for a living."

Despite claims that she was not a natural performer, it's plain that Fleming possesses the twin talents of making a career and maintaining it. The first, as in most professions, calls for ability, ambition, hard work, and luck. She is no stranger to any of them.

Two daughters are the source of yet another juggling act—that of working mother.

Longevity demands other gifts. For vocalists, it means not yielding to desire (or poor advice) which goads them to build a career at the expense of their instrument. To preserve the voice, singers must be careful at choosing roles right for that voice. Careers are prolonged by refusing parts that are too heavy; they are shipwrecked by singing the wrong ones at the wrong time. The diva's dilemma becomes one of durability over performance: More years or more concerts? Make a mistake, and the voice will pay. Misjudgment has strewn the vocalists' graveyard with bones of the prematurely mute.

Maintaining one's singing life can also be a question of brand. Fleming is not afraid to stake out turf others shy away from. Her European tour, for example, featured a seldom-heard 1979 work by American composer George Crumb for soprano and amplified piano, with text by Walt Whitman. The piece scored with audiences from Scandinavia to Bavaria. Hitting this bull's-eye, Fleming feels, demands daring, and her gambles are paying off. It's as if a second genius—adroit management of her voice—is shielding the first, which is her voice itself.

Yet the voice remains an enigma for Fleming, even though hers has found the ultimate balance. Emotions, acoustics, diets, and fellow performers can all affect it. "We all know it's ephemeral," she murmurs softly. "Singers don't have that much time." Then, more loudly, "I want to be the one who decides when to quit." No doubt she shall.

You once said, "Singing takes ten years to accomplish and ten minutes to explain." Can you explain it in five?

The five-minute version is: the concepts are not difficult to understand, but the physical coordination, in addition to the art of interpretation, is next to impossible to accomplish. This is a process which is made up almost entirely of involuntary muscles, muscles we don't consciously control. For breathing and support, we have to try and effect change through the use of muscles we can control: the abdominal wall, back, and intercostal muscles.

The five-minute version is: it's a mass of coordination. A process which involves almost entirely involuntary muscles, muscles we don't control. For breathing, we have to try and effect the right change, and that's through the use of muscles we do control. The balancing act of all these things is what's so difficult.

Start with breathing.

That part is already complicated. I separate breathing into three parts. Most people agree with me on the first two, but the third is a bit controversial. First is the most advantageous taking in of breath: breath capacity. Then there is controlling the rate at which it goes out, which is called breath control. The final item is the concept of support, and it's something about which people have vastly different ideas, both on what it is and how it works. Not just singers, but politicians, teachers, and actors have to support their voices. I just witnessed this in London—I love theater and go a lot. Actors who don't find a technique for support combined with optimal use of resonance end up hoarse after two or three weeks. And you worry for them. You think, Are they going to make it through?

That's breathing. And after? You mentioned trying to effect the right change. Change of what?

That's part two: the use of resonance. In a perfect world, in terms of pitch, we make a sound from bottom to top which is even, consistent, and smooth, with no obvious break. The quality doesn't change in a way which is unattractive or obtrusive. That's really difficult to learn. One has to use imagery to blend the different registers evenly and without tension. Because I can do it now, I understand it well. But when one is learning how to sing, it's impossible to understand fully. It's just one of those enigmatic things.

And you're sure, along the way, that you're going to eventually get to that point?

Most people don't. A fortunate few are born with the ability to sing naturally—a little tweaking here and there is necessary, but basically they have it all together. But most people never really figure it out—I mean, all of it. I had a strange trajectory because if I didn't have a vocal problem I seemed to try it anyway, as if wanting to explore every corner of the voice, even the unhelpful ones, in the first ten to fifteen years. Which is why it took me so long to learn how to sing. In most sports, one learns about the concept of muscle isolation: using a muscle or muscle group without bringing in others unnecessarily. This is at the heart of the difficulty of learning how to sing. The trick is, there has to be enormous energy and a certain kind of tension, but only the right tension. Any unnecessary tension can make or break a phrase, a vocal climax, or a sustained pianissimo. One also needs strength and stamina. This program I'm singing here is, with encores, two and one-half to three hours long, and it's just me. That's tiring. It's a long, demanding program. But it's fun, and I love doing it. It's also challenging musically for the audience—Purcell to Crumb, with Berg songs, Schumann songs, Handel. It's all music I love. And it's also music which has a certain evocative sensibility. A lot of mysticism to it. It's difficult to describe. When you see it on paper you think, "How on earth is this going to work?" When you hear it, it all fits together and makes sense.

Did you choose the songs in the program?

I do all of my own programming. It's a labor of love which takes into account my calendar and the audience. I will hopefully find something which everyone will enjoy on any given concert. Operas, too. I have to decide what I want to sing. I try not to sing as much opera as I used to, so I choose very carefully.

How do you stay in shape for three hours of singing?

This program takes every shred of technique I have to be able to get through without killing myself. I've built up a lot of stamina for singing, but I also have become a pilates fan in the last two years, which is helping. I try to train two to three times a week when I'm home, and I have a trainer who's demanding. I love that. I've just been home for two months, and she really did her job. I've noticed a big difference in my ability. I sang *Manon* at the Met, and usually I'm exhausted by the end. Beverly Sills said to me, "It's the *Götterdämmerung* of French opera." It's very long. But I was fine at the end, not nearly as tired as when I've sung the role before.

Do you sing every day?

I'm always singing. It's rare that I get time off. Not by design; it's just my work schedule. I'm not one of these people who is so disciplined that I feel I have to vocalize absolutely every single day. But I'm working all the time, preparing something, researching, or rehearsing.

The program sounds risky. Would you say you like to take risks?

Yes. In fact, I don't see how you can maintain the interest of the public more than twenty years without taking risks all the time. It's so boring otherwise. It's funny, because I don't think I have that risk-taker gene. I guess it's a calculated risk, to try something new in what I know well. The audience has to be surprised and excited by what I'm doing, and, frankly, so do I. It's more that it's in my nature to want to be continually challenged.

How do you achieve that?

There are two schools of thinking on this. Some believe you should do something better than anybody else in the world. Do five or six roles extremely well and continue to fine-tune them over time; Alfredo Kraus comes to mind. That's the school of specialization. Another school of thinking embraces newness, an ever-growing repertoire; obviously more Plácido Domingo. My sensibilities lean towards the latter, although after fifty-one new roles, I'm longing to repeat more.

Is that your recipe for longevity?

Longevity is really about maintaining the voice. Sing repertoire which is within the realm of what's appropriate for your voice type and temperament, accounting for issues of drama, tessitura, and the volume of the orchestration. Emotional health and career stamina are equally important.

How do you know what's right for you? How do you make the proper choices?

I'm fortunate because I found mentors who were great singers. I have been privileged to spend time with Beverly Sills, Leontyne Price, and Marilyn Horne. I could go to these generous artists and ask, "What do you think about this? Should I sing this role?" And they may have had some experience to be able to tell me what to watch out for and what to think about. This idea of sharing knowledge with the next generation is a truly magical tradition. We all know this gift is ephemeral. Our careers don't last nearly as long as an instrumentalist's or a conductor's. They can work until they retire, but most of them never do. They simply never stop. And we're forgotten relatively quickly when we do stop.

You really believe that?

Other than by a core group of people who really love history and love to hear older recordings, which is a small group, and of course, by young singers. But for the larger public, sure.

Luciano Pavarotti chewed ice to keep his voice. Does that work for everybody? Do you?

No, most of us drink warm things. He's the only one I know who did that. In a way it makes sense, because you'd use ice against any kind of swelling or inflammation. Everything works better for me when I have herbal tea or just hot water. It's the steam that is important.

Does "marking" help preserve your voice?

Marking is a technique one uses in rehearsals sometimes. I don't mark as much as some singers, especially if it's a new role, because I believe in singing the role into the voice and into the body. I also believe in keeping the singing mechanism fit through training, and that means singing. However, if I'm tired, I mark either by singing the music down an octave, or by singing more softly. Dancers to it, too. I just saw a rehearsal of *Romeo and Juliet*, and they mark by not lifting and by taking it easier during the hardest passages.

How far ahead do you schedule?

Concerts are booked, generally speaking, eighteen months to two years ahead. Opera is planned up to eight years ahead.

Does it happen that you tell an opera house you'd like to do a certain work, or that you and a conductor have an idea for a production, and the opera director says, "No, thank you—we decide what to put on"?

Sometimes my suggestions are taken, and sometimes not. Sometimes they say, "What about this?" We negotiate. It's a collaborative effort. There are operas I keep bringing up. I want to sing André Previn's *A Streetcar Named Desire* again and am finally having luck with that. It's a very dramatic piece and wonderful theater, which is one reason it works—besides being music I really love. And it's a great role.

Is it hard to plan ahead?

It's different, depending on what the item is. It used to be, literally, five solid years in advance. But that's not fun. First of all, it's difficult to know exactly what you should be doing that far ahead; and second, it doesn't leave room for anything else. There are other professional things you've got to leave room for: television, publicity, things that come at the last minute.

There's a world that goes hand in hand with having a career, and that's promoting that career. You seem to have accepted TV, press interviews, and the business side of things. Isn't that a risk—maintaining your image in our TV age?

I don't think that's part of the risk. We have this strange conflict that has existed for a long time. We're always between a rock and a hard place. How do we satisfy our core audience—the real intellectual aficionados of classical music—without losing the sense of integrity we have, or pandering to the audience, and still garner the largest possible audience? If my audience were small, I wouldn't be able to make any records at all. The record firms would just say, "Sorry, it's not worth it." In music right now, it's very difficult because everything has become about profit. Very little is subsidized or supported anymore.

Let's talk about balance, personal and professional. First, personally: How do you balance being diva and mother?

I think I'm finally getting the personal balance. It's not easy for any working mother. The problem for me, and for anybody who's a classical musician, is that we can conceivably travel every day of the year if we choose. Some do, and love it and thrive on it. The lifestyle suits them. But often these people have no children. I have two daughters, so that's not possible for me. I adjusted my schedule several years ago to include far less opera and far more concerts and recitals, and that has worked wonderfully. It's even enabled me to actually travel more. In these three weeks I'm traveling to ten cities. If I were doing an opera, I'd be in the same place for six weeks or two months. The daughters are in school, so I can't just bring them over. My oldest is in one of the most demanding schools in the country. I can't even take her out for a week. As a consequence, I'm home more. They come with me on school holidays. This year, we're going to Hawaii. Next year, the Far East. But this new arrangement is working out really well. I'm home more, then leave for short periods of very concentrated touring during the school year. In the summers, I'm almost always in Europe with the children. I never go anywhere for Christmas; it's too hard to move. I usually stay home with the girls in New York.

Do people—opera houses and programmers—understand your priorities and this new schedule?

It's a reality of my life, and people are understanding. But the Met is an obvious place for me to work a lot, because I can be home. And it's a great house, my home theater. Paris has been my second home for the last ten or fifteen years, but that's changed. Now I'm singing all over Europe. I had opera in London this summer. In 2006, I was in Japan almost all summer, with the Met and Seiji Ozawa and the world premiere of an opera by Henri Dutilleux which Seiji Ozawa commissioned. Dutilleux is a great composer; it was very exciting. I was with the Orchestre National de France also and brought the piece to Paris. The summer after that, I was in Vienna. It's changing now; I'm all over.

Do you feel you have to sacrifice to be with your daughters?

Never. It's a sacrifice to be without them. There's no question that leaving my children every time, even for a week, is a huge sacrifice and the most important one I make. However, I'm teaching them you can be a good mother and still do work you absolutely adore. They know they're my first priority and know I'm crazy about them. My mother did that. She worked and was passionate about her teaching. I don't think it's a negative message.

How do you find your balance professionally—onstage, between the right amounts of emotion and technique? How do you stay real in the role without losing virtuosity?

That's all going well for me right now because in the last couple years my technique has really stabilized, to the point where I can, for the most part, forget about singing. It's so wonderful now. I want the audience, in a sense, to forget that I'm singing and become involved in the drama, the story, and the character. Perhaps this isn't as easy in a recital as in an opera. If the music catches them unawares, and it's an emotional experience for them, great. That's been working. I've been able to make my voice an expressive tool entirely, and be in control of it, rather than it being in control of me— which was the case for years and years and years.

When you listen to older recordings of yourself in this period, do you cringe?

No, but I can hear I've grown. I saw an old video of *Otello* I did some time ago—I sang the role again last summer—and could hear places where I was clearly struggling or having to think really hard about what I was doing. Now, it's second nature.

Would I be able to hear those places where you were struggling?

I don't think so. It's not an easy thing to do. Lots of people would have a million opinions on what I was doing that night, but they'd probably all be different from mine. Singing is a very individual thing. Even my colleagues and I, after a performance, could share how we thought it was going, and we'd have differences. It's personal. In my book, I say that my road is just a template; it's how someone did it, it's not necessarily the right way. It's so subjective. But you can tell when someone's voice cracks. You can see when they're afraid. The audience picks up on obvious problems. I heard a performance recently where a world-class tenor came to grief at the end of the opera, and I'm sure everyone in the house knew it, not just me.

Who was it?

I'm not going to say. I won't even tell any of my colleagues. I'm too politically correct, sorry! [*Laughs*] Actually, I'm superstitious—I figure I'll be next! [*Laughs*]

How do you deal with critics? Is it a good idea to only read them at the end of a run?

That's something everybody has to learn to manage. It's not easy to be criticized publicly every time you get up and do your job. I don't read them all now. I don't have time; I'm performing so much. A sports psychologist who works with Tiger Woods and top tennis players recommended something that I have taken on. He said it's incredibly important to have the right support around you. You've got to protect yourself. One of the things I do now is, if I know I'm in a city where I'm likely to be reviewed unfavorably, I'll have other people read the reviews for me. Then they tell me if they're okay, or advise me not to read them! [*Laughs*] A lot of artists say they don't go near them. But I like to know in general what's being said because I can learn from that. And I have learned over the past ten years. There were a few years where so-and-so said I was too bland, then I swung the pendulum the opposite way and was putting too much on the music. It's good to know those general things, if they're consistent.

But again, it's subjective—just one person's opinion.

Of course. And it's a person who is trying to sell newspapers, so who wants to be colorful. I empathize with that.

Everything must seem mild after critical journalism in New York.

London's much worse. They have seven newspapers there. All competing. New York is mainly the *New York Times,* for classical music.

You say you can forget singing now, but audiences would probably say you've always been able to communicate that.

My acting is much better now. It's really improved. Experience and focus have helped. Also, getting my voice in hand enough so I could just focus on that. It took me ten years to not stop thinking about this when I was onstage. In the beginning I'd get bad reviews and have off-nights, and my voice teacher said, "You have to give yourself time. You're learning on the job. Don't be so hard on yourself."

Unfortunately, you often don't get a second chance.

True. You have to stay at a decent enough level to keep getting work! [*Laughs*]

What's the most important thing spectators need to know about singers?

There are two major points. It's important to point out that we're the only singers in the Western world who aren't amplified. That's something we all take for granted. Even street singers have their own traveling PA systems. That's a huge distinction. It means we have to physically be able to create a sound loud enough to carry over the orchestra and the chorus in a hall that can seat two thousand or four thousand people, without any help. That's really important, and a lot of it is technique. And it can't be screaming—it has to be a beautiful sound. Second, most of us have to be versed in many languages. Some people specialize. Luciano Pavarotti never really sang in anything but Italian—maybe a bit of English. Some can specialize, but most of us, and certainly most of us who are English speakers, absolutely have to sing in several languages. I sing in eight—ten if you include the two dialogues of Elvish which I sang in the film of *Lord of the Rings*. That's a lot of study. We also have to understand style. We need to know the difference between French, German, and Italian music, and the difference between the Classical, Baroque, and Romantic periods. What I'm saying is that the training that goes into what we do is intense and takes a long time. My best fans are people who sing or who are amateur singers in choruses and so on, because they have a kernel of understanding of what's involved.

What can spectators do to enhance their appreciation of opera?

Any knowledge would enhance it. It's the same with wine, jazz, or all things worth knowing well: they require a bit of effort. For opera, people certainly need to know the performance history of a piece, the story; all that is useful. On a really basic side, I think people should simply listen and do a bit of research in advance. The problem is nobody has time to do this anymore. People used to read the libretto before they went to an opera. Now we have supertitles, so it's really not necessary—thank God!—because they're wonderful. They're the best thing that's happened to opera in a long time. Some people still take the time to listen to the opera in advance, familiarize themselves with it, maybe know a bit of the story, maybe even a little about the composer.

In your book, you say there are two ways to get started as an opera singer: get an agent and do the rounds of auditions, or try and make yourself known on the competition circuit.

I went the competition route. I lost three times as many as I won. So it's not a perfect way to go. And it's incredibly subjective and arbitrary.

What advice would you give someone about competitions?

Don't put your heart on your sleeve. Just do it and wait to be lucky. Obviously, if you're weak in areas, then you probably need to go back and work. You always have to keep working. I would always go to the judges for comments. Sometimes they were very helpful and sometimes not. To anybody entering competitions, I'd say, Don't invest yourself in winning or losing based on your quality. Because very often it's political. It's just one day, and rarely in my experience have competitions been consistently great predictors for great careers.

Is there commercial pressure, from record companies?

Not that early. If you're doing competitions, chances are you haven't even been noticed by a record company yet. No, that doesn't happen. It's a great way to get exposure, though. It was a great way for me to have enough money to pay for my lessons and coaching in those years when I wasn't really working yet. So it's useful. The other route, of course, is that you can somehow get an audition with someone, and they hire you, and you just start working. But that's not easy because there's a catch-22: not being able to audition unless you have management, and you can't get management unless they've heard you sing professionally.

Or unless you have a sample recording to show around.

Demos. I don't know if they take the time to hear them. They probably want to hear you live. Which is why competitions are an option; they can come to the finals. Also, if you've won, they think, "Aha! Other people thought this artist is worthy, so maybe she is."

You sing a lot of jazz. Have you found any crossover techniques from jazz applicable to classical, or vice versa?

Listening to jazz is still a great hobby of mine and one of the ways I unwind. There's no question that singing jazz has greatly affected both my own style and what I bring to music. I have a desire not to sing anything too metronomically straight, and I sometimes use vibrato as an expressive tool. There are lots of elements that come from my jazz background which affect my classical singing. Certainly the improvising I did for two years has made me enjoy bel canto, Handel, and the baroque repertoire much more, and it made me into a much better musician in general. One's ear has to be incredibly developed for jazz, because the tune is just the beginning for making something that's completely unique. It's liberating to use a melody as a starting point and create something new from there.

What music is important to you at this point in your career?

Right now, my central composer is Strauss. It's a combination of my own personal taste and the fact that his music suits my voice really well. The roles are a perfect match. I recently recorded *Daphne*. The three central Strauss parts for me are the Marschallin in *Der Rosenkavalier,* Arabella and Die Graefin in *Capriccio*. Beyond Strauss, my repertoire is broad, encompassing French, Slavic, Italianate, and American opera plus orchestral and song recital literature.

Some singers believe Strauss and Mozart are the two composers who understand female psychology the best.

Strauss loved to write for the soprano voice. He wrote the most beautiful, the most arching, linear music. I say it's good for my voice now because it's a question of where the music lies and the kind of quality it wants. It wants a silvery rather than a gold timbre—the gold being better suited for the Italian *verismo* repertoire and Verdi. Mozart is also in the lighter, silvery category. But it still needs sumptuousness and warmth. It's a great fit. The tessitura is right, as are the long, high-flying phrases.

You began with Mozart.

It was more circumstantial. It was suited to my voice, but my career started in the Mozart year of 1991—the two hundredth anniversary of his death. All theaters were programming so much Mozart that I got started as a Mozart singer, in the role of the Countess in *Le Nozze di Figaro,* and then I stayed with it for ten years. I credit Mozart in part with teaching me how to sing, because it's trial by fire: enormously difficult and demanding a crystalline perfection of timbre, pitch, and style, not to mention nerve.

Do you see yourself evolving toward Wagner?

I sang Eva in *Die Meistersinger* in Bayreuth, which I very much enjoyed. There is one other Wagner role planned for the future, but I am not at liberty to speak about it yet.

It must be fulfilling to be able to go from one role to another and span the history of music.

It's wonderful being able to sing in music that spans four hundred years. I could probably, from today until I retire, never repeat anything and still have music to learn, especially in the song literature. Less so in opera. Although Plácido Domingo is still going strong, having sung well over one hundred roles. And he counts everything, too, which I find fascinating [*laughs*]. He can rattle off even the numbers of every time he's performed a certain role in a certain theater. I have no idea and perhaps I don't want to know. I must be in schedule denial.

The great advantage now must be choice, the reward for all the hard work.

Definitely. No question, in every way. What you sing and how much you sing. Those are the two crucial things.

You wrote, "Stress, fear, emotions, hormones, acoustics, colds and other health problems, diets, relations among singers and conductor can all affect your singing."

That's true. Everything can affect it. It's your body. It's your emotional life, your mind. We can't divorce ourselves from our instruments, unfortunately. There are many days, believe me, when I'd like to trade mine in. Not so much now, but earlier. It was so frustrating. It's a long road. I always say it's a miracle that anybody learns how to sing.

On days when you wake up, or woke up, frustrated, did you give yourself a pep talk? How do you overcome that feeling?

I have to constantly diagnose the voice. It's different every day. I'll have three good performances, then on the fourth something will go wrong. It'll feel strange; then it will take a while to come out of that, to figure it out, diagnose it, and prescribe a remedy. I'm my own voice doctor now. There are a few trusted people whom I'll ask about a phrase or a sound. We always need outside ears. Gerald Martin Moore has worked with me on every recording since my Handel disc. He has a terrific ability to address vocal issues through musical means, and he would be the first to tell me if he thought I were headed in a wrong direction, vocally speaking. I am also still reliant on trusted language coaches. Singing in foreign languages requires nuance and fine-tuning which can never be good enough. And finally, I work with pianists who help with style, learning and memorizing music, even repertoire. But I don't really have a voice teacher.

Are you looking for one?

You know, if I don't know how to sing by now, then it's maybe too late.

Private photo / Veronica Klose

Ferruccio Furlanetto,
or functioning as a filter

A showery Saturday in Paris, at the Opéra Bastille, early summer. Ferruccio Furlanetto is in town to close the season as King Philip in Verdi's Don Carlo, *a role he has sung for nearly thirty years and one he's most known for. He discusses it at length.*

After our interview, we stand outside, waiting for a break in the rain. Even when it comes, the chatty basso continues talking for twenty minutes more. The longer we wait, the more it feels he appreciates the connection, however brief, that has formed between interviewer and interviewee.

But that took some moments. As the interview opens, he seems wary, even weary of talking, and the frequent shifting in his chair suggests, if not back pain, the expectation of another series of questions he's heard a hundred times. He even volunteers the answer to "What are your favorite roles?" a question I didn't ask and never would. This, I assume, is prepared boilerplate. It is followed by more information which, one imagines, was readied against the stock question "Who has helped you the most in your career?" but Furlanetto wasn't asked that, either.

He changes soon enough, begins enjoying himself, then recalls times past with Herbert von Karajan, Jean-Pierre Ponnelle, Cesare Siepi, and Ezio Pinza.

He is dressed all in brown and speaks with a quiet humor and languid manner. This slow, almost dreamy facade was perceptible everywhere—in the body language, in the voice—but not in the eyes (brown as well), which

look at you directly, almost challenging, and seem to be where his energy
residues. "I'm not a workaholic," he drawls, guessing he averages fifty per-
formances a year and can remember colleagues who overworked them-
selves into early graves with twice that much.

Born in northern Italy, close to the Austrian border, Furlanetto is based
in Vienna, where, between the Staatsoper and the Salzburg Festival, he
has spent most of the last twenty-five years. Following Don Carlo, *he's*
looking forward to a month off "in a cottage by a lake, five minutes from
where I'm a member of the golf course, five minutes from my favorite fish
restaurant, less than fifteen kilometers from Salzburg. After twenty-one
Salzburg Festivals, I have more friends there than anywhere." His German
is good, though he claims his French is better. We speak in English, and as
the lazy, deeply echoing bass fills the small room, you could almost at
times be listening to Henry Kissinger.

King Philip is one of your better-known roles.

This role was extremely important for me, because it changed my life. It was
at the Easter Festival of Salzburg in 1986. I was there for two concerts with
Karajan—*Coronation Mass,* Mozart, and *Te Deum,* Bruckner—and a contract of covering King Philip. And it happened. I had to jump in, with notice
[*checks his watch—it is 11:20* A.M.] at *this* time of the day for the dress
rehearsal and premiere. At the dress rehearsal, the public was in black tie
for television. Because with Karajan there was always television, telecast,
laser disc at the time. He was ahead of his time in communications. I jumped
in at four o'clock. And the day after, everybody in the world knew I existed.
Because when Karajan touched somebody, it was with a magic wand, like
in fairy tales. I was in good health, knew the role—I had already done it—it
was the right moment in my life, the right place. The big lottery. Everything
fell together.

It's become one of your signature roles.

It's one of my favorites—at the moment. Because ten years ago I would
have mentioned a lot of Mozart, Giovanni or Figaro. They belong to a specific time in the life of a singer. You need to be a young man. You need to
be jumping around, you need to be athletic. It was pure happiness to do
these Mozart roles. And they opened all the doors. Now, though, the three
favorite roles are King Philip, Boris Godunov, and Don Quichotte. They are

roles where the vocal part is important, but the *acting* is as important. And I love this. I love to be involved vocally, but also dramatically, in the role.

Is the acting part as important in influencing your decision to sing it?

Absolutely. Now and always. I did all these years in Mozart, and in Mozart you cannot be only a singer. You need to be an actor. I was lucky, again, to have people help me. The two who really helped my career were Karajan and Jean-Pierre Ponnelle. Ponnelle was a sensational stage director. I did my first *Figaro* with him. I did a lot of *Giovanni*s, the movies of *Così fan tutte* and *Rigoletto*. Jean-Pierre taught me to *live* the characters, out of my own skin. He taught me acting, basically.

Many of your colleagues talk about him. Why is he remembered?

He was purely an opera director. He wasn't somebody who landed in opera from movies or theater. He started as a set and costume designer. Then, when he would see his sets destroyed by some other direction, he said, "Enough. I'll do my own." He spoke sensational Italian. In Mozart, the *recitativi* were alive, so beautiful. He inspired you. He used the music for the staging as nobody else I know.

Any examples come to mind?

I will never forget my first *Figaro*. In the beginning of the fourth act, Figaro realizes that Susanna, dressed like the Countess, is Susanna. In the Ponnelle production, it was always a system of games. I was grabbing her ankles, hiding under her skirt. It wasn't easy for—not a beginner, but a young singer—to jump in this kind of acting concept. But he showed us, and if you have a model, it's easy. Jean-Pierre was also a friend. He meant a lot not only to me, but to two generations of singers—the one that was ending and the one that was starting. I was lucky enough to spend six years of intense work with him.

Have you done much acting? Did you ever take lessons?

No. That's why I was lucky to have this kind of help. Ponnelle, unfortunately, died in '88 at fifty-six. We could have done so many things. When I did something with . . . not his "replacement," that's a bad word, but with somebody else, I was lucky, again, to do three years of *Don Giovanni* with Patrice Chéreau in Salzburg. Patrice is another genius. Totally different from Ponnelle. Patrice speaks Italian with no accent. He was a pupil of [Giorgio] Strehler, lived in Milan working at the Piccolo Scala. Patrice uses the Italian and the text in the *recitativi* in Mozart like a god. For an Italian to find somebody who teaches you that the recitative could be done also *this* way, and you never thought about it—it's fantastic.

Which way was that?

For instance, Giovanni arrives in the country wedding where Zerlina is getting married to Masetto. Normally, you see Giovanni saying [*sweetly*], "O cara la mia Zerlina! [*Brusquely*] O caro il mio Masetto." Patrice said, "No. If you really want to get to her, you flatter the husband." And this [*laughs*] is true! In life it happens like that! [*laughs*]. That *Giovanni*, with Barenboim and Patrice, was supposed to open this theater, the Opéra Bastille, in 1988, but the project collapsed. Patrice was desperate because he really wanted to do it. Luckily, Gérard Mortier [then head of the Salzburg Festival] decided to do it in Salzburg. Patrice told me he only accepted the idea of doing *Giovanni* the moment he found a solution for the end. Then he started from the beginning.

Why was that?

If you don't have a *coup de théâtre*, or something for the ending, everything will collapse. This finale was a sensation. It was a ten-meter wall, and behind the wall was the huge head of the Commendatore on a kind of catapult. And on the D-major chord of the Commendatore's entrance, this big head—built in something not exactly light—was catapulted over the wall. The wall broke in pieces and this head came in. I had to stop it sometimes. The floor went down a bit, to help, but the last one who could save the orchestra was me! [*Laughs*] The finale was under this big head, and then everything went down. I tell you, every night, for three years, in that moment, I *knew* it was going to happen, and every night, in that moment, I was like this [*freezes, tense*]. And the audience were jumping on their chairs. It was a sensational *coup de théâtre*.

Are there any roles where you really don't have to act?

Zaccaria, in *Nabucco*. It's very demanding, probably the most difficult Verdi role. But from the acting point of view, it's zero. You just stand there with your stick and sing out.

No director has ever wanted you to do something new?

There's no possibility. The singing doesn't allow you do jump or do crazy things. It's so hard, you need to just stay there. You can't make any comparison between a role like that and Philip or Boris—the personal satisfaction these roles give you when you're onstage. Boris and Philip are historical characters. For a few hours, you're allowed to be somebody incredible. This, together with the acting, fantastic music—it's the greatest privilege you can have in this career.

We've talked about directors you've worked with. Can we discuss conductors?

Karajan was like an alien from another planet. He was amazing, incredible. Demanding, but at the same time he allowed things. When I jumped in on that *Don Carlo*, for instance, fifteen minutes before the beginning, I went to see him. We came to *Ella giammai m'amo* [third act aria], and he said, "You sing it. I will accompany you." I tell you, I never heard that phrase from any other conductor in my life. It's very humble to do it. But it's very clever, in a situation like that, if you trust the singer, to follow his contained spontaneity. It could be the key to success. He did, and it was sensational.

What do conductors normally say?

They ask you to follow them. And they're right, maybe—sometimes. But if you have a good professional onstage, in that aria, I assure you, it's better to give vent to the spontaneity of the singer rather than impose a tempo or an interpretation that doesn't fit the sensibility of that performer.

Don't most conductors understand that?

I can think of very few who really are supportive. They always try to give their print. It's understandable. But often you don't feel comfortable with it.

So what do you do?

Compromise. If you really want something, you discuss. Normally, they follow what you ask. But sometimes you see there's a kind of resistance. Like there's a resistance on my side, of course. It's difficult to say who is right. But when you have somebody who understands deeply what you want to do, it's pure joy. Many conductors don't understand much about voices. Not necessarily young people. They sometimes do not understand breathing necessities. They do not understand the ideas of the economy of a phrase. That you need, for instance, to have a sort of suspension in the tempo, because it will be helpful to breathe, but to breathe in a way that it will sound like an interpretation breathing, not a necessity. The universe of singing is very complicated. And very few conductors are on the same wavelength.

How can somebody get to be an opera conductor and not know about the voice? But I suppose conductors counter with, "You don't know anything about tempi or orchestral phrasing."

Okay. But in an aria like "Ella giammai m'amo," everything should come after the singer. Because when you have "Dormirò sol nel manto mio regal," you must allow the performer not only to sing, but to express the feeling of the most powerful man on earth in his solitude. Historically, he had a very good relationship with Elisabetta. Unfortunately, she died young. They had two daughters, and he loved them both. You have to romance the piece a bit. In history, there was this lovely, quiet marriage. In Schiller, not at all. In Schiller's play, the king is very dry. There is no space for any passion. He's a bureaucrat—as he was, actually. Verdi wants you to be in love with this girl and to have all this pathos and desperation that comes from a presumed betrayal. And if you have a good performer, you have to let him go. Luckily, 90 percent of the time you have great conductors for *Don Carlo* because it's an important piece.

What other conductors do you particularly remember?

I was lucky to start my career when the great old ones were still alive. I sang with Bernstein, with Giulini, with Solti—the most beautiful *Nozze di Figaro*, with Solti, and he was eighty. The tempi were sparkling, fantastic. With Giulini, the most incredible series of Verdi *Requiem*s you can imagine. That man was a god. In filtering this incredible piece. Then I was lucky to start with the already young but already powerful conductors, like Muti, Abbado, Barenboim, Maazel. And the new generation, like Bychkov, Gergiev, Gatti. In the Salzburg years, the first *Figaro* I did with Ponnelle was with Jimmy Levine. I started singing at the Met very young, in 1980, mostly with Jimmy Levine. Jimmy is probably the greatest opera director.

He knows all the singers' parts.

Not only that. He was always with us, onstage. Conducting by heart, as do many colleagues, but he was always *with* the stage. And this is a fantastic feeling. It gives you the liberty to not look constantly toward a conductor, but to feel it.

Some people say this generation of conductors are less musically knowledgeable than previous generations.

You cannot say that. There are products of this mediatized world. Sometimes, you see somebody not even thirty projected on big stages to do *Don*

Giovanni. This is wrong. Because *Giovanni* is something where experience and age will help. I'll never forget the *Giovanni* Karajan did. From the death of the Commendatore to the very end, Giovanni is just death. His main concern is death. A young conductor, a young person, has an aggressive attitude towards death, maybe violent. Karajan was already close to death. And there was a kind of acceptance, and it was much more interesting.

For whom?

In general. Also the way he was filtering the music. I will never forget the trio at the death of the Commendatore. Karajan wanted three different kinds of fears of death. Leporello is a simple person. Every time he faces death, he's scared, in a normal, human way. The Commendatore is scared because he's dying. And Giovanni is scared because at that moment he feels his destiny is starting. Karajan achieved this, the three different fears, and everything in *piano.* It was magic; you were hypnotized. A young conductor would have been aggressive, and it would not have been that way. It was sensational to have these opportunities with Karajan in *Giovanni* and *Don Carlo.* There were moments in the orchestra that I never heard again in my life. With Giulini, I told you, the Verdi *Requiem* was incredible. He was filtering this masterpiece in a way . . . he was suffering, you could see that.

What do you mean by "filtering"? You've used that term three times now.

Our function in this profession is to be a filter between the masterpiece and the audience. We filter, through the interpretation, through our feelings, sensibility, and musicality. Singers, conductors, even directors.

So it's not just a question of if you can sing the notes.

No. You must *live* the notes.

Can you do that for every role?

There are roles I sometimes do because it's part of the business, let's say.

For example?

Barbiere di Siviglia. Basilio. I do it . . . [*shrugs*].

You don't particularly love it?

Nah. Not at all.

Musically or theatrically?

I don't like the character. I don't like the grotesque—I don't feel it. You do it because you're a professional. But if you ask, "Am I happy?" No. I've been happy the times I did the Mozart roles. Now I'm extremely happy, in heaven, when I'm in the third act of *Don Carlo*, starting with the aria and through the Inquisitore, the duet with Elisabetta, the quartet. Or the monologue in *Boris Godunov*, the death of Don Quichotte. These moments make this profession not a profession but a privilege.

You've said your voice is in good health these days. Has that always been the case?

I've been lucky. When I started, I was not thrown onstage with important roles. I had the first five years growing up, getting experience, doing not important roles, where you're not exposed.

What were some of those roles?

Sparafucile, in *Rigoletto*, or Tom in *Ballo in Maschera*. Last night, a gentleman waiting at the end of the opera for autographs told me, "I was in Aix-en-Provence in the summer of '76 when you were the Doctor in *Traviata*. Big career since then." I don't say it wasn't important to do these roles. I had this gap of five years where I was working a lot, earning—which was important—building experience, becoming involved in this profession. What we call *gavetta* in Italian [rising from the ranks], when you start small and then go up, is fundamental. Today you see young people, without experience, thrown onstage to sing a major role, without this period of routine, of minor roles. I saw, during those years, many good voices starting, and disappearing, in a matter of two, three years. It's sad.

Things like that happened with Karajan and his favorite singers.

This was the only risk—I wouldn't say defect, because Karajan didn't have defects—a singer could have, belonging to his group of favorites. If he asked you for something not exactly right for you in that moment, you couldn't say no. It happened, unfortunately. I remember there was a moment when it could have happened to me. But I was extremely clever.

Tell us.

We were rehearsing *Giovanni*. One day, during a pause, he was sitting onstage and told me, in Italian, "You know, there is something you should do, and we could do, one day: it's Escamillo." Which is very hybrid; it's a bari-tone role. I never did it in my life. And in a split second, I said, "Maestro, did you see the new Porsche that just came out?" "Yes, of course. I ordered one." And Escamillo was finished [*laughs*]. This was very clever. Because I couldn't have said, "Maestro, it's not for me." Because it would have meant, "You are wrong." You could not. That Porsche saved me! [*Laughs*]

And you never sang it—not even in a recording?

Never. When somebody does all the Mozart roles, sometimes they start to think you are a bass-baritone. And if you're a bass-baritone, maybe you can do baritone roles. It wasn't my case. My voice was allowing me to do that repertoire. But I could never have done Escamillo. I remember [Carlos] Kleiber once proposed for a recording, Iago [*his eyes go wide*]. And I was lucky again, because the project dissolved; they couldn't find other singers.

You would have done it?

Yes, because in a recording you do it, little by little, then you put it together, and you have it. And doing this, you allow the entire world to think you could sing it onstage. It wasn't the case.

What would prevent you from singing it onstage?

It's too high—it's a pure baritone role. And I'm not a baritone. I'm not even a bass-baritone. I was born, vocally, a bass. I could do the Italian Mozart roles. But this was a very specific box. My first role was Sparafucile; the first role I learned for a competition was Sarastro. When I'm singing, say, Padre Guardiano in *Forza del Destino*, or a typical, cantabile bass in Verdi, I'm at home.

Can you recall any other moments when you've come close to singing something that wasn't right for you?

My first appearance at Glyndebourne, in 1980. I was there for two operas, *Fedeltà Premiata*, Haydn, and the year after, *Barbiere di Siviglia*. I went one night to a performance of *Falstaff*. A Ponnelle production, which was splen-did. I was a kid but looking at these singing-acting roles like goals. And the Falstaff was Renato Capecchi. And he was a baritone, but he was very dark. And I thought it could be done by a long-ranged bass and wanted to do it. Now, San Diego Opera is a theater where I go often, and Ian Campbell [the general and artistic director] put on a production for me. So I started to study the prologue—this was three years before. And I said, "My God, I'm dying here. This is not possible for me." I spoke with Renato Bruson, I spoke with Leo Nucci, and they both told me the same thing, separately: "Listen. We're not exactly dark baritones—on the contrary. But after the prologue, we are dead." So can you imagine a bass? I phoned Ian Campbell a year before and told him he'd better find somebody else now, rather than a month before. I could have hurt myself. The choice of repertoire is fundamental. If a young singer doesn't have this clear idea, from the beginning, of the repertoire he should do, and starts to do the wrong thing, for two or three years, it could be deadly.

Why would it be possible to do Iago in the studio? Using the tricks you mentioned?

Yes. You can record just little parts.

And that's okay?

Of course not. It could have been the only possibility. In all the recordings I've done, you sing your part because it's your role, then you can make corrections. But if you want to do something that is almost beyond the edge, you could do it in a recording. *You* could make a recording, if you want! [*Laughs*]

Can you tell if that's the case, by listening?

If I know the singer, yeah. In tenors you can tell whether high notes have been added. It happens all the time. Of course, now the recording world is finished. Dead.

Why? Too expensive?

Because of Internet; the free downloads you can get everywhere. Classical recording was a kind of flower you put in your buttonhole in the record industry. The big companies were living splendidly on pop. But pop is in crisis. They are not earning the money they were. And they cannot afford to throw all that money at classical when they know that money will never come back. In the past, an opera could sell one hundred thousand copies. Now, if they reach twenty-five thousand, it's a success.

Opera was the luxury item for record companies.

Absolutely. I was lucky again, because, in the good times of Salzburg, with Karajan, it was an Olympus of opera and classical music. This system collapsed. The Salzburg Festival is not what it used to be. When it was big, it was led by great, charismatic musical personalities: Karajan, Böhm, Furt-wängler. When that finished, Mortier did well, I must say, for his ten years. He had to change from the Karajan time. After Mortier, that was the end. It's sad to think what it was and what it became. How long it took to create this Olympus and how short a time it took to bring it down.

Maybe something will revive it.

There's only one key: a big, charismatic, musical personality. Not accountants.

Is it the same for opera houses?

No. A festival lives for a month and a half. It's a reduced program, and they work all year for it. You need somebody special to attract the attention of the world. In a big opera house, where you perform every day, you need a system. You need complex administration, like here—it's a big machine. But a festival needs somebody [*snaps his fingers*] special.

How do you see the future of opera?

I think it's in good health. There is a good group of young conductors coming up. There is a very good group of young singers, very professional. The big problem in opera is stage directors.

Why?

Because in the past, opera directors were opera directors, *e basta*. They were specialized, they were professionals. Now opera has become television, it's become movies and DVD. Showbiz and money. It's attracting people from different fields that don't necessarily have anything to do with music. And, too often, stage directors are totally uninterested in opera. They do not speak the language of the piece they're going to perform. They direct with a translation of the libretto. With Da Ponte, for instance, you simply *cannot* not understand, deeply, the text in Italian. It's like a director who pretends to put Shakespeare onstage without speaking English. It's ridiculous.

Sometimes they're friends of the opera house director.

Yes. And because it's show business, they try to fill the halls because they must sell tickets, and tickets are becoming more and more expensive. So they have to attract people, and to attract people you need names, and sometimes the result is not important. Then they boo. "It's okay, they paid. They are there." If it's a scandal, they will boo, they will protest, but then others will come, because they want to see how awful it is. Today, to be demanding means to be difficult. This is the problem. Instead of searching for a director who is demanding and professional, they search for somebody who is easy, who won't create problems, and then if they're booed, who cares? It's his problem. It makes things desperate for us sometimes. Because we are professional. We love to do what we do. But to be a professional in the hand of an amateur is a disgrace.

Besides that, what else do you dislike about opera?

Opera can have many defects. But sometimes defects make a woman more beautiful. So it's okay. But I cannot stand a lack of professionalism. This is really what hurts.

We're seeing a lot of Asian and east European singers in roles traditionally sung by Westerners. Some say this globalization will mean the death of singing traditions, like bel canto. Do you agree?

When I started—and this was thirty-four years ago—I remember going to a great voice teacher in Mantua. He taught most of the great Italians, Pavarotti, Scotto. I remember there were hundreds of Japanese coming to lessons there, so it's not a phenomenon of today. The east European countries, yes; they opened after the Berlin Wall. Before, they couldn't come out—or very few could, and only with two KGB guards. Now there is an enormous group of very good singers from Russia. And in Russia, there is a tradition of singing that is amazing. They have beautiful voices, the school is good, and Russia is too small. If you want a reason there are many young, east European singers, it's because they are cheaper for the theaters to hire. They can fill gaps saving money. It's a matter of budget. But to say they are cheaper economically doesn't mean they are cheaper in quality, of course.

I've heard you talk about Cesare Siepi. Did he mark you, like Karajan and Ponnelle did?

Well, yes, of course, I cannot forget Siepi. When I was starting, I had a "latinity" in my voice, as he had. I adored his way of singing, and the roles. If I started to go towards Mozart, it was because I was inspired by what he did, by his Giovanni, his Figaro, and knew I wanted to go in that direction, his direction.

When you say "latinity" in your voice, what exactly do you mean?

It's a matter of color. If you think a Siepi voice, you have a clear image.

He was a wonderful actor.

It's for that reason I focused on that direction, because Siepi was the beautiful voice accompanied with sensational acting. This was the model I grew up with. I had another I loved, but it has nothing to do with affinity, and that was Boris Christoff. Boris Christoff was a sensational interpreter, a sensational actor. My second opera was *Don Carlo*; I was singing the Monk. And Filippo Secundo was Boris Christoff. He was so charming, so sweet. Sixty-six and singing like a god. Why? Because he had a technique that was perfect. So these two: Siepi, yes, number one, by far. But Christoff was a big inspiration, especially when I started to go into the Russian repertoire.

Let's talk about that. You were the first non-Russian to sing Boris in Russia.

That was *the* event of my career. To do Boris on the stage where it was born, at the Mariinsky, was amazing, amazing, amazing.

Is that a natural path for a basso, from Mozart to the Russians?

I would say so. The Russian repertoire, for a bass, is enormous. The roles are complex. They are all roles where the vocal part is enormous, but the acting is also.

Is it easy for you to sing in Russian?

I took two years to learn it. I was in New York for four months one year and had a teacher coming at home, four times a week. It was a full immersion. But it paid, because when I came to Boris, everything was there. Russian is splendid for singing. It doesn't have anything to do with Italian. But both are based on vowels. And vowels carry the sounds. And the consonants, both in Russian and in Italian, are not strong and fluty like German. For an Italian it's easy to go into that direction. I suppose it's the same vice versa. But for the same reason that an Italian goes easily into Russian, there's great difficulty going into German.

You're an Honorary Ambassador to the United Nations and sang benefit concerts to raise money to rebuild La Fenice in Venice after it burned.

I went back after the restoration for the New Year's concert and was touched, almost to tears, because when I went in—of course, it's a bit more shiny, but it looks *exactly* as it was. It's the place where I saw my first opera, because I'm from that area. For me, it's the most sensational theater in the world. To see it back to life and back to its beauty was a joy. Because I sang

Don Carlo two months before the fire. The emotion I had the first time I put my feet onstage at La Fenice was comparable to the emotion I had when I put my feet onstage at the Mariinsky.

Can we end the interview with pop music? I understand that when you were a kid you played in a band.

Yeah. We're talking about the second half of the '60s. A magic moment in pop. Everybody was playing an instrument, everybody had a group. We had a lot of fun. Every week, there was a new release; the Beatles, Rolling Stones, hundreds of groups.

You sang?

Of course. Lead guitar and lead voice! [*Laughs*] I did it kind of professionally, because I made two or three recordings with CBS—not a small company—with television in Italy, but I never liked the ambiance. Even at that time, pop was already in drugs. For a country boy, this was a kind of scary world.

You gave it up for opera?

I knew I had a voice, but opera was light years from my mind. A sister of my mother's sang a bit of opera. She told me, "Why don't you try it?" I didn't want *not* to try and do something with the voice. So I went to see this maestro in Mantua I told you about.

That was your first voice training?

Yes. With a recording I learned Fiesco's aria from *Boccanegra*. He didn't want to hear it. He just went to the piano and said, "Let's see what your range is." We did that, and he said, "You're a bass. You have to study, it's a beautiful voice." Then I started. I went to Mantua three times a week for lessons with him. I think I started in April '73. And in March '74, I had my debut in a very tiny thing in the province around Vicenza, a lovely old theater. And I did Sparafucile, my first role. Then I was hired in Trieste, which is an important theater. And did *Bohème*. Then it started and went by itself. It was extremely easygoing. It went in the right direction, into the right repertoire. After so many years, I can look back and say I've been quite lucky.

Do you still listen to pop music?

In the car on my iPod I have a huge collection of oldies. I love them.

Do you ever sing pop today?

Two years ago, I was in San Diego doing *Boris,* and got the most amazing offer. "Would you like to do *South Pacific* on Broadway, for its sixtieth anniversary?" I said, "My God, I'd love that." After sixty years, to redo it on Broadway, after Pinza, another Italian, would have been fantastic. I said, in principle, yes. We met in New York with the director, but then everything collapsed because I didn't know the world of Broadway. They asked me if I could be available one year and a half later for five months. I don't have five months in a row for five years! "Can't we have two casts?" It didn't work because of this. I loved the idea. But it could have been very difficult. They perform eight times a week. Wednesday matinees. If I had accepted, at this very moment I'd still be there, singing the same thing eight times a week. That's a bit much.

But an easy night, compared to Don Carlo.

[*Sighs*] I don't know. It was a charming offer. But eight times a week—whew!

You might have won a Tony award.

Pinza became a superstar at the end of his career through this. There must be a reason, no? [*Laughs*]

© Henrik Engelbrecht

Kasper Bech Holten,
or the emotional fitness center

The surprising thing about Kasper Bech Holten is not that he's in charge of one of the world's major opera houses and he's only thirty-five. What's remarkable is that he's already been running the place for more than eight years.

Named head of Copenhagen's Royal Opera when just twenty-six, Holten, a stage director, came into the job, as youth will, questioning its very existence. He began by looking for answers to basic questions like, "What is opera?" and "Why do I do it?"

"I needed a story I could tell myself, my artists, my staff, and the audience. I wanted to tell people why we're here, why we spend the taxpayer's money, what our contribution is, why you should buy a ticket."

He devoted his first half year on the job to finding answers and has seen them through various incarnations, refining his story steadily ever since. He has now emerged as standard-bearer of a new generation of opera directors—thirty- and fortysomethings who are aware that every performance is up for grabs in today's media markets and who, as a result, are courting a new crop of operagoers to survive. After explaining how he administers the opera, he discusses various survival strategies and especially how to lure younger spectators. This is an objective preoccupying most opera directors today, and Holten is particularly vocal about it.

He calls opera an "emotional fitness center." "You have to use your love muscle and your hate muscle to get something out of it. You have to invest your own emotional life."

The emotionally engaged operagoer is a vivid image, one that strikes a chord with audiences wherever he goes. It is the business of directors to find metaphors for the stage, and Holten's conception of opera as gym, where anyone can exercise empathy and emotional fiber, communicates well—particularly with the young.

Copenhagen—one of the rare major operas to still work as a company— has a new opera house that sits grandly on an island facing downtown. It is with a resolute, not relaxed, step that the shaggy-haired, open-shirted but plainly driven Holten crosses the threshold to his office at the heart of his emotional fitness center. From his seat overlooking the sunshine dappling the surrounding blue-green water this warm spring day, the blue-eyed, youthful leader of the 250-year-old Royal Opera describes the reworked metaphor he has fine-tuned to proud perfection. It's one that others might want to borrow. It is plainly working for Copenhagen, where attendance figures have risen 77 percent under Holten's watch.

How did you come into this job as director of Copenhagen's Royal Opera?

They advertised for a new opera director when Elaine Padmore left for London's Covent Garden [where she is now director of opera]. They couldn't find the right person. They asked me whether I would do it.

Where were you at the time?

I had been working as a freelance director for seven years. I had revivals of things here for the Royal Danish Opera, so they knew me. When they asked whether I would like the job, I said yes. It was my dream job! But it came a bit earlier than I had dared hope for. I hadn't even applied, because I thought, "I'm never going to get it." I was also at a point in my career where directing meant a lot to me. Since Elaine Padmore wasn't a stage director, I had a difficult time imagining combining the two jobs. On the other hand, it's been seen before, and maybe is a good combination. I'm not saying every house should do it.

What advantages do you see in the combination?

It gives some authority to my decisions. If I reduce the chorus or cut the prompters, they know I have to live with the same conditions when I go onstage.

You don't do all the staging for all the operas in the season?

No, one or two a year. This season I did Nielsen's *Maskarade* and *The Secret Songs* [Elvis Costello]. Some of my stuff is revived. I get to do something outside Denmark once or twice a year.

As part of your contract?

Yes. I was in Moscow this year, where I did *Lohengrin,* and last year *La Traviata* in Stockholm. It's difficult for me and for the house when I'm gone, but it provides new inspiration, fresh input, you meet people and get a stronger network. It's also to see what other houses do. Nobody has a real company of singers anymore. Ensembles don't exist any longer.

Why is that?

With globalization, all the good singers started traveling and didn't want to be stuck in one place. The reason we've been able to maintain a large ensemble of high-class singers is that the best ones, who have offers from all over the world, must do fifteen performances a year here. We plan around them several years ahead. We spend a lot of time and energy planning their careers with them. We're flexible and take care to keep them; we want to make sure everybody develops over time. We get them at a fair price; they get health care and the benefits of belonging somewhere, having a pension, and being steady with someone. And at the same time, they can pursue an international career.

Other major houses work on the star system, not the ensemble system like you do. Is that a budget thing?

It's a combination. First, it's ideological. I don't think we want to be—even if we could—an international airport opera, where people come in and go out, and you have only the best freelancers. That has, of course, some good things. You can always cast the ideal singers for every show. Having a company means you have to compromise. You have to use people even though they aren't exactly right for that role or style. But it gives us something else: a possibility to develop relationships among the artists over many years. Conductors and singers coming from outside all tell us there's a unique family feel to this house. I know as a stage director that when you work in a house where everyone is freelance you have to spend a few weeks getting over that, getting to know each other, maybe showing off to each other.

Sometimes you don't even have a few weeks to do that.

When we did the *Ring* [Copenhagen's first complete *Ring* cycle in one hundred years, which opened the new opera house], we built it over five years, with the same people, developed a sense of style and detail that I think would be difficult to achieve in many houses. People here know each other, they've been lovers onstage, they've killed each other onstage, they know each other's children, they've cried together and laughed together. It makes us, I wouldn't say unique, but relatively unique in the opera world today.

What other houses work on the company system?

Stuttgart, Stockholm. There are a few. Not many.

It's something you didn't bring to the opera house.

It was here when I came, but I wanted to develop it. It's something I believe in very strongly. I'm a child of this house, too. So it's in my blood. I find it hard to see us not working this way.

What's the top price you pay singers? Some European houses say their maximum is fifteen thousand euros per night.

We're lower than that, even with our top fees for guest singers.

How difficult is planning in a repertoire house like yours?

The detail that goes into planning several hundred performances every season makes it very difficult. Sometimes people have a picture of the opera as a kind of anarchistic, artistic house where we come in every morning and say, "So, what are we going to do today?" I plan premieres five years ahead, and once I plan them often they cannot change one week. Everything has to happen on the day it's set for. In my nine years, we've never postponed or canceled a premiere. We've canceled two shows in nine years. That's much less than 0.2 percent.

How many performances do you put on?

At the moment, it's 170 opera performances a year. If you include ballet, it's 270.

And what's your budget for that?

This institution, the Royal Theater we're part of, also includes drama. So we have drama, ballet, and opera. If you take them all, we do one thousand performances a season in the three houses. The total budget for that is about ninety million euros.

The Paris Opéra gets five times that much, for opera and ballet alone.

French houses are rich [*laughs*].

People's conception of Denmark is that the government takes good care of everyone, including opera.

We try and use the money effectively. Not all one thousand performances are big ones. We send small things on tour. We get a lot out of the money we're given.

That's enough on practical matters for now. We'll come back to them. Let's talk ideas. You call opera an "emotional fitness center." What does that mean?

This idea came from the question I had to ask myself when I was appointed. I was twenty-six. I had worked in and directed opera, but had to simply ask myself: "Why do I do opera? What is it?" Our orchestra is supposedly the world's oldest—five hundred years. The Royal Danish Orchestra played for King Christian IV in 1601 when he had parties. Not the same musicians we have now [*laughs*], but that institution. In the bigger, national artistic institutions that have been around for years, people sometimes take their being there for granted. We tend to think everybody accepts an automatic authority. In a modern media landscape nobody has automatic authority. You have to fight for making people interested in every production. People don't just buy tickets to the Royal Opera anymore. They go if we put on something they think might be interesting.

You're fighting for your place in the market.

It's one of the reasons many houses are scrambling. They're afraid because the competition is changing. I don't think that's bad. It forces us to think about why we're here, what we're doing, then telling that story. That's what many opera houses don't do well enough. So it was very important for me to find answers to that question—What is opera, and why do we do it?— answers I could tell myself, my artists, my staff, and the audience. And have it be one coherent story I tell behind the scenes and to the public. You can tell it in different languages and lengths, but you have to be able to tell the story about why we are here. You need a vision for why we exist. Why do we spend so much of the taxpayer's money? What's our contribution? We think that since we've been here 250 years, we're secure for another 250. I don't think it's like that. That's why I thought long and hard about my story and came to the conclusion that opera is basically, in many ways, impossible and ridiculous. It's a terrible business to put that few people in a room with that many performing, highly trained artists.

Opera is not good business?

It's never been good business. You lose a lot of money every time, wherever you are. It's the same at the Metropolitan Opera, but they have rich sponsors. Here the taxpayers pay for it. Opera isn't really an art form; it's the world's oldest multimedia. You take all the forms and combine them. And that's difficult. Not all performances are good. But with my vision, I try to remind ourselves why it is important to try hard every time.

Was this vision conceived when you came here at age twenty-six?

I had an idea but had never been able to put it in words. That's what I spent my first half year on. I've been developing it ever since.

How do you do that?

Through telling it. Every time you tell it you get a little closer to the point. Each time people ask a question, every time you get challenged, you refine it. At the beginning my metaphor was "The Emotional Laboratory." I figured the opera house was a kind of lab where you experiment with emotions. But I realized that was too clinical, too cold. It made it sound like something we're standing outside of, looking into. I wanted my metaphor to include audience participation. That's what I like about the refined metaphor "The Emotional Fitness Center." If you don't get on the machines, if you don't contribute, it doesn't work. You can go to all the fitness centers you want and look at the machines. That doesn't help; you won't get slim or trained. You have to invest yourself and your own emotional life. You have to use your love muscle and your hate muscle to get something out of opera.

Do you think your average spectators have difficulty investing themselves emotionally?

I think their primary prejudice is, Why does it have to take seven minutes to sing "I love you," or five minutes to sing "I'm dying now"? I always say, "But that's extremely fast." Not in realistic terms, of course. But if you go to opera and expect realism, you're really stupid. It's not realism, obviously—even if we build a realistic set. Trying to express yourself about love in five minutes is fast. It can take two years to say that or to even understand that. Saying "I'm dying" in seven minutes is fast. Thinking about death occupies people from puberty through the rest of our lives. It's the biggest existential question there is. So yes, in real life we don't lie around singing for seven minutes when we die. But to *express yourself* about the feeling of dying, or the anxiety of dying, in seven minutes is actually pretty fast. My point is, in one evening, you go through in two and one-half hours what the rest of us spend our whole emotional lives living through. That's why I say it's a fitness center. It's a workout, intense and focused—if you look for the emotional dimension and not the realistic one. Opera tries to show life as it is, not as it looks.

What would you say to people who, hearing that, would still say it's too long?

The reason it seems long is that we spend time on what's important in life. When you look at your life, what's going to define what it was? Not the everyday business, but the emotional highlights, disasters, or triumphs you had. That's what we focus on in opera. And that's because we have music.

For a theater person like yourself, how important is that dimension—music?

Extremely important. Music can communicate something that's not intellectual. When you read the stories, they look banal. Opera is really not about the story. It's about how quickly we can put people in a position where they love or long, are jealous or desperate or afraid of dying. We fast-forward over everyday life. And when we get to the point where they say "I love you" or "I'm afraid," "I'm jealous," or "I'm dying now," we press pause and spend five minutes. Through the music, we not only look at the person feeling that, but try to zoom into *what* it feels like. When music works, it's not an intellectual exercise. You really feel the lump in your throat or the butterflies in the stomach.

As a theater person, did working with music in opera come naturally to you?

As a stage director, I represent the theatrical dimension of opera. But opera has always been my thing. Music is what we use to express ourselves about emotion. We express something that words can't. We live in a society where we speak a lot, where we talk about emotions, and that's great. But how can you tell someone what love feels like if they've never felt it? How would you express that? You have butterflies in your stomach? Yeah, how many? When is it real love? How do you tell the difference? What is sorrow? Should I feel more sorrow now? Is it enough? Is this the right feeling? All of that you have to find out. I compare it to skiing. You can read all the books in the world about skiing, and it doesn't help one bit when you're out there. You have to find out with your body what it's like. It's the same with emotions. You can read about it, but once you're in it, that doesn't help. That's what opera can do. It's an emotional fitness center, where you live through love, being jealous or desperate or losing someone. You train your emotional muscles and your empathy.

Do you yourself feel pleasure in going to the fitness center and dwelling on your emotion—love or hate, say?

Sure. I think it was Stuttgart Opera who had a fantastic slogan: "Enjoy other people's pain—go to the opera." That's basically it. You can live through all these painful emotions without having to live through them. An important value in modern society is empathy, and that's something opera helps develop, too. I'm not saying opera is the only place where you use your love muscle or your hate muscle. But it's very focused on that. That's why taxpayers should pay for it.

Can you elaborate?

It's important for society to have a place where you spend time and energy on that side of life. We Scandinavians live in a society where everything is based on Ibsen's dramaturgy; you go from A to B, then there's a reason you go to C. Our public discourse is always about this. Everything is rational or logical. How people have the motivation to do this, then that. We have to remind ourselves that life often differs from that scenario. People are illogical, irresponsible, driven by passions and fears. Imagine what fear of dying can do to some people's decision making. We emphasize that in opera.

Is this vision your own or something belonging to your generation? Would you say you represent a new breed of opera directors?

The words are mine, but it's inherent in opera. I'm not reinventing anything, just pulling out an essence that's always been there, trying to find out from myself what the essence of opera is.

To survive, like any opera house, you have to find ways to bring young people in. How is your vision communicating to the younger generation? At the performances I saw, average age was maybe fifty-five.

Like most houses, most of our audience is older. To be honest, I'm not sure I regret that. As long as we have a big audience.

That sounds contradictory. You say to survive you need to find a younger audience.

I say we need to continuously find a new audience. They don't necessarily have to be young, as long as there is always an influx. And I've never been one who preaches, "We must bring in all young people to survive." I want to bring young people because I think they're missing out on something. Because they should experience opera.

How does one find a younger audience?

You have to make something really good, insist on quality, then tell the story about why you love it. Then they'll be curious. My generation can smell far off a desperate, sixty-year-old opera director thinking, "I have to try and speak in the young people's language and be smart and sell them opera." It sounds phony. Don't even try. Please tell me why you love opera. Tell me your story about opera. Opera is unashamedly big, spectacular, emotional. It's much in tune with our times. If we believe in what we do, it's going to be in high demand.

What part of the younger audience are you targeting?

There's a natural balance in life where from your mid-twenties to your mid-thirties you have small children, you're raising a family, your finances are a bit under pressure. We'll never reach that group with theater or opera the same way we do teenagers or people in their twenties who are experiencing life's emotions for the first time. They find an interest in opera and come back. We know that if we don't catch them in their early twenties it's much more difficult getting them back when they're forty. We should focus on seeing that people from fifteen to twenty-five come here at least once, because they'll return.

Do you have a strategy for this?

It's centered around a community on the Web that we've built. People under thirty-five can join free. We hoped to get five hundred members, and we have over seven thousand.

This was your idea?

Yes. I thought to myself, "What could have kept me from going to opera?" I was a bit nerdy, so did it anyway. But I thought, What *could have* kept me from going when I was sixteen?

You were nerdy?

[*Laughs*] I was a nerd, a huge opera nerd.

So you're a "former" nerd?

I've turned into a more open nerd now. Directing has taught me to be more open. But I was very shy; good in school, but had a difficult time believing I could have any value in social contact. The thing that could have kept me from going to opera at sixteen was that I felt so alone with it. So I asked myself, "What do we have to do to make them come?" The answer was, "Give them friends." We believed having friends would help build the community. So we put this club on the Web to show them there are other young people out there. You can meet them, share your experience, discuss it afterwards. It's horrible when you go but don't have anybody to share it with. If we make people self-confident about their interest in opera, they'll bring their friends and more people will join. It seems to have worked. Yes, our audience's average age is still over forty. But we're creating a solid interest in the future because we have a lot of fifteen- to twenty-five-year-olds coming while they're young. And they'll be back.

How does your approach differ from ways the opera house used to try and find new audiences?

Twenty years ago, the Royal Theater could focus on talking to people who were already coming. Subscriptions passed from generation to generation. People inherit them. If you were the son of someone who went to opera, when you were fifty you would also start coming. We didn't need to focus on a broader audience in those days; we could take this automatic authority for granted. Today, you can't. People nowadays go to the Royal Opera on Monday, a rock concert on Thursday, and a restaurant Saturday. A lot of houses are afraid of that. They think, "Now we have to compete with restaurants and holidays and football and art museums and rock concerts and everything. We have to fight for our place." I think that's healthy. I'd like to break the whole circle of complaining. Opera houses cry, "Poor us! The future is horrible, the Internet is going to steal from us." On the contrary, opera offers a chance to be unplugged. Your phone is off, for three hours it's a fantastic luxury. I'm not afraid. I think the electronic media should be afraid.

You say opera houses should stop complaining. What else could they do to bring in new subscribers?

We take the wrong approach trying to get people interested. When we bring new people in, we always start telling them the story of the opera, which is really stupid. If you went to a movie and started telling them that in the end Scarpia dies and Tosca kills herself, the audience would be really mad. Why did you spoil the suspense? But we have another approach that is arrogant: People feel that if they don't know when to applaud, don't know how to dress, haven't studied music literature for ten years and don't know the text by heart, they're not allowed in. Nowadays we have the text machine [supertitles]. Most operas are simple stories. You can follow it. We need to tell people what to look for. Because if you go to opera and expect realism or logic, like you get in theater, you'll be disappointed. We have to put people's antennas in the right direction.

How would you do that?

We should say, "Put on nice clothes, sit down, drink some champagne—not to impress anybody, but to make it something special for you." Because going to the opera should be special. The glamour and the gold, the big foyer, the expensive ticket, your dressing up, and the social dimensions—all that isn't there to inhibit you. It's not there to tell you, "Sit down and be quiet." It's there to celebrate that you go away from everyday life. Here, literally—since the opera house is on an island, and you take a boat and leave the city. For a few hours you celebrate the fact that you deal with what's really important in life, which is, as I said, what we focus on in opera. That's what I want to tell people. To turn their antennas in that direction. Some get inhibited by the spectacular, grand gesture of opera. I want to tell them, "No, that's all about you liberating yourself. So you can cry, you can go into this adventure and free yourself from the inhibitions of everyday life."

Did taking over the Opera at twenty-six and having to find and develop a vision present any difficulties?

Sure. But it presented a huge advantage in that a twenty-six-year-old opera director is unusual, so the sensational side of it gave me access to a lot of media that normally wouldn't have bothered. They wanted to speak to me, because, Who the hell are you?

Which I hope you milked for all it was worth.

I tried to. And tried to tell my story in the media in a way that made other young people think, "Whoa. He doesn't look like an opera director. What he says sounds interesting. Maybe I should go see if it's something for me."

How about the disadvantages?

They were more internal. Having to be director of 230 people and responsible for the big budget. Having to do all the stuff that requires heavy personal strength. You have to develop singers, develop their careers when it's not going the way they expected, you have to sack people and make the unpopular decision. That requires a strength you don't necessarily have at twenty-six. It's something I had to learn. In the beginning I was much too focused—sometimes still am—on pleasing people instead of doing what I feel is right.

Do you ever tire of the administrative part?

People ask, "Don't you long to just be an artist?" Yes, there are days you think that.

What part of the job is administrative?

About half. It's difficult to tell because if you put together the rehearsal schedule that will ensure a good production, is that artistic or administrative? Making the right administrative decisions ensures great artistic product. And the other way around.

Met Director Peter Gelb says the blueprint for marketing is in artistic planning.

It's true. That means if you think, "The administrative business is boring, I'll leave that to someone else," you miss out on factors that will influence whether you have good artistic output. And vice versa. If you don't respect the artistic quality and say, "We can cut this, rearrange that, and they'll have to live with it," in the end you'll lose income. People will sense it's not a good product. There is a balance. Having to develop a house, a company, 230 people who are working for me, take care of them, make the popular but also the unpopular decisions, is something that develops me personally, both as director of the house and as a stage director.

What will you do after you contract runs out? You'll be thirty-eight.

I don't know. If there's one thing life has taught me, it's that I can't predict. If somebody had told me fifteen years ago that you'll not only work in opera, which would have been a lot, and that you will have directed an opera, which would be a lot, but that you will have directed the *Ring* in a brand-new opera house in Copenhagen, where you are the artistic director, and you will have worked with people like Plácido Domingo, I would just have laughed. That would have been my combined life and dream. That it would have happened in fifteen years, I wouldn't have thought so.

Have you any plans?

This summer, I am going to make a film of *Don Giovanni*, with the title *Juan*. It is Mozart's opera, but we're going to try to make it really work as a film—to try and have opera and film get the best out of each other. For many previous opera movies, I think the opposite has been the case. We're going to shoot on location in Budapest. We've shortened it to 105 minutes and will sing it in a new English version—which is quite special. But it is all the original music, mixed with the sounds of the action on screen.

Have you changed the story at all?

The story is told in a contemporary, globalized city and is a portrait of modern, Western man: restless, selfish, but also seductive and energetic, with incredible persuasive powers and strong empathy, but fulfilling his life through consuming other's people's dreams. Juan is a visual artist who is making a special project out of all his seductions, documenting them. In the end, his work, his art, becomes so important, so much the meaning of his life, that he has to stay loyal to the project, even if it costs him his life. It's a movie about how closely connected are the energy and appetite for life—that makes us become artists and want to conquer the world—to destruction, eventually self-destruction, if it's not controlled.

Who is singing?

We have a very strong cast: Christopher Maltman, Mikhail Petrenko, Elizabeth Futral, Maria Bengtsson, Katija Dragojevic, Eric Halfvarson, Peter Lodahl. We will prerecord the orchestra music with Concerto Copenhagen, conducted by Lars Ulrik Mortensen, but the singers will be singing live as we film, so the sound will be rough, energetic, live, and authentic. If they are running, they will be out of breath! And you will see in the pictures that they are really singing. The *recitativi* will be recorded live through an elaborate setup with in-ear pieces for the singers. We'll take advantage of the differences within this global cast. For instance, Leporello [Mikhail Petrenko]—Juan's assistant and cameraman—is Russian, and we won't try to hide his accent. We'll use it. In the same way, Elizabeth Futral's Elvira will be American. The main point is to try to make opera and film stimulate each other, Not through glossy, superficial big images, but through film's ability to create identification and come close to the characters, and through opera's ability to express life's extremes. I hope it will be as exciting a result as it is to make. I have been working on the script for five years now, with Mogens Rukov, who wrote *The Celebration*. It will be released in about a year.

Just a few final questions. What do you like about opera?

[*Laughs*] That it reminds you life isn't so controllable. In Scandinavia, we're always trying to tell each other that you can control life, that you can plan—that was my point about the future a moment ago—that you can do this, and then this will happen. We are control freaks. Opera is wonderful because it reminds you of the opposite part of life, the huge turns and leaps it takes.

Has your way of enjoying it as a spectator changed at all?

Having worked with opera and having come to know the workings of productions has inhibited me in experiencing opera. When you know the crafts and the technicality of what goes into it, you're always thinking, "Aha, he did that to solve that problem, that's interesting." When you know how the machine works, you get obsessed with the single parts instead of seeing the whole. Opera is about all the single parts melding into one, and experiencing it. The more you know about the workings of an opera house, the less you can actually experience it.

To sum up, can we say your vision of opera as emotional fitness center is working?

I think so, but it's going a bit far giving me the honor of everything. Remember that in the end I'm not on the stage. My vision is working in that it has created a steady, growing interest in opera. It means people come: When I came in 2000, we sold 130,000 opera tickets a year. In 2008, it was 230,000. It's working in that it makes everybody in the house, for a relatively small budget, perform a lot, on a high level, and that brings us recognition for our art. But in the end, it's the artists doing the show. If they do a good one, people will come back. The frustrating and strange thing about being a stage director and about being the manager of anything is that you're the most important person maybe, yet at the same time you can't do anything because you're completely helpless. I can sit here and say all these nice words, but if the singers aren't good, if my people don't work well, it's nothing. That's the dilemma of being a director. You're important.

Your vision drives everything. But at the same time, you have to remind yourself that you're nothing. Really, you're nothing.

How big a role do leadership and motivation play?

That's what I mean. Motivation is everything. In the end, it's the only real management tool you have. The only thing you can do is try to tell the story the right way, and that story has to be authentic. The most essential tool any leader can have is to go into your heart and find out why we're here. What is it we're doing. If you can communicate that, I think you can get people to come along.

Keenlyside getting help with the score from newborn son Owen (Simon Keenlyside)

Simon Keenlyside,
or a workingman talks
about traffic control

The youthful, spirited Englishman bounds into a room in the fourth-floor press headquarters of the Royal Opera House, Covent Garden, immediately filling the small space with his great energy. He's wearing tennis shoes, dark shirt, Levi's, a big wristwatch, and a pale blue muffler, which he removes at once, thus beginning the interview. "I'll just be myself," he says. "Ask me anything you like. Anything you like! I'll do my best to answer. I never like being given anything in advance. It's more fun—and more truthful."

And so we are under way. Trained as a biologist, Simon Keenlyside has left his beloved farmhouse and fauna and flora in the Welsh country-side to appear—backstage—at the opera where he made his 1989 debut (Pagliacci).

Despite earlier written press reports ("He says he has nothing to say"), Britain's bird-loving baritone converses easily with an expressive and many-colored speaking voice. He is relaxed, accessible, thoughtful. Obviously changed since the days when he fled interviews, today he has plenty to talk about. If his voice is clear, his thoughts are often abstract, and to help him along he has a habit of rubbing his close-cropped brown hair with both hands while thinking about precisely how to phrase his answers.

He plainly possesses the English national trait of modesty. Though his career has taken off internationally, if the interview is any guide, he hasn't changed his hat size, nor will he need to anytime soon. He still calls him-self a "workingman." He is, among other things, refreshing.

We sip red wine at the opera house where the workingman has sung Don Giovanni, Billy Budd, Hamlet, Papageno, Valentin (Faust), Pelléas, and

Winston (1984)—a pleasant enough way to spend the second-act inter-
mission of Götterdämmerung. The sole intrusions come at regular intervals
through the backstage PA system, as an efficient-sounding woman with
an English accent barks orders. ["Stage cleaners, to the stage, please, with
Hoovers, thank you."]

The interview contains a minor dose of suspense at its ultimate mo-
ment. As the woman on the PA calls the five-minute warning for the last
act, and we're still talking, we realize we'd better wrap up. Keenlyside, who
had recently married, has to get home to his wife (Royal Ballet principal
Zenaida Yanowsky), and I have to return to my seat. Suspense heightens as
we lose our bearings in the royal confusion of corridors backstage and can't
find the elevator. "I thought you knew your way around," I say once we
finally locate it. He just laughs. No sooner does that dumb remark escape
than the lift doors part, and we step out—onto the stage. Where else would
he go? Thankfully, the curtain is still down. He takes off jogging in the half-
dark, and I follow, stepping around boxes, coiled ropes, and other Wagner
décor. When I catch up with him, he is smiling, holding the door open, and
I look through it, out into the seats. "Enjoy it," he says, and is gone.

From what I've read, your career doesn't sound like the typical trajectory.

I'm seeing everything in retrospect, of course, because you make sense of
it afterwards. But in reality, you're just bobbing around on this current, which
you have no control over. You might get a bit of luck sometimes. And if
you're prepared to take advantage of any luck that may come past you,
well, you may get a chance. That's all it is.

That sounds too modest. What about talent? And isn't it a question of
instinct, knowing how to grab the luck when it comes by?

Yeah, but I wasn't good enough. Until I was thirty-five, and I'm forty-eight
now, I couldn't do what I wanted. I had lots of arty ideas. But in actually
getting the engine of expression, the diaphragm and your voice, out, I was
a very long fuse, a slow start.

Thirty-five doesn't seem that old.

I wouldn't say I could do anything I wanted when I was thirty-five. Things
were a lot different after forty. But after thirty-five, things started to settle
down. In my twenties, I read that Ghiaurov hit the ground running at twenty-

three. Then I read it was much later that Birgit Nilsson started doing her big stuff, or Corelli didn't settle down with his top register until after thirty. I've been a workman from the beginning. In a way, that's been the biggest privilege.

Why is that?

You have any number of ways of making a career. You could do the old way of carrying your five roles around the world. You make a load of money and do those roles really well. But it never would have happened for me, because I wasn't talented enough to do the five roles I'd like to do now ten years ago. Not to mention that two of those roles would have been Pelléas and Billy Budd, both of which I've had to give up because I'm now too old for them.

That was your choice.

Yeah. Men are luckier than women. I can't think of any other roles I'll have to give up. But that meant all sorts of surprises came my way. Monteverdi and Gluck. I would never have looked out for those. They were a really interesting challenge.

You lived abroad a lot. Would you say yours has been the atypical career for an Englishman or a baritone today?

Maybe the point of that is "today." If you look at careers of singers in the '50s or '60s, their repertoire is enormous. In that sense, my career—and I'm not saying I'm in the same bracket as these people—is an old-fashioned one. It's very broad-based.

That's a rather humble résumé. Does it sum up your career to your satisfaction?

Pretty well. You've got to be realistic.

Is it hard to maintain a career nowadays?

People are pushed too soon. A normal, healthy, busy singer does between forty and forty-five shows a year—concerts, lieder, opera, altogether. But we all know sublime talents that have been too impatient. Often your *spinto* character with a lyric voice is not a good combination. Some singers blame managers when the voices blow up. Or the marketing situation, which is horrible nowadays. But you only have yourself to blame. You can say no. Of course those temptations never came my way.

You're being modest again.

No. Mine's been a fantastically interesting time. The fact that I wasn't doing all that opera in my twenties and thirties gave me more time for German and French song, which have been always really important to me. You can't build that up; you wouldn't have the time. Hundreds and hundreds of songs, over twenty years—it's a good base. In any case, if you're singing all your blue-ribbon roles when you're thirty-five, what are you going to do at fifty-five?

We'll talk about concertizing and lieder in a moment. Why do you like to sing opera?

I like the theater. Of course, there are bad singers and bad actors; a couple of big, fat birds give opera the reputation of being sung by overweight people who can't act. But the form is a fantastic vehicle for theater. Mime is acting. Opera is acting. Dance is acting. It's just stylized.

What's the singer's role? Is it stylized interpretation?

I don't want to bore your readers rigid and don't think it would serve any-body to tell them the nuts and bolts of how you do it. All I'd say is, it's a mirror to life. Why is it theater? Because it's focused. It's an aspect of our common humanity that's focused by the playwright or composer, added to by the director, producer, singers, or actors. You choose an angle, and, if you're good, you remain in that focus. Because to give too much informa-tion at any one time is to show nothing.

What are you supposed to show, then?

It's important to keep a half pace back from total involvement. That's es-sential to retain technical vocal and physical control, and also to better focus whatever you want to say and show. But you still have to be honest. You've got to be raw; you've got to show yourself. That demands exposure of uncomfortable aspects of our human nature, and as filtered through our personal experience of that nature. You've got to take that risk, to show something that might be uncomfortable. If you don't risk exposing yourself as a conduit, as it were, a bottle blown over by the wind of that piece, you have no chance of showing anything but a pretty sound. If you stay within the comfortable, tried-and-tested methods of getting through an evening successfully, sooner or later that won't be enough; it's bound to be a little boring. You don't want to semaphore the technical aspects, either. Mostly you want to be a conduit for whatever it is that your masters—the com-poser and librettists—want to say.

That seems easy to say but might be hard for somebody not involved in opera technically to understand about keeping that half step back.

Okay, put simply: if I were doing *Billy Budd,* as I was in Vienna, and somebody gives me a kitchen carving knife, barely blunted, for a fight scene, you've got to say, "Sorry, this is theater, not real life. Give me something else." When you do a fight scene, it's got to *look* dangerous. But it isn't. I make it look difficult—as long as I don't hurt anybody.

How do you do that?

I make sure I've rehearsed it, that I know exactly what I'm doing. If I'm coming down a slippery ladder from way up top, I'll have my own safety things going on. I don't want the audience to see that, of course.

Is this what most singers do?

I have no idea what anyone else does. I've always been insecure. As I said, until I was thirty-five, I couldn't get the juice out of my voice that I needed. So I fell back on stagecraft and all sorts of things. Because I was insecure, when everybody else was going out, I'd be back in the theater, working, working, working, if there were physical roles, to get my feet right. Now I have a reputation amongst my colleagues as a risk-taker. Nothing could be further from the truth. When they go home or to the pub, I go back into the theater and practice. I want to make sure I nail it down.

Can we say that you're not insecure anymore?

Of course I am. Any artist is insecure, or he's not worth it. If you think you're the bee's knees and can do it every time, well, I've got news for you.

Do you rehearse so much because you don't get enough time before opening night?

It's limited. A recession means less rehearsal time. Less rehearsal means more dangerous situations. Basically, the theater is a building site without yellow hats. You've got to watch yourself.

You fell through a trapdoor once.

It was here at Covent Garden, during *The Magic Flute.*

Can we talk about that?

It was three days before I was to go to Paris to do my first *Eugene Onegin.* But it wasn't to be.

How did it happen?

I made a mistake. The trapdoor was open, and I wasn't expecting it.

There was no light coming off the stage?

The dangerous place in the theater is in the wings. Coming off or going on the stage are trapdoors. *The Magic Flute* was designed by Schikenader to show the workings of his new Theater an der Wien. Nothing's changed; people want to show off our fabulous, modern machinery. *The Magic Flute* is the perfect vehicle. They show all sorts of nasty things that can trip you up.

Were you hurt?

I was busted up really bad. Tendons in the back of my hand, cracked rib, cartilage torn, black and blue. Luckily, I hit the stage manager on the way down, otherwise it would have jammed my spine. You just have to get up, not make too much of a fuss. Theater is a contact sport, like football.

So if I asked you what's the most important quality you need to do your job, would you answer "physical stamina"?

For a singer, consistency. And your worst on any given day better still be damned good. Because in my world, if you're just visiting, not fixed in a house, you've got to do your job well. Even if you're in a company, you haven't got more than a couple of times before people start to think, well, that's not good enough. It doesn't matter what's going on in your life. You've got to make sure you nail it. Technical consistency is very important. Knowing what you're doing will help that. An aspect of that is knowing how it works.

Does that mean a solid technique?

It certainly does. Knowing that with a certain preparation, *that* will work. And you have options if it doesn't. If you've got a cold or something, you can do something else.

You are fond of quoting Piero Cappuccilli, who said singers have to "act with the voice." What does that mean?

Actually, I tell that story against myself. He took a shine to me here. It was during my first job at Covent Garden. I was Silvio in *Pagliacci*, and he was Tonio. He took me out and told me, "Don't leave your Italian stuff too late."

I said, "Maestro, if I do it now—I was in my late twenties—I'll blow my voice up." He said, "You might. But if you leave it till it's too late, when your voice is absolutely ready, your name isn't Italian, and you won't have done the repertoire. It'll take you too long to get it." And he kept saying, "Prima la voce." Now I understood that, in my ignorance, to mean: stand and sing. Of course he didn't mean that at all. He meant if you're speaking to somebody in their own language, you're talking about inflection, about those arrows of inflection that pin people to their seats with intensity. You don't need to cartwheel and mug and wink at an audience. If you were reading a Walt Whitman poem, you think a cartwheel would help anything? You'd be doing the color with inflection. I don't see why music should be any different. I didn't understand, when I was a youngster, that's what he meant.

Wouldn't that depend on the audience? Different cultures or countries?

Yeah, but do you really want to go down to that level? If they don't speak the language, do you want to have to semaphore everything you're saying, physically? I think that's a very retrograde step. You don't underestimate an audience. They may or may not have done their homework. You have to expect them to know something about it before they come. And trust the judgment that they wanted to go in the first place. They have supertitles nowadays. I don't think you need to wink and nudge at the front of the stage and hide behind tricks.

If the director wants to go in that direction, what do you do?

Yeah, good question. I think now, at my age, that you can, as a singer, live to fight another day. Many times I've done it in a way I really didn't want to. But I thought to myself, two things. First of all, if I do what's asked, it may just be that I'll learn something. Even if I don't like the production, it will reveal something fundamental about the piece, dramatically or musically. So it's worth a risk. Secondly, unless you do that, you are condemned to a golden birdcage of your own making. Every time you do the role, you do the same. And that would be boring. You can never be more than the sum of yourself. Whereas you might learn, even if it's boring or frustrating sometimes—which, believe me, it is.

How about if you really don't want to do it?

Sometimes you'll say, "Could we try another way?" if you really find it objectionable. You choose your battles, you don't fight everyone. A nice director will say, "Okay, show me, I'll tell you whether I like it." But if they come with a vision of the overall thing—costume, lighting, and everything—you undermine their work.

Can you recall an instance when the director said, "I want you to do this," and you really didn't want to?

In Zurich, I did Schumann's *Faust Scenes*, which is not an opera, it's a concert piece. There was a famous Austrian painter, Hermann Nitsch, whose work is, to my mind, about blood, death, sex, and more blood. He showed blood the whole time. And I said, "I am not going to disembowel a real animal and use real blood," which is what he wanted. I did everything he wanted with synthetic blood, synthetic organs, slicing a pig open—it was a synthetic pig. I'll spare you the details. But I hated it all. It had nothing to do with the piece. But I thought to myself, "Look: if I treat it as an installation, either I do the job or I don't. If you really don't want to do it, just resign."

But when you signed, didn't you have an idea of what to expect?

No. I knew he was a provocative painter. And I thought, "Let's have a go." But what I loved was when he came up to me at the end and said, "Thank you for doing everything I asked. I didn't think you would. Thank you for giving me the opportunity to show my paintings." That's all he cared about. He said, "I don't care about Goethe"—it was Goethe's text. "I don't care about *Faust*. I don't even know *Faust*." I was a little irritated but kept it down. But the thanks at the end from this old man made it all worthwhile. He couldn't destroy the music. It'll live to fight another day.

[Announcement: "Götterdämmerung. Call for Mr. Rydl. Mr. Rydl, we should be ready for you to come and have a wander around the landscape in its upstage position in about five minutes."]

Kurt Rydl—he's been around a long time.

When I did my first performance in Vienna, he had just celebrated his thousandth.

Does he count them, like Plácido Domingo?

He does, doesn't he? [*Laughs*]

You don't do that?

Of course I bloody don't.

You only sing in languages you know, is that true? [Another announcement: "Calling for Götterdämmerung. Gentlemen, this is your half-hour call to act 3. You have thirty minutes, please. Thank you."]

Sorry about these announcements.

That's all right.

French, German, and Italian are the languages I speak and want to work in.

And English.

What English opera is there? Not much I'm interested in. *Billy Budd* is a joy.

John Adams?

I don't want to be a specialist in anything. I've done my fair share of modern stuff. Loren Maazel's *1984* and Tom Adès's *The Tempest.*

How was the Maazel?

Well, you know, I cannot be the arbiter of anyone's work. I can't judge the piece. But I can say it was a good evening in the theater. I had a nice time. I got to work with Robert Lepage, the director. I got to see the workings of an incredible technician and conductor—Maazel. He was great.

Seems to me you're being discreet here.

You can't do what you want all the time. The chances of having a good conductor, a great orchestra, great singers, a good production, and good lighting are really slim. But if you can find something positive about it, I think that's a good way to live, because the alternative is not worth thinking about. It's definitely a great way to work in the arts, and particularly if you're in opera. You asked me what it was like to do Maazel's opera. I got to work with Maazel and see that amazing conductor. I got to work with Robert Lepage, who is a genius. And I found the whole thing interesting.

Are you saying singers can learn from conductors? ["Calling Mr. Rydl, this is your call to the stage, please. Mr. Rydl, thank you."]

You can learn a great deal. Because they're aware of so many things. They say, "Look, I'm asking you to do this because the horn is doing that while you're doing it, and it's reflecting what you say."

And you wouldn't necessarily know that.

I wouldn't necessarily know that.

But you would have studied the score.

Yes, but more than likely—increasingly less so—I'm a great deal younger than these people. When I was with Abbado and Muti I was thirty, thirty-five. Not only that, I'm working in their language. There's all that. One of my friends, a colleague, said something which is fundamental to my own approach about working. Susan Graham, when we were kids, said, "I wish we had a bit more traffic control." She meant instead of art.

You're talking about onstage?

Yes. If you've got a five-week rehearsal period, what I like is traffic control. Where am I, when, and why? Give us the parameters to work in, instead of the hand on the chin, earnest, going into the heart of the first bar, one at a time—it just doesn't work like that. For me, anyway. I'd like broad brush-strokes. Then we'll add to it.

How does that help?

In the performance, everybody knows where they're supposed to be and why, or roughly. If you just are spontaneous all the time you might screw up someone else's ideas—someone who has an overall idea of the production. But if you're open and know roughly where you are, anything can flow out of that.

Logistics before interpretation.

I want art, but not on Day One. Practical issues. The logistics of the opera are enormous. We need to organize them before getting down to which side the hat's going to be worn on.

That echoes what you said about directors who have an overall vision. Some bring the piece to themselves, whereas often the better ones go the other way. Dominic Dromgoole [director of Shakespeare's Globe Theatre] says that three things actors must do are: find out who you are, learn your lines, then get out of the way of the play.

That's why I kept saying "conduit" or the wind of the music blowing over the bottle of whoever you are. That's exactly what I mean. Don't show all your toys in your box every time you go on the stage; (a) it's boring, and (b) it's disingenuous. If for example, you are doing Pelléas—young man—or Billy Budd—young man—use the colors for a young man. It'll be in the score; it'll be done for you. Don't use your wide-throated, Italianate, *Don*

Carlo type of Rodrigo singing. Because you'll be too old for the role. Yeah, you'll impress people, but you'll be doing the piece a disservice. And you'll be doing yourself a disservice.

It sounds like you're thinking of serving the composer.

The piece.

But it also sounds like you're not serving the audience, in a way. Maybe they would like this, or that.

I said don't ever underestimate an audience, and I believe that profoundly. If somebody's doing something entertaining, people will love it. If somebody fantastic is doing it, an ignorant audience will still know on some level. Even if it's because the master knows exactly what to do to get them. An example is Jussi Björling. The way he sang naturally had a sob in the sound. The audience feel that; it was his natural voice. But a good professional will use a quality of sound which you know will affect people. It's not cynical. Because what you're doing is getting the traffic control pillars, the parameters, the frame, of your role in that piece, of your personality. When you've got all those pins in place, it's like those things you had as a kid with nails on a glass, and you put your hand on it, turned it upside down, and you had your handprint. Within that frame you can do anything.

And it's not manipulative?

I don't think so. My job is not to go and nudge the audience. My job is to use them as a fourth wall, with focus, as we said at the beginning. But the coat I wear is defined by the play, the music, the director, and my own ideas. If I've got those pieces, and we're all in agreement, roughly, about what they are, then within those parameters, anything goes. If we've got all the borders, I can really inhabit the role and there's room for spontaneity. Where do the audience come in? That's the professional aspect. How much do you engage them? That depends on the agreement you've made with your director. That depends on the nature of the production.

This notion of traffic control is important, and I want to make sure I've understood it. Would it be right to say that freedom in a role comes once you've defined your limitations?

That's what I meant. Traffic control is putting the big bollards on the road to say, "This is the area we're working in." Then we're going to move them in, define them a bit more. Then we're going to put more pegs in, so before you know it, when you're nearer the production you can see the outline of what you should be doing. I was a biologist by training, and it's one of my deepest loves. My brother, who is an entomologist, told me that if you could take a photograph of all the nematode worms in your body you'd still be able to work out the outline of the human being pretty well. That's sort of what I mean about traffic control and parameters. There are very many. In an ideal world, you take some of those parameters with you to the next production. You can't reinvent yourself every time. But you may be working with people you've worked with before. That nematode worm is the ideal that you've put your posts in. You know where you're supposed to be, in terms of this character and the production. Within that, you're free.

[Announcement: "Attention, calling for Götterdämmerung, *ladies and gentlemen, this is your call for act 3. You have fifteen minutes, please. Thank you."]*

We'll have to go soon. Do you like working in a new production?

It's great to explore something quietly and have the time to experiment in rehearsals. But you have to be careful; you've got to be disciplined and use the time well. Even in a four-week rehearsal, the last week is chaos—the last ten days, really. The difficult thing is when there's no rehearsal.

That's what I was waiting for. I was at last summer's Festspiele in Munich and a couple of funny things happened onstage.

They always do.

This was in the opening of The Marriage of Figaro. *I spoke with Heidi Grant Murphy the day before your first night there. Remember that? She sang [Susanna] with you [Count Almaviva], and told me you had no rehearsal time with the orchestra or on the stage for your two performances. The principals, she said, had all been hired because you had sung the roles often and could be dropped into a new production blind. I was at the first performance and saw two things in the second act. One, you couldn't get your sword out of the scabbard; and two, you fell on your behind over a chair. Was that on purpose? It wasn't clear to me.*

Of course it was! *[Laughs]* It was a pratfall.

I wasn't sure.

I know exactly where this was. It was the chair, left of the settee, and it was stage right, standing, backwards. If you noticed, I'd shuffled ten seconds earlier: I made sure I dropped the pliers and the hammer a bit further to the right, otherwise I would have cracked my head on them.

I didn't notice that.

Of course not. I could never have asked them if I could do that. It's enough to do the production. They would have told me, absolutely not. At the time I thought, "Dammit! I'm gonna give this a go; I think it's a good idea." But it *wasn't* a particularly good idea. I thought to myself, "Where should I do this, in a comedic moment?" Actually, what I did was not in the most comedic moment. As I got up I was thinking, "Well, I should have thought that one through!" [*Laughs*]

Did anybody say anything afterward?

No, because I said it was an accident. But of course it's not! [*Laughs*] They're lovely there, they really are. But if you try and bully your way, you make everyone's life difficult. You work within the parameter. When I did that, I didn't get in anybody's way. I didn't ruin anybody's lines. I was the one to speak after. So I wasn't disturbing anyone's art. I feel that's fair game. And I was within the parameters of the production.

Were you within the parameters of the character?

A little outrageous, maybe.

Because my first reaction was, it's out of character for Almaviva.

Of course it is. It's ridiculous. But it was a spontaneous decision. And they're not always good ones.

Did you do it in the subsequent performance?

Yeah. I tried it again in an earlier place. And it didn't work. My first idea was that the funniest place to do it was against the wall. But then I realized it's not a wall. It's only material, and I would have broken the whole set. Everything would have come down! [*Laughs*] You've got to take risks sometimes. Not physical risks necessarily, but musical risks. You've got to see if you can get through that phrase in one breath. Because you think it might be interesting. You might not make it. But it's worth trying.

Are these things you try in rehearsal?

I try them in the shows sometimes. But you don't want to be flying by the seat of your pants, all the time.

Are you on anybody's blacklist for these sort of things?

No, no, no! They wouldn't notice what I was doing. If I tried to do a phrase in one breath—I just made up that example—for a reason I thought was a good one, at the time, in character, as we were saying, those are the parameters, and you're free within that. Then something may occur to you in the middle of this glove shape, as we were saying, that you think, Well, that's a good idea. You don't have time to think about it. You either do it, or you don't. That falling off the back of the chair was a bad idea. I didn't think it through. But I thought I'd give it a go.

Do you remember the sword being stuck?

Yeah, I did that on purpose, too. It wasn't stuck. It was just a bad joke. Because he's supposed to be . . . so . . . furious! [*mimics an enraged Almaviva trying to get a sword out of his scabbard which won't budge*] . . . and it doesn't come out!

You had problems with the doors, too.

The doors *all* got stuck.

But that's a minor thing.

The door thing was really embarrassing because there's a whole door scene. Like Heidi, I'd never done their production. And we had no rehearsal. Nothing.

How is coming into a situation like that? Even though you know the role well?

I thank God I know the role.

But you land like that in a new production, with everybody else in the same boat.

I think it's fun. You know, your life isn't at stake. You know your notes. You know the character. You speak the language. You know who relates to whom. What's the worst thing that can happen? You make a bad judgment call. As I and many of us do, from time to time. But sometimes they're good calls. I found it fun because I've done so many revivals that I've got used to finding ways through it so I enjoy them.

You don't really mind things going wrong onstage, then?

I love them when they go wrong! Because if I'm with people I know, or I know the piece, then I'll have options. And sometimes surprisingly wonderful things can happen which you could never have rehearsed and never repeat. And if you're sensible, you'll keep your mouth shut and say nothing, and people will think you're a genius and you worked it all out! [*Laughs*]

There are superstitions in opera houses, aren't there? In Copenhagen, you're not allowed to wear a jacket onstage.

Vienna's the same.

What superstitions are you aware of?

[*Laughs*] I'm aware of a lot. I couldn't give a fig about any of them.

But you respect them.

Exactly. I would respect them if by not respecting them I would upset any of my colleagues. We all know them: there's no whistling in the theater because the scenery was handled by sailors and that was their land job.

And for sailors, whistling is an alarm. They might drop the sets on somebody.

Yeah. So it's for a practical reason. But nevertheless, many of my colleagues are superstitious. And if I were to whistle, or leave a bent nail on the stage, or say "Macbeth," or wear my hat or coat in Vienna, somebody might be upset. It might upset their performance. So I would never want to do that. But I couldn't give a stuff about any of it. I think it's nuts.

[Announcement: "Calling for Götterdämmerung. Ladies and gentlemen, this is the five-minute call for act 3. You have five minutes, please. Thank you."]

We'd better go.

The more normal you are in your real life, the more chance you've got. I was working with a young soprano in Munich, and she said, "Oh, I don't speak much the day before, and I don't have milk, and I do this and don't do that." And I said, "Darling, you're going to build a very expensive gilded cage for your life."

So you don't have a favorite pair of tails, cufflinks, or anything?

No. If I did, I would go out of my way to throw them away! [*Laughs*]

© Wilfried Hösl

Waltraud Meier,
or the sweatshirt must fit

Like others in this cast, Waltraud Meier takes a few whacks at stage direc-
tors. There seems to be a reaction among opera professionals these days
against the over-the-top, or underprepared, mise-en-scène artist. Perhaps
we are hearing the first sounds of a crumbling idol: the Stage Director as
Star. Meier, however, has some kind words about one director in particular.

She is shorter than an audience imagines—nothing like the towering
Teutonic divinities, Venus or Isolde, she incarnates onstage. Pale pants,
white shoes, turquoise top and scarf, lipstick a pale red, and hair cut short,
hardly hiding the collar of her black raincoat. Though it's a chic coiffure, it
is vaguely reminiscent of the style worn by those in mourning, and you
can't help wondering if it's for Tristan, *because the interview is happening*
in another empty, echoey dressing room—not her own—at Paris's Opéra
Bastille, where she has returned for a reprise of Tristan und Isolde. *We dis-*
cuss this opera and its composer.

She is happy when she realizes we will be speaking in English, not French,
though she is comfortable in both. As we talk, and she shuttles among
three tongues, including her native German, she always speaks unhurriedly
and chooses her words with concentration. During her recurrent pauses,
she connects with the eyes, staring straight at you to make a point, so the
silences that follow and frame her words are as captivating as her speech.
When excited, she not only switches in her chair but, at one point, actually

climbs around in it like a small child. Feisty, instinctive, and emotional, she is someone who knows what she wants, as you will hear.

She is staying in an apartment near the opera, and has spent much time in this city—three years, she tells you, if you add up all the visits. Born in the north of Bavaria, Munich (Schwabing) has been her home since 1986. She also has an apartment in Berlin, "But my heart and everything is in Munich."

The soprano is carrying the current copy of Pariscope, *a weekly entertainment guide to the French capital. She likes to go to movies and plays, she says. Do I know of a good one?*

You have time on your hands? Tristan und Isolde *opens here next week. How much rehearsal do you need?*

I did this production three and a half years ago and needed one rehearsal for every act. *Basta.* For the third act, I'd say, "Let's talk about it," because I just enter, go forward, then sing my stuff and do my expression however I feel it. For every act, one rehearsal—maybe one orchestra rehearsal per act. That would make six.

That's enough for a reprise?

For me, absolutely.

How about for a new production?

More—but not as much as they do nowadays. Because most directors come and don't have any idea or are not well prepared, or—what I had a couple of months ago—they don't know the music. We have to deal with that.

You're not the first to condemn this. Whose fault is it?

I don't exempt theater managers because more and more they think it's fancy to take somebody who comes from outside.

But often they're from theater.

If it's theater, it's already something good. But if it's somebody that's done nothing, maybe a film . . . [*shrugs*]. And if they don't read music anymore? In any other profession, you let experts do the job. Only in opera now does this happen.

How do you handle that?

I meet a lot of directors who don't know anything about music and think they can direct a great opera masterpiece. I tell them, "You're creative. Why don't you have the courage to write your own opera, then work with a good composer? Then it's really something out of yourself; you are on top of your own work. Otherwise, you're below it." I'm fed up—no, that's too strong—say I'm *through* working with somebody who is not on a high artistic level. It's taking over—I would say it happens a good 70 percent of the time.

On major stages?

More and more. Then you work with somebody like Patrice [Chéreau] and feel like you're in absolute heaven. For the reprise of his *Tristan* at La Scala, we will rehearse four weeks again, because you change, and he will change a lot of things. That's what I love about him, it's really work-in-progress. He develops things, he's free, and he waits for you to develop. Also, his German is perfect. It's a pleasure to work with him on the text.

What's the future for opera, if so few directors are really up to par?

Incha Allah [it's in God's hands].

You often sing at the Munich Festspiele. Do you get enough rehearsal time at events like that?

Last year, we did *Tannhaüser*. When we performed it during the year, we had rehearsals. Maybe one for the Festspiele. You get the same pieces you see during the year, with mostly the same casts, only for much higher ticket prices, and less rehearsals because it's every day another piece, and we don't have time to rehearse properly. The famous *Meistersinger,* which is always traditionally the last day—never rehearsal! One day! Munich is not a real Festspiele. Maybe I'll get killed for saying that. Others are *real* festivals. They have special operas they put on during that time, with preparation.

Like where?

Salzburg. Even if they have revivals, it's for only two or three years. Bayreuth.

Some singers can describe their voices. Can you?

Difficult, because I don't hear the same things other people hear. I hear it from *within* my body. How would I describe it? I would say it has a . . .

[*pauses*] . . . dark color, maybe copper. Instead of silver. My ideal for a soprano voice should be silvery. Like . . . [*thinks*] . . . in *Der Rosenkavalier* you have Octavian und . . .

Marshallin.

Nein.

Sophie.

Yes. *That* should be silvery. My voice, I consider more copper.

Does that mean it lets you do, or limits you to, a certain repertoire?

[*Thinks*] . . . Well, I wouldn't answer that question so easily. It's not so simple. Because singing a role, or not being able to sing it, has other reasons. I think I have quite a powerful voice but also a very sensitive voice. At least I try to range it from the most tender expressions to the most powerful. That was always my goal.

Why do singers use metals—gold, silver, copper—to describe their voices, anyway?

Because metal shines. Its brilliance gives a different sound when you push it out—different than wood, say. You have wood instruments, like the xylophone, but metal creates more of a *vibrating* sound. That's why we say metal.

How is a vocalist trained to produce sound?

We use the expression that you "grab it," very tightly, where you produce it [*points to her mouth, then pauses and stares*]. . . . If I give you a voice lesson, I should really give it in German.

Keep going. You "grab it, very tightly" where?

Difficult to say. You grab it, then make it develop, outside. There is a place, above your palate, above your jaw, then there is the "third eye," as we call it [*indicates forehead*], and then over your head. It's like a candle you think is there. Then you should have the feeling that it's spread out in front, like—how do you say—a bow and arrow. The place where you put the arrow is very small. Then with the bow, you stretch it quite far. Then you can let it go, and it goes far.

It's not easy to describe these things, is it?

That's why it takes so long to learn it. Otherwise you could do it in a week.

What do you like about opera? Why do you sing it?

First, I would like to say I don't consider myself an opera singer. I see myself as a *singer*. I like to sing opera, but opera is not my favorite. I prefer concerts and lieder.

Has that always been the case?

Not really—for a long time I was afraid to sing lieder in public. Of course, I sang it at home, I grew up with lieder. But when you sing lieder, you're totally alone in front of two thousand people. That's a different thing, and I was scared to do it for a long time.

Scared because you were alone?

Yes. Because it was just the text, the voice, the music, and me. There was nothing else I could hide behind. I had to stand there as myself, not in a role, where I play something I'm supposed to play. In lieder, I'm really myself, with my personal interpretation of a text.

Do other singers feel that way?

There are both types. Some are the other way around [*laughs*]. I've talked with some *lieder* singers who would never *dare* go on an opera stage. But I lost that fear totally.

What happened?

Getting more mature, more self-secure. Knowing what I have to say, and being sure it's something that could interest other people.

You took a whole year off from opera, during the 2003–2004 season, to do only concertizing.

It was great! I didn't miss opera. That's why I say I'm a singer, not an opera singer. Of course, most of the business, and most of the time I spend in my profession, is opera. But that's also because it *takes* more time: rehearsals, then you have a series of performances. Out of the whole cake of a year or a season, I always have to cut a big part where I do only lieder and concerts. I prepare that quite consciously. I do lots of concertizing now.

And enjoy it more, I hope.

My attitude has completely changed. I look *forward* to going out onstage. Now I'm much more the missionary, saying, "Hey, audience: I have something to tell you. And I think you will like it. So listen carefully." And that's a joy. The thing is that I can have control of everything.

You choose the repertory, the pianist . . .

And choose if I sing it *piano* or *mezzopiano,* in what tempo—always in accordance with my pianist, of course. And I can concentrate more on the . . . [*pauses*] . . . on the real stuff, the substance of things. I'm not distracted by . . . so many things that, in opera, are going on at the same time. I want to concentrate on a moment where I can really dive into . . . [*pauses*] . . . into poetry, into text. Before, my concerts were always *between* an opera series. I realized it's not fun.

You can't "dive into text" when you're in an opera?

Not to that extent, because I'm too busy with what we're playing onstage. I'm not a reproducing-type singer. I'm always trying to do different things from the last time. Even every performance. So for some directors I'm good; they have time for me because I'm creative and constructive. Others are afraid of me because I always change.

What are you changing in this Tristan?

I change it every time! And I will always negotiate. I'll say, "I've thought about this phrase. And in this context, and if it's like that onstage, then the context is different, and we have to play it like that this time." I keep discussing, and for me it's always alive. I will never, *ever* do the same thing the same way. Because every day is different. I wake up differently. Sometimes I'm in a more joyous mood and think life is easy; then of course you can link better with joyous things in the text. Then, on another day when you are moody, you think, "Ay, death is near," and all that. I am convinced it is important to have that freedom onstage. Because then it's convincing. Then there is really something . . . [*pauses*] . . . authentic in that moment. I'm not answering your question directly, I'm going a bit around.

That's all right. A last question on concerts: you change your performances in opera all the time, depending on how you feel. Is it the same for lieder?

Yes. And that's fun, because often we go offstage and say, "Hey! What was *that* today?!" And . . . [*thinks*] . . . I'm looking for a word in English . . . you need to be more *aware* of what is happening in the moment. Because you live much *more* in the moment. My pianist is also a creative musician, and when I feel the slightest change from what we did last time, I have to pick it up and follow that logic. And this is interesting, because you enter into another . . . [*pause*] . . . a world which is inside and outside of you. So you connect with something, and you have something. And still you're totally aware of it, under control and not under control. That's great!

You needn't mention names, but can you recall times when you were creative and changed, as you say, in opera, and the director or conductor didn't like it?

Of course. At those times, I feel like the director wanted me to put on a sweatshirt that is absolutely not my size, not my color, and a fabric that itches. And I have to say "thank you" for it.

If you're in a mold like that, do you think the audience can feel it?

[*Raising her voice*] Absolutely! That's why I will *never* do it onstage. And directors know that. I will never, ever do anything that is totally against my conviction. Because when I'm convinced, people see it. They see, on the other hand, if I'm a puppet. And a lot of singers act like puppets.

Why do you suppose that is?

Often they have stopped *asking*; they just *do*. Then they stop thinking about it in bigger contexts. They say, "It would lead me to something where . . ." [*shrugs*]. So they feel it's better to just accept what they're asked to do. I see that when *I* go to the opera! That's why I'm really not an opera fan. When I have to see a performance, I'm always very critical. It's not pleasure for me. It's difficult to judge *why* that is, and maybe it would be presumptuous. But I can only see what comes *out*. And I'm disappointed. I see when somebody is not convincing. I say, "He does this and that, but it doesn't *come up from inside!* It's not really *born in that moment.*" At least I see it; maybe the majority of people don't.

You said once, about choosing roles, "Does the character speak to me or doesn't it? It's like turning the dial on the radio: nothing . . . nothing . . . suddenly there's a signal." Is that what you mean?

It's still true! [*Laughs*] It has to vibrate. Of course, that changes. A year later, all of a sudden, you can think, "Hey, I have an approach to this role now. There's something there; I can feel it."

Are there roles you once felt and no longer feel?

Absolutely.

For instance?

Octavian. I did Octavian I don't know how many times. And there was one performance—in Stuttgart, and a good production, I remember—I was on-stage in the third act, and realized, from one second to another, "What am I doing here? I'm not feeling it. This is ridiculous!"

It's a question of age?

Yes. It's not me anymore! [*Laughs*] There's nothing where I can *enter* into it.

Do you mind if I ask how old you were at that time?

[*Thinks*]

Roughly.

I must have been thirty, thirty-one, something like that.

So can we sum up by saying that to successfully perform a role, you have to believe in the character? And in the text? In other words, you must be convinced to be convincing?

Yes. Always take seriously what is written. It's not nonsense. And no irony.

And you're saying there are performers today who don't do that.

Absolutely. On the other hand, I can see clearly when it's an artist and when it comes from the inside. Then I'm overwhelmed. I'm taken and I'm happy. I want the audience to laugh with me, suffer with me, hope with me. I want them to be sad, cry, have all the emotions I show them. I want them also to get into it, and feel it themselves, in the moment. That is most important for me.

You are known as a Wagnerian. Have you pretty much given up the Italian roles?

No. I would like to do more, but the market is getting . . . how should I put it? . . . [*Thinks*] Artists with a more . . . overall range have fewer possibilities in this market than before.

You have to specialize.

It was always like that, but it's getting even more ridiculous.

You're talking about the recording industry?

Not only recordings. Engagements for opera houses. You know how it works now: young singers have a success in a certain role, and then they go—boom!—from opera house A to opera house Z with the same role. And this is insane.

It could help explain what you said before about how singers won't take risks.

Often, it's not only that they *can't* ask. They *are* asked, but sometimes you have to follow the market. I think the business has become more brutal—on one track, and going faster.

It sounds like you're almost typecast. You have fewer opportunities to do the Italian roles.

Vienna still asks me, and Berlin. But they take people now for certain roles; it's mainstreaming. I think it's destroying a lot in opera. It's a big problem in all opera houses.

Is your concentration on Wagnerian roles then a result of the situation you're describing, or did you get there consciously?

Both. I'm lucky because my voice suits some of Wagner's roles perfectly. Especially those I call the "in-between" roles, like Kundry, like Venus. They can be sung by a mezzo and a soprano. My voice was always something in-between. I was never a real soprano and never a real mezzo.

That hasn't changed over the years?

A little. The high range has become more firm, more secure. But I always had more ease in singing those roles. And my approach to them was a mixture of "Do I feel it? and "Does it vibrate in myself?" But there was also a strong intellectual . . . [*pause*] . . . "approach" is a stupid word . . . *Beschäftigung* . . . occupation . . . with it.

Is that also what you look for?

Yeah. When we were preparing *Tristan* with Patrice [Chéreau] for La Scala, we met for five days in Aix-en-Provence, half a year before we started stage rehearsals. And we only went through the text. And analyzed it. And went from here to there. And proved every phrase on its content, and on the real inner truth in it. I love that! I do it also, on my own.

Without a director?

Yes. For instance, I was here in April, doing *Parsifal*. You know how many times I've done *Parsifal* in my life? I don't know—uncountable. And many, many different productions. So I have big input from all these ideas. But I remember, I sat here, not with the score, but with the text, reading it through, again and again, and again and again, finding out—even more—what lies in the text, the truth in it.

What do the Wagner roles—text and/or music—allow you to do that other roles don't?

You cannot separate one from the other. It all goes into the music . . . [*thinks*] . . . Every time I compare a Verdi text to a Wagner text, I think Verdi is maybe ten pages. And the Wagner, [*laughs*] sixty pages.

More text means more profound?

You declare yourself more. That's just in the words. But then, also in the music, with all the counterparts, leitmotivs, and what he does with the language in the music. For instance, a lot of harmony changes are on a consonant. So if you have rhythmic text with a lot of "t" or "p," he uses it musically, to express something very specific, where you need that rhythm in it.

And Verdi, no.

Less.

Does that pose any problem for non-German singers?

Once I had a *Tristan* whose text was horrible. The "r" was horrible. At the end of every phrase he expressed too many consonants, wanting to make everything clear, but the result was nothing was clear.

Why didn't you help him?

You have to have a relationship where there is confidence with the colleague. Then, I can. But if somebody makes a wall around himself, then who am I to say anything? They have to give a sign that they are open.

Have you come to appreciate Wagner more as a result of your specializing in his work?

I can say that, as an opera composer, he is right after Mozart.

Mozart is first?

Different. It's difficult to compare apples and pears. It would be unfair.

But the two major composers—

—in opera.

—are Mozart and Wagner.

Yeah.

Mozart because of the dramatist, the musician, or both?

Also in how the music takes, picks up the drama.

What's the one quality a singer must possess?

[*Thinks*] . . . Integrity. To yourself. To music. To life. *Wahrhaftigkeit.*

Anything else?

You asked me for the main thing, but everything else comes from that. Because if you follow your integrity, you know precisely the power you have—your physical power—your physical . . . *faiblesse* . . . weaknesses, and you're not pretending. You're clear on what you are.

Is this something you learn along the way?

Of course. I think I've always had a healthy mentality. Franconian, down-to-earth.

"Franconian"?

That's north of Bavaria, where I come from. Those people are very down-to-earth. Honest—not diplomatic, but straight. And deep. They will always say, "No, that's not true. Let's go behind it and find out."

Is there an experience—maybe in your Franconian background—which marked you, which you remember as being strong, or fundamental to the musician you became?

My upbringing. My family were absolutely nonprofessional musicians. But music was always present. You made music for your own amateur pleasure.

Classical music?

Everything. Folk music, classical; when I was young, there were the Beatles. Music was around. And played a total, normal part in my life. My father played the piano, but just for fun.

But you said your family were not musicians.

Not *professionals*. It's difficult to explain to people, because now when you say you come from a musical family, they think it's so *serious*. In those times, it wasn't. We had no TV. I remember my father came home with a TV someone lent him so we could watch the moon landing. He had to bring it back the next day. So with no TV, what did we do? We played the flute, we played piano, we sang when we did the dishes, we sang canons in the car. Things like that.

How many in your family?

We are three sisters.

And you played the flute?

I played the soprano flute and a little piano. But manually I'm not very talented.

How important is playing an instrument for a singer?

Anything with an instrument is important, because you should have the feeling of how you produce a sound. And what happens when you strike an instrument or when you blow into an instrument. What's important is to educate your ear. That is what happened in my family. But it was joyful play—in the real sense of "play."

That was the fundamental experience.

Yes, and it was at home. And with a lot of joking. I remember . . . [*laughs*] . . . here's a typical scene: us three sisters, doing the dishes after lunch, and somebody starts to sing [Mozart's] "Das Veilchen" [*sings*]: "Ein veilchen auf der Wiese stand . . ." And all three of us tried to sing it with our personal expression. And it was so funny! It wasn't Mozart anymore, it was nothing, it was just us. That's what I miss now. The approach for young kids to music is too serious. There should also be jokes.

If I may say, with your steady diet of Wagner, I don't see how you can get many jokes in.

[*Sitting up*] A lot!

Really?

You don't know! Go to a cast of Germans doing Wagner. You're *in pain* afterwards, you laugh so much!

Tristan?

Always!

Hard to believe—inside jokes, maybe.

Of course, but there are a lot of opportunities! [*Laughs*]

Any examples?

I remember the last performance in Bayreuth of *Tristan* [*laughs*], I even surprised Daniel [Barenboim]! He looked at me like—[*opens her eyes wide, in astonishment*]. Because at the end of the first act, there's a bit with Tristan, "Mein Herr und Ohm, sieh die dir an: ein sanft'res Weib gewännst du nie" [My Lord and uncle, look at her! A gentler wife you could not discover]. And I sang instead, "Mein Herr *Marquis* sieh die dir an" which is a line from an operetta! I took another text from an operetta and put it in there! I've always wanted to sing that—once! It rhymes better! "Mein Herr *Marquis* . . . gewännst du *nie*."

But that was in rehearsal.

That was the last performance in Bayreuth!

Who noticed, besides the conductor?

Well, of course, my *Tristan*; it was Siegfried Jerusalem. He *laughed!* [*Laughs*]. He knows about these things. Because in the second act, there are all those long phrases, and once he completely lost the text. So he started to sing about spaghetti and I don't know what else! Yes! And when he finished, I looked at him and said, "No kidding?" [*Laughs*] He turned away and laughed!

Can I use that story?

Sure, he knows about it.

Did any critic notice?

No.

You said earlier that music is serious. Now it sounds like you manage to have fun with what you do.

I think the complexity of life is that there is always everything. You know yourself that you never laugh as much as when you're at a funeral. There's always the ridiculous in the serious. And no tragedy without a joke. So it happens. I do it sometimes.

I'm going to be watching you at the next Tristan. *Do you want to talk about conductors? How important are they for you?*

Very. I can name some. For me, the top, for influence and everything, it's Barenboim. My other favorite is Jimmy [Levine]. I *love* to make music with him. Or Muti. Very passionate, very good.

What have you learned from these people?

It's difficult to say precisely, because everybody has their own . . . [*pause*] . . . personality. Maybe generally I learned . . . [*pause*] . . . that there is this inner truth in music, but still there must be . . . a certain personality, and it resonates differently.

In each performer?

Yeah. And can still be true. So there is no objective one way. But still it's not total liberty. There is a frame. If you go outside it, you lose the truth. And this is very difficult to define. I think a lot of artists have destroyed their heads over it.

Can we talk about the public? What false ideas do you think they have about opera?

Well, the audience isn't always the same. I notice, for instance, that an American audience . . . [*pause*] . . . receives an opera in a . . . more like a good meal.

That's good or bad?

Not good or bad; it *is*. They like the *sound* more. My theory about that is—except for some Britten operas or modern composers—they are not used to understanding the text. So they don't care about it.

When you say America, do you mean New York?

Not only. San Francisco, Chicago, and so on. They receive beautiful *sound* more. So they are more receptive to the beautiful voice. So if you know that, go to America, hold your high notes a little longer, sell yourself in a different way. Berlin is different. There they absolutely pardon you if, out of expression, you miss a note, or something. They would much more appreciate that you do something out of the *text*. It's a more . . . theatrical expectation they have.

Would you say they are a more thoughtful audience?

Different. They don't think so much about the beauty of the voice, or the beauty of a sound, things like that.

They are closer to the text; it's in the culture.

Exactly. Even when it's in a language that is not German—in Italian opera, say—they know the text is important.

What about opera do you not like?

[*In a deep, Marlene Dietrich voice*] A lot.

Where do you want to start?

I hate when it's exaggerated. I hate fake feelings. Anything that's fake. That's most of it.

Isn't there a bit of exaggeration because it's theater? Movements have to be a little broader?

No. Watch Patrice's [Chéreau's] operas. It doesn't have to be like that.

Anything about opera that has defeated you?

Well, I'm still waiting—maybe it'll come in my life, or maybe it's over, I don't know—but I would like to do a *Carmen* where I'm really convinced. *Carmen* is the most difficult thing to do. Ask eight people at the table how they see *Carmen*, everybody will have a different opinion.

Will they all say it's difficult?

No, because they don't know it, but they are convinced of their opinions: "I see *Carmen* like this." And the other sees *Carmen* like that. To me, all those expectations make it absolutely impossible. I saw a production on TV once in France, and I don't know who did it, but I liked it because it was in the *opera comique* style, the French style. Because Carmen has to sing, mostly, *chansons*. Only the fourth act gets dramatic. Until then, it's chansons, it's easiness. And in America [*Dietrich voice again*], you like those women who are . . . femmes fatales. She's not! *Carmen* is about *liberty*. And the joy of living in liberty, in the extreme sense. So I would like to find a director once with whom I could realize what *my Carmen* would be. But I have to hurry! [*Laughs*]

You've had a long career. The secret of longevity?

I'm in my thirty-third year. What's the secret? Don't go with mainstreams. Always go . . . [*thinks for a moment*] . . . always be reasonable. In anything you do . . . [*pause*] . . . in success, or in exploiting success. For instance, several times I had the possibility for much more marketing. And refused. Because those names on the piles of CDs next to the cashier are promoted very much. And when you are on top, you can never hold on to it. Life changes. From a pedestal, you fall really low. But you fall a lot higher from the top. So if you're always a bit underneath, it's better.

Are you saying you're prudent?

I am. But I also dare things . . . [*thinks*] . . . As I said before, I think I have integrity and never was afraid to tell the truth. If it's always about the art and not about your own person, that's good. And people feel it; I think that's the most important. I don't want to put myself, as a person, in the window. It's what I *do* that I put in the window.

What do you do on a typical working day, when you have a performance?

I wouldn't give an interview. I shut up. I talk at home on the phone but of course have to reduce it. Here we start late for a *Tristan* [6 P.M.]. I'm used to *Tristan* starting at four or five o'clock, so I try to have a good sleep, a good breakfast, a little—not a nap, because I don't sleep—it's more like . . . relaxation. An exercise I do; not meditation. I relax and go through the whole body, mentally, to relax.

How long have you been doing that?

Years. I do that on the day of a performance. If I have the chance, I do my workout. When it's at home—Munich or Berlin—I have a cross-trainer machine. If I'm in an apartment where there's a gym, I go there—even before a *Tristan*—for half an hour. Then I go to the performance. I want to be in the house two hours before it starts, to have time to warm up the voice.

No matter what the production is?

Two hours before I begin. Mostly I start at the beginnings of operas—*Tristan*, *Parsifal*, Ortrud, Venus, Sieglinde; *Fidelio* is almost the beginning.

Do you prepare for interviews?

No. What should I prepare?

Maybe your management gives you a message to communicate.

No. It's my opinion. Aside from, "What's your favorite role?" the other question I *hate* is "What is next?" But I've learned to never react to anything stupid in the newspapers.

Some singers answer e-mails on their Web sites. Do people write to you?

Not on the Web site. I'm very cautious in separating the business Waltraud from the private Waltraud.

And the private Waltraud is what? Married, children?

No [*laughs*], *private!*

We can stop there, then.

Because when I get too close with fans it doesn't lead to anything.

Their expectations are too high?

They want to see you only as the *artist*. They are not really interested in who is the *person*.

I'm surprised fans wouldn't like to see the other side. What you do on a Sunday.

Yeah, but then they say [*whispering reverently*], "The artist does *that* on a Sunday!" or "Take care, it's windy outside!" At home I don't feel *at all* like an artist. My being me is a human being.

© Jennifer Gasparian

Heidi Grant Murphy,
or sopranoed—with children

Heidi Grant Murphy looks extremely relaxed as she walks smiling into the lobby of her hotel, dressed in black Capri pants and sandals. Her bright blue eyes match her turquoise top and abalone earrings, which dangle lazily. It's a lazy day. It's hot. She is tanned. With her chestnut hair tied up behind, she looks like she has just put down her book and crawled out of a hammock for a short spell at interviewing.

She seems relaxed because she is. The soprano is taking it easy this afternoon between two performances of Mozart's Marriage of Figaro. *A brief moment of calm.*

We're at the summer Festspiele (opera festival) in Munich, where, for four and one half weeks in June and July, fans of the lyric arts can revel in an orgy of operagoing unparalleled in Europe: as many as seventeen operas staged in three theaters, written by thirteen different composers spanning three hundred years. People attending the festival can, by adding concerts, ballet, and recital evenings, see more than fifty performances in thirty-five days. This includes world premieres.

If it sounds like a lot of work, it is—for Festspiele organizers. Staging a different opera every night is no easy task for a big theater like the Bayerische Staatsoper. Fortunately, labor strikes are not part of the culture here, or it wouldn't work—as it doubtless wouldn't work farther south. But all that is not even a remote worry to Heidi Grant Murphy. For her, it's all vacation because her kids aren't here.

She lives with her husband, pianist Kevin Murphy, and their four chil-
dren in New York. Her family—and in particular, her children—are a key
subject of our interview. They appear early, weave in and out of her talk,
recurring time and again. Her children seem as present as she is. So much
so, in fact, that you begin to wonder how she actually manages to juggle
her two jobs of singing and being a mom.

Her voice chirps merrily like a bird's; her words are punctuated through-
out with easy laughter; she is pleasant and easy to talk to. She pronounces
the Italian names of composers and musical terms in a very American ac-
cent. She is no pushy, intellectual type; she is winsome and uncomplicated,
and though still quite young, stands at the midpoint of her career on this
midsummer afternoon—a convenient vantage point from which to look
back over, and contemplate, her professional life.

How did you start singing?

My father was a minister, so I grew up singing in church. I didn't really know
I could do it for any other purpose, other than accentuating my father's
sermons. I loved the idea of finding out what he was speaking about and
finding something appropriate that would accentuate through music what
he was trying to say. Twenty-five years later, I still try to do this.

Are you saying there's a religious or spiritual side to your singing opera?

Not religious. It's about communicating something through music. I started
singing at an early age, using singing for a reason: it was a communicative
purpose. I think this is the difference between a good singer and a great
singer. I don't mean to imply I'm a great singer! [*Laughs*] But the people I
admire as great singers are in tune with the ability to communicate what
they want to say. The ability to put aside the thought of your technical abilities and speak through your voice and your heart and head is a gift. This
was the beginning of my evolution as a singer and is an integral part of who
I have become as a singer.

Do any colleagues come to mind who, as you say, are in tune with the
ability to communicate?

Christa Ludwig. Bryn Terfel is remarkable, because he has this amazing
voice, and yet he really does throw it aside in order to communicate what
he's singing. And it always comes from this enormous store inside him which
is full of joy, rage, love; it's very apparent.

I don't suppose "putting aside the technique in order to communicate" is something you do consciously.

To be able to do all we need to, with range, stamina, and floridity, we singers have to learn how to hone our instrument. That's one tricky thing. Then you have this communication side. People who can do it best have such a fabulous technique, or natural technique, they don't have to think about it. The people I think really are fantastic are people who *do* have to think about it, but don't. And sometimes you get a big, fat crack. Or an awful sound. But I'll take it, any day.

It's more human.

Yeah. Much, much, much more appealing than a perfect performance.

What kind of training did you have?

I was an education major. I wasn't thinking about singing. Actually, a high school choral conductor is what I was sort of planning to be. But don't tell my conductor friends! [*Laughs*] My last year at Western Washington University, I had a teacher who convinced me to try singing. So I went to Indiana University, about the biggest singing school in the country, where I met my husband, so I'm happy I did. I did the Met auditions that year, won, and ended up at the Met the next year. I came into the Met apprentice program very young. Very inexperienced.

Do you regret not becoming a choral conductor?

Not really. I love kids. I get my fill of them because I have four! [*Laughs*]

You live in New York. Can we assume the Met is your home stage?

Absolutely. I've been at the Met twenty years. That's remarkable! [*Laughs*] The other day, I realized I am getting older. How do you go from being the youngest person in all your casts—which I was for a long time, because I started early—to all of a sudden having twenty years behind you?

You say you started early. How early?

I was twenty-two, maybe, twenty-three. My voice was on the lighter side, so it developed naturally and easily, as opposed to some which are heavier and take longer. My career jumped out quickly; not just in opera, but in concerts and recitals. By the time I was twenty-four or twenty-five, I had a solid concert career and a beginning opera career at the Met and around the world.

Were you young for that size stage?

It wasn't the usual thing. For most singers, by the time you arrive on the stage of the Metropolitan Opera, you have performed your role many times all over the world. And the reason you're singing at the Met is because you're the best at what you do! [*Laughs*] So for me to have someone like James Levine pick me out, coach me, push me in the right direction, give me the opportunity to sing Barbarina while Kathy Battle or Dawn Upshaw was singing Susanna was a fabulous opportunity. I was very lucky. At the time, I took it for granted.

Was it hard for you?

It's not easy for a young singer because that stage is very exposed. There are a lot of people watching! [*Laughs*] A lot of critics. And it's scary. I'm glad I was a bit ignorant. It's the best way to do something like that! [*Laughs*]

Do you remember your first voice lessons?

I wasn't particularly thrilled with the music I was singing. But the pieces my teacher picked for me suited my voice. When I look back, I can't believe I sang them. I was about nineteen. My teacher gave me the Constanza arias from *Die Entführung aus dem Serail*, "Caro Nome" from *Rigoletto*, and an aria from *Martha*. They all had high E's and lots of florid runs and difficult tessituras. And I never knew they were difficult. My favorite was "Qui la Voce" from *I Puritani*, which is also kind of a tour de force. Now I know that! [*Laughs*]

Do you remember your first recital?

It was in college. My voice teacher and I had worked on my songs, and I kind of went along. All of a sudden, the day of the recital, I went in and said, "Forget this, I'm going to sing them however I want to." And I sang them, and I'm sure I scooped all over the place and did my little thing, you know, and I thought, "My teacher's going to kill me!" And she didn't. She came to my dressing-room and said, "What happened? That was so amazing! That was a whole different thing." So I figured it out: "Okay, I can sing this type of music with my own voice, the way I want to."

Are there two opposing approaches here? Do some say, "Sing by the rules," while others urge you to free the voice within?

They don't have to be opposing. I think—and I say this to young singers all the time—you have to find your inner voice. And you have to let it out.

Hopefully, you'll have a teacher who understands this. However, it's also important to have a teacher who knows when you're straying too far off the path. Our instrument is very delicate—if you do something technically inappropriate because it feels good to communicate, you can hurt your voice. That's a tricky barrier. Singers have struggled because of this.

How do you choose the roles you sing?

I'm sort of in a repertoire where I don't have the problem. "Do you want to sing Desdemona?" [*Laughs*] People wouldn't think of me. My choices are slimmer. A lot of roles have chosen me. I started out really bel canto–ish. I learned *Rigoletto, I Puritani, La Sonnambula*, that direction. When I started at the Met, because I was a light voice and a young singer, they were very careful with me. Also, honestly, at that time I couldn't have sung those roles because my voice was not developed enough to carry over the orchestra and into the house. The roles which suited me were Mozart and Strauss. That's where I started. And that's where the rest of the roles sort of caught on. This year I branched out. I did my first *Elisir d'amore*, which was a real blast.

You moved to Donizetti from Mozart.

Those things are not so far apart. Donizetti, particularly *Elisir d'amore*, has more ups and downs, and middle and fat notes; where Mozart has more line and lyricism, with the complication of having to struggle to make it sound simple and lovely. And trying not to complicate it, which is my biggest trouble! [*Laughs*]

Can we talk about that? How do you complicate things?

The more you do something, and the more you love something, it becomes part of you, and you tend to want to find something else in it. So you add your thing, and this thing, and that, and change the tempo, and pretty soon it becomes something else. When Jimmy Levine sits down at the piano—he's done this a few times with me—with a Mozart aria, and I hear him play it, I go, "Right. That's the way it's supposed to sound. Uncomplicated. All on the page. It's all there." Once in a while, he'll say to me, "No. *Just sing it.*"

You say you've branched out. Are you going consciously in another direction now?

Not really. It's difficult because my life crosses over with my art. The problem is partly that I have four children! [*Laughs*] I have a very, very, busy, busy, full, full life. I can't even begin to tell you! [*Laughs*] The problem is I don't have time to try to consciously push my career in a different direction. Often I find myself saying, "Okay, I have this much time to prepare this role and this recital and this concert. Or I can do this. But I don't have time to try that." So I end up saying, "This fits with my son's schedule."

Does this mean you are—I don't want to say stuck—but concentrating on a group of roles you know because you don't have time to learn new ones?

No. There was a time, for five or six years when I was starting out, that I felt I ought to try harder to get a job singing Gilda. Or in *I Puritani*, or someplace else other than the Met, a smaller stage someplace. I never did that because my career took off in a certain rep.

You mentioned Mozart and Strauss. You're not the first soprano who seems to specialize in these two composers. Why are they often linked? What have their roles got in common?

It could be the tessitura they're often written in.

That's technically. Psychologically, would you say they both have insights into the female persona?

Certainly. Those female roles for Strauss and Mozart are fabulous. I learned this when I was in recording sessions for three days, where I would record twenty songs and do them over and over and over and over. By the third day, your voice is just exhausted. I found that if I went into a dressing room and picked a Mozart song or a Strauss song and sang them for a while, my voice would come back, feel healthy and rested again, back to where it should be. There's something about the way they're written, the tessitura, the way you have to sing, that is extremely healthy for the voice.

Anything you want to say about how you prepare for a role?

I think I prepare pretty much like everybody else. I start with the text, then learn the music, then put them together. As a kid growing up at the Met, I was trained that way. I figured out early how well you have to be prepared. So generally, I'm always very well prepared. If it's a new piece we haven't all done, I feel I need to be extra prepared. This particular kind of preparation comes from the place where, in the beginning, I was the youngest person in the room. I had to prepare extra well, so people didn't look at me and say, "What's up with you?" [*Laughs*]

Describe your typical day when you have an evening performance.

My typical days are very different, depending upon where I am—if I'm home with my kids or here, for instance! [*Laughs*] The tricky thing about being a singer and a mom is you don't get to do what normal singers do for their days and performances. Our voices are delicate instruments which have to be in shape and rested, so you must strive for a balance of working it out, singing, practicing, honing it, resting it and keeping it hydrated. Lots of things. As a mom I don't really get to focus on me and my instrument as much as I would like and as much as I should. So my typical day is not . . . ideal! [*Laughs*] It's usually whatever I have to do: Get my kids up, feed them, get them to school, go to the grocery store, run the errands, pick them up with a friend or two in tow, run them home through the playground. . . . and then head to the concert hall.

You don't get enough time for yourself?

Generally, when I'm home with my family, I'm running to get to my opera or concert just as I need to get there. If you can imagine, there was an occasion where I acted as first-base coach for my son's baseball game, swallowed about a pint of dust, made my way to Carnegie Hall and sang Mozart's *Mass in C* with James Levine and the Met Opera Orchestra. When I get to the concert hall, I take my fifteen minutes and settle down, drink my water, and curl my hair, warm up, and I'm out on the stage. But I love it, or I wouldn't do it! And I love my family. I don't delegate well [*laughs*]. I can't say "no" very well. So I probably do too much. But my kids are only little for so long, and then I don't get it back. So, yeah, it's a struggle sometimes, and I'm really tired at the end of the day. But I'd rather have it this way than feel like I didn't do something I should have.

How old are they?

Twelve, nine, four, and three. The older ones go to school and the little ones are with me.

You have no nanny?

I have a babysitter who I've had for years, but mom is mom! [*Laughs*] And no matter how hard I try, on a day where I have a performance, and try to say, "You guys, it's time to go to the park! So I can rest and look at my music," inevitably, one of them will have a meltdown and decide they're not going! [*Laughs*] So the rest of my day is spent with the three-year-old.

That must not be easy to manage.

I've learned over the years what my limit is, to be able to do my job well. How tired I can be, and what I can do. There have been times where I've crossed the line, and I have known I haven't given my best. Thankfully, I've never had someone tell me that! [*Laughs*]

You mean critics?

If a critic didn't like me, it usually wasn't because I didn't have a great night because of my kids. It was generally some other reason. A matter of taste or style.

Do you read the critics?

I don't generally. Recently there was something I did that really didn't go over well with someone. And I didn't know it. And I was really glad, later! Because it spoils it for me. You work so hard with your colleagues to put something on. And then to have one person say something not nice about you. And another person will say you were a goddess, or something. But one person really can color how you feel about the rest of the run.

Do you find yourself being a critic when you attend someone else's performance?

It's hard for me to not judge. Sometimes it's obvious that something is good, or mediocre. But generally, as a performer, you can sympathize and come away with the positive part of the performance because you know what the performer you're watching has gone through to get there.

How do you like singing in a festival, like here in Munich?

The Festspiele is interesting because many operas are presented in a short period of time. They hire very talented performers who are familiar with the operatic roles, so they can put the show together quickly. We had three days to put together two performances of *The Marriage of Figaro*. I think one person in the cast had done the production before and the rest of us were doing it for the first time. There were some scenes we had basically touched one time which might not have worked out just perfectly. . . . [*laughs*].

What didn't work?

Thursday night we bumped into each other a few times. We hadn't rehearsed any of the production on the stage, so weren't sure how some of the doors worked.

You had no stage rehearsals?

No, and nothing with the orchestra. But we had [conductor] Lothar Za-grosek, who does this piece wonderfully. It was, musically, very easily done—the orchestra was great. We had a couple of moments where we had to slow down or speed up, but not as much as we could have. There is such a high level here, they can produce very good performances. This is a good house for such a recipe, which might not work in other places. The Festspiele has fabulous directors who know how to work quickly and efficiently. Our stage director was also the assistant director, and he put it together in three days. I don't think he stopped talking the whole time. As well as singing all the parts, and all the *recitativi*, by heart, in English, German, and Italian.

After the performance, do you come right back to the hotel?

No, I love to hang out with the other singers. It's not a matter of rehashing the night; performances are such that you pour yourself into it. You work for that moment and for those few hours. You concentrate and expend so much energy that you can't just say "Bye!" and go back to your room. First of all, I can't ever go to sleep. I'm just buzzing. And no matter how many years I have been doing this, it is always the same. It's nice to go out with colleagues and wind down for an hour or two. That's a lovely thing about opera. When you get to a certain point, you know at least one or two people you've worked with before. Or you've worked with them so closely for three days that you feel like you've known them for years. But it's also a curse, because you leave the job, and you've made a good friend who you might not see again for two or more years. But the beauty of this business is you can pretty much pick up right where you left off, because you're poured back into something else in the same way.

If I were to ask you what are the main qualities someone needs to do what you do, what would you answer?

To be a great singer, you have to have talent. But talent only takes you to a certain point. Something else needs to kick in. You need a certain kind of psyche. Singing, and constantly being evaluated by people watching you—critics, voice teachers, conductors—is very difficult. You need a brain which says, "Okay, I've got to be prepared and know my stuff." But you also must be able to take what is thrown back at you—whatever that might be—in the right way—and keep on going. It's not a small thing. I believe this is the difference between somebody who sticks around and somebody who lets it get to them and eventually makes a mess of it.

What would you call that quality? Resilience? Armor?

I think it's an ability to process the feedback.

That's while you're coming up, and once you've made it?

Once you've made it, you have to think about what might happen when you're on the way down. Then, perhaps those same people I described above: voice teachers, critics, conductors, patrons, whomever, begin to criticize you for being not able to do something, for whatever reason. Then there is the person coming up behind you who starts getting the role. Being able to process such things in the right way and not let them make you bitter or destroy your insides so you can continue honing and refining your craft the way you've always done it. It's a tricky business. I find it's even harder for females—single females. Especially when you reach the upper echelons of the business. People focus on you in a different way. You're either worshipped or torn down.

Do you get both?

Yeah.

But you go into this job saying, "If I ever get big, I'll expect that."

You don't think such things when you're young, or at least I did not think such things. You think nothing is going to ever upset you. You don't think you can get a bad review. Thankfully, many critics are kind to young singers. You start out getting love.

You sing around the world. Anything come to your mind about how different audiences can be?

They're different all over. The Met, Paris Bastille, here, Salzburg, they're different in the way they express themselves. In France they like to boo. To them it's saying, "Eh, not so good." People express their opinions; if they don't like something, they'll tell you. It's not necessarily meant as a personal attack. As singers, we're spoiled because the rest of the world doesn't generally do that to us. I've never sung at La Scala, but I understand they do that and can be quite difficult. Here they tend to be polite. But they express themselves. And they're very well informed. They know their music, know what they're listening to. Houses that have a long history are the ones that have more character. They have their favorite composers and affections. If you mess those things up, they'll tell you! [*Laughs*]

Also on the subject of audiences, what false notions about opera do you think people have?

Often, what an audience takes away from a performance is not what we're actually giving.

How do you mean?

When you're singing—even in voice lessons—my husband has always said it, Jimmy Levine said it, too, and it was something I had to learn: "You love to sing. You're really enjoying it. But nobody's getting it." There's a point where you have to learn how to sing, and put it *out* there—not keep it so precious and personal. There was a point where I had to kick it in and take it to another level. I had to sing a little louder, get it out of my own space, and give it to the people listening.

It's as basic as that—singing louder?

Well, perhaps ramping it up, as it were, and connecting with the audience. You see, I want *that* lady out there to get what I'm trying to say, and I need to connect with *that* lady and take it to the next level.

Can you see that lady?

Oh, yes. Especially in a hall like this. The audience is on top of you.

So you focus on one person in the audience?

Sometimes. Often your eyes are led back to a certain person. I don't know why—their hair, or what they're wearing.

Wouldn't that happen more in a concert environment?

It does, generally. The Met is really big and tends to be dark, so you don't often pick out people. But here, the other night, I picked out some.

And felt you were communicating better because of it?

Yeah.

And at the Met it doesn't work because you can't see them?

You have to work a little harder in a bigger house. It's not a matter of exaggerating, it's a matter of focusing. Of intensity. In a place like this, well, I had fun the other night, because I could be a little more subtle, sing a little quieter, a little more intimate. And try and draw in people that way. At the

Met, I don't have that luxury. I have to do it with focus of the sound and focus of intensity and intention. I don't want to say "singing loud," because that never works with my voice. And I don't think it works with other people. I've been onstage with singers who don't want to be labeled a voice that's "not big enough." So they're singing as loud as they can, and you see their veins popping out, and you hear their voice spreading, and think, "It's not working. It's not about volume. It's about focus and intensity."

Do you think audiences are aware of that?

The one thing I feel opera audiences really miss is that when an aria ends with a bang, they stand up and scream and yell. It's always after those big arias. And, as a result, they often miss some of the most beautiful, subtle moments. Maybe the aria or duet ends quietly or subtly, and yet it was this point where the music found its highest level—not in the big aria.

Can you give an example?

Some of the moments during my duet with Simon Keenlyside [Count Almaviva] here, which is a duet that kind of passes by; people often don't clap. Another was when Anja Harteros [The Countess] and I were singing the letter duet. We came offstage with goose bumps in awe of Mozart's genius. But I am not certain if the audience registered the moment, because what really seemed to grab them was "Dove Sono," which is the only moment in the opera where the orchestra ends with a *Da! Da-ta-da!* And they jump up and scream and yell. And they remember "Dove Sono" at the end and don't necessarily remember some of the gentler moments. I'm not certain how you would cultivate such a thing and get people to understand.

You mentioned the older houses with long histories, like this one. Are you aware of that history?

At some, like Salzburg, or here, or the Musikverein in Vienna, the history does kind of wash over you. It is amazing. I tuck those things in the back of my mind, and I count myself lucky. When I was young, it didn't occur to me.

When you're in your dressing room or onstage at one of these places, are you ever conscious of the, shall we say, spirits of your illustrious predecessors?

Definitely. The structure of the stage is almost identical to what it was way back. So when you open the doors to your dressing room to go into the stage area there is a certain smell, a certain darkness, a certain . . . thing that happens. It's all there still. The tradition of singing is there. When I look out into the audience, I see the lights, whatever it is. There is an enormous history which is preserved and a part of what I'm doing.

How do you see the next generation of singers?

Things in this business are changing so much, I'm praying the level of singing stays where it is. I think there is enough competition out there among young singers that it will.

Is the level today better than a generation ago?

Yes and no. There may be more singers competing for the same number of spots. But there's a whole other element, because personal appearance and weight have become important factors in determining the kind of career a young singer might have. The television age has arrived for opera. Gone are the days where you can be thirty or forty pounds overweight. All over the world, it's becoming an issue because there are so many singers out there, if you look hard enough, you can find a body type to fit the operatic role.

And who have the voice?

I'm not so sure about that.

I thought that was more a concern of filmed opera.

It used to be, but a lot of the houses now really pay attention to what the person looks like, as well as their singing. There is a great deal of competition out there. Except for roles that are extremely hard to cast, like Tosca—you've just got to find someone who can *sing* Tosca—but in many operatic roles, body type is definitely an issue.

Do you think that's a good thing?

I think on one level it will take opera forward. Because when average people come to a performance, it's easier for them to relate to the visual if the character looks like what they're supposed to look like. Gone are the days when people sit, close their eyes, and listen. They want to see something if they're paying three hundred dollars a ticket.

Do you have any personal fetishes—something you always wear? Any rituals you do before singing? You mentioned your fifteen minutes before going on, and drinking water.

I don't really get a chance to. I'm sure I would have a ritual if I didn't have children! [*Laughs*]

Is this going to become an issue, balancing the kids and your career? You bring it up a lot.

Well, you know what? I've always had to make choices. It has not always been the best for my career. I've had to forgo a lot of things.

What things?

I've been pregnant four times! [*Laughs*] So there have been a lot of jobs where I've had to say, "Sorry, can't do that."

Anything particular you regret having to turn down?

I really, desperately, wanted to sing with Simon Rattle in Berlin. I had to say, "Sorry. I'm going to be eight and a half months pregnant, and you don't want that!" [*Laughs*] I don't often get to do new productions that take me away for two months, unless I can bring my family. The kids are getting to a point where I have to make those choices. It's not always easy.

Is that the fault of not being well organized on your part?

No. It's just that you get to where the things which are important to the children sort of trump what is important to you. For example, my twelve-year-old son is a good athlete. He really loves his sports. Ridiculously. He loves being on the school soccer team, and the basketball team, the football team. Every time I take him away for three weeks, he misses that and can't be participating. So I have to weigh what I do, and how much time I can spend away from them, and how much time I can take them away from their lives.

You can't really raise kids on the road.

There haven't been loads of female opera singers who have. It was not a big trend in the generation before me. Some, like Frederica von Stade, and a few others, did raise their children on the road, and they did it well. Clearly, because I have more children than most female opera singers, I had to make careful choices. I was always feeling it out with my kids, and I wasn't sure if it was working or if it was particularly good for them [*laughs*]. I remember once I was with my son in a strange town in a strange hotel with a strange babysitter—and as I was headed to the concert hall I just couldn't leave him with this stranger—lovely as she may have been. I had to grab him, pay the babysitter, let her go, and head to the concert hall with an infant in tow. I got to the concert hall and just handed my baby to the artistic administrator, whom I adored. He took care of my son while I went out and did my thing. Looking back, I realize it has been a pleasure and a blessing for my children to have had this experience. They can walk into any situation, any diversified place, and relate. It doesn't bother them if they can't speak what everybody else is speaking.

At this point in your career, is there one lesson you've learned about singing?

The importance of listening. When you're young and at what you think is the top of your form, you have so much to say, and "I do it this way!" When somebody says, "But can you do this?" or "It would be nicer if you did it this way" or "Can we do it a little faster?" you're put off by that, you're taken aback. But at some point, you start to listen. Then you decide, "Oh, it goes nicely that way!" And so, here I am, twenty years later, and I realize that most people are where they're at, when they get to a certain level, because they have something to offer. They don't get there for just any reason. They're there because they do what they do in a professional, good way. And they have something to say. So it's important to listen. Often I come away and have learned something new, even if it's a concert or opera I have performed many times.

How do you see your future—the next twenty years?

My goal for the next few years is to continue to do what I do, at the highest level I can, in a fulfilling way, and still make my family work. I don't know if it works all the time, but . . . [*laughs*]

How about 80 percent of the time?

[*Laughs*] Eighty percent! What else can any normal person ask for?

© Enno Kapitza

Kent Nagano, or remaining relevant

Heroes in the Grimm fairy tales were given such impossible tasks as slaying giants, capturing unicorns, or bringing back hairs from the devil in hell. They might as well have tried to get Kent Nagano to talk about himself.

It's not from any sense of contrariety. He's an unpretentious man and doesn't relish self-marketing.

He even looks the modest part this morning as he rehearses Munich's Bayerische Staatsoper orchestra, where he is music director. Thin-waisted, graceful as a dancer, he peers out at them through large, round glasses. Dressed in Levi's, his dark hair flows generously over the collar of his crisply pressed shirt, which floats around him like a sail.

He seems at home here in Munich, and maybe he is. He speaks to his players in German and English but mainly German; he's made progress in the local language, an effort they appreciate. Though his style is casual, the 140 members of the Staatsorchester know, as any observer in the underground rehearsal hall can see today, that he's boss. After twelve years at the Opéra de Lyon and stints at Hallé, Berlin, and Los Angeles, the man whom Olivier Messiaen chose to assist Seiji Ozawa in preparing the world premiere of Saint François d'Assise *now commutes between Munich and Montreal, where he heads the Montreal Symphony Orchestra.*

We move to his top-floor office in the gray stone and glass New Rehearsal Building behind the opera house, and here the California-born conductor will outline his strategy to keep opera relevant, a key driver in his

Munich activities. In particular, he will relive an intensive, three-year study plan he undertook before even starting the Munich job. It included a six-month sabbatical devoted solely to the Staatsoper's five hundred-year history, during which he stopped all conducting.

Few people know this because he doesn't talk about it. Laying down the baton to pick up books is a pretty rare twist for any globetrotting podium star.

One reason Nagano seems modest is that he chooses his words carefully. He pauses frequently when talking, searching—or perhaps waiting —in the silences, for the proper phrases to be delivered to him. He is soft-spoken and serious, respectful and precise. His language is often scientific. You get the feeling he would make a wonderful surgeon. I felt he'd be a good one to talk about acoustics; I had no idea his father was an architect.

The Staatsorchester members say his style differs from that of his predecessor, Zubin Mehta. He knows what he wants and sticks to it, they tell you.

"Kent's very precise," declares a brass player. "He has a vision and wants us to play in a certain way. Less so than with his predecessor, who let things happen." Adds another Staatsorchester member, "We play more accurately and to the point now."

Ask Nagano if he is satisfied with this, and he gives, as expected, the graceful, self-effacing answer. "It remains a challenge," he replies. "Every day, every month, every year, you have to challenge yourself. The moment you say you've succeeded, you've failed somehow."

The Staatsoper players enjoy saying their orchestra has a "warm" sound. "If you're talking colors, it's dark red," explains one. "Very round. Not forced or aggressive." They are extremely proud of this sound. Only now they report—just as proudly—that a new, "transparent" element, inspired by Nagano, has added something to their famous timbre. For five centuries, the Staatsoper has been solid. Now, they say, it's acquired some grace.

What were the challenges you saw coming in as music director of the Bayerische Staatsoper?

The challenge is, was, and will be the one that faces everyone who is part of a leadership team of an opera house, which is to ask the question, "What is the relevance of opera today?" And to ask it in a way that you have—not necessarily an answer—but communication, both with the house and the public.

Why is this a challenge?

The tendency for everyone is to slide into a routine or into assumptions. Dialogue with the public is sometimes not effective enough. That's why we hear, over and over, "Is opera relevant?" "Should there be a place for it when we are facing so many other economic crises?" "Is it a form that is only for a select part of society?" These questions come out of misunderstanding or from a public that can't answer what is the relevance of opera today. In this house, the question has been asked over and over. Opera has been redefined and rediscussed in such a way that it does remain relevant. Munich, more than any other opera house in Germany, and more than almost any opera house in the world, has a history that can give us the keys to saying, "Not only is it relevant, but perhaps today it's more relevant than it has been in a long time."

Tell us about that history.

One of the strongest and unique characteristics of this house is its glorious and musically important tradition. Not only a consistency of excellence and service to opera, but also, in this house, important developments in the history of Western music have taken place. Orlando de Lassus's experiments in developing *colla parte*, where instruments began to double the voices, which led to an expansion of polyphonic singing to where concepts of theater and opera began to germinate. From there was derived the symphonic form. That took place here with de Lassus. His monument is just across the street. *Idomeneo* was premiered across the way, in the Cuvilliés Theater, under Mozart's hand; *La Finta Giardiniera* also premiered here. One thinks of what that provoked out of Mozart; the great Da Ponte operas came right after. And what happened to the world when *Tristan und Isolde* was premiered here with this orchestra. Not only did the entire concept of how we think of harmonic structure but actually how we think of form began to be discussed and redefined. *Die Walküre* was premiered by this orchestra. And all the great Strauss operas and his involvement with the house. Munich has one of the oldest traditions in Europe—nearly five hundred years—certainly one of the oldest in Germany. I want to continue this, to be a house which looks forward and is courageous in embracing evolution. And in the other direction, the Bayerische Staatsoper has always made a commitment to new commissions in music.

Why do opera houses keep commissioning? You know you're going to lose money on new works.

Because we believe in the art form. That's how it can continue to grow. And through growth, like in anything, you have a chance to remain relevant. The reason Mozart, Wagner, and Strauss are important to the Bayerische Staatsoper, and to the world, is not because they lived one hundred or 250 years ago, not because they were creative geniuses. These composers speak to us today about humanity through their music, which allows us to realize it's relevant to the tensions and complications we face in our world. These composers are important to keep active in our repertoire because they are contemporary composers: they speak of human themes that we think and feel and work within today. That's why it's important to make sure we continue careful and responsible commissioning, to make sure the art form continues to serve humanity.

Humanity, yes. But you are doing the commissioning, so how much of your-self comes into it?

Careful and responsible commissioning also has a great subjective point to it. It would be difficult for me to agree to commissioning a work unless I profoundly believed in the composer and believed the music was important. If we, as a house, didn't believe that, it would be nearly impossible for the public to believe it.

What is the last new work which became fully integrated into the reper-toire?

It's constant. *Saint François d'Assise*, which is now being performed so often, is slowly finding its way. Many of the Shostakovich operas—*Lady Macbeth. Nixon in China* has found its way into the repertoire. Poulenc's *Dialogue des Carmélites*, which was premiered in the late '50s. It happens all the time. The last commission we did at the Opéra de Lyon, *Les trois soeurs*, by Peter Eötvös, has received many performances, so I hope, since it's an ex-ceptional work, that it'll find its way as well.

You mentioned the social questions, questions of human nature with Mo-zart, Wagner, and Strauss.

Humanity.

Do you think the average operagoer comes with those antenna out, waiting to be touched and moved? Or does that happen unknowingly, on an unconscious level? This person doesn't know the score by heart like the professional does. Can that same kind of connection exist as it exists for the musical insider? To whom are you communicating when you are on the podium is, I guess, my question.

The opera house and the symphonic orchestra belong to the public. The concept that there is detachment is relatively new—the idea that it might be for an elite, or only for enthusiasts. If you look historically, in the great cities of Europe, the opera houses and symphonic halls are generally in the center. Why is that? Because these were platforms where society would meet, where issues would be discussed, examined, shared. Not directly, as in politics, but through the abstraction of the fine arts. Through this abstraction it opens up, so people on all levels, from all backgrounds and experiences, can participate and find a relevance.

You actually believe that?

You can't argue with history. This is what has happened to the great tradition.

You can't argue either that traditionally, the great masses have shifted to another art form—the cinema, for example.

What are these points of contact? A football stadium? A cinema? Certainly in the fine arts, the operatic medium, we play to the public because the music and the art form belong to them. That's where tremendous responsibility lies upon us. It's much more complicated than, say, an entertainment form, where—and I don't want to imply in any way that it's simpler—the definition of success is maybe easier to see. Entertainment forms can be rated in statistics, what the numbers are. In art forms, you deal with many more levels. This is what I mean, really serving the public in a more profound way.

You feel that, personally? This sense of public service? This tie?

Part of the definition of a performance is the realization that you can't have a performance without a public. You can rehearse without a public. You can even do a dress rehearsal. But it's still not called a performance. A performance is an art of communication and a dialogue which happens where there is a public and interpreters. That's what makes a performance;

the community or the public. Society is an integral part of the performing or fine arts; that's what makes music special. It's one of the few mediums today in which we can all experience a miracle. Nearly every one of us—certainly everyone I know, including myself—has gone to a performance where we've arrived with the weight of our lives on our shoulders—cell phone ringing, 150 emails backed up, a schedule that's impossible to meet, running late, stuck in traffic. And if the performance is really a great one, we can be taken out of our seats, and for periods of time we're in some other world. Maybe an ideal world. Who knows where we were? At a certain point, we return to the concert hall. Where were we during that time? Who were we during that time? What happened? What happened to the environment around us? Where was the person sitting next to us? In a sense, it was an existential miracle in the real sense of the word. That is the power of music, taking us into a different world where the perspectives are different.

The last time a miracle like that happened to you, were you in the audience or on the podium?

The one I'm referring to was as a public member. I love going to performances.

What makes a miracle?

That's for every person to find.

Again, it's very subjective. Is this the sort of thing you aim for when you're conducting? You want the audience to experience a miracle?

Yes.

You're on the podium, trying to create a miracle.

That's actually not the objective. You are trying to serve the music in the most honest and truest way. It comes from the music; it's not man-made. It's not a question of individual control. It's actually common sense. It sounds funny, to put it in words, but that's why we're music lovers.

Emotion comes into it.

Emotion is very much a part of it. But not only emotion. You can become very, very close to music emotionally, intellectually, spiritually—there are many levels of consciousness which are active at the same time. Even physical. How many times have you just felt the power of the *Nabucco* chorus, or the physical presence? This all combines to make it a human experience.

You say intellectual. Would you say some twentieth- or twenty-first-century music, like atonal music, is more intellectual? More for the page than for the stage?

Unfortunately, we today tend to load up words with all kinds of connotations. I meant it in the most simple way.

Okay. That's a nice way of telling me I'm full of shit.

No [*laughs*], as in being aware of a structure, being aware of a form. Being aware of harmonic progression.

Just the same as in Mozart.

Yes. That's what I meant by intellectual.

There is, however, the argument that Schoenberg, or atonal music, is—not a dead end—perhaps a parenthesis in musical history, because it lacks what the more traditional forms have: repetition, memory, anticipation, suspense, fulfillment, which are basic human emotional needs. That's what I meant by intellectual: the older forms can communicate in a way that atonal music can't. Am I still full of shit?

[*Laughs*] It's sometimes important to realize that if we don't thoroughly comprehend things today, it doesn't mean we're never going to comprehend them. That goes on a personal level as on broad perspectives as well. The kinds of comments one read after the premiere of Beethoven's *Ninth Symphony*, for example. Olivier Messiaen himself told me about the reactions he had to bear for the premiere of *Turangalîla Symphony*. The reactions to *Le sacre du printemps*. I'm trying to cite works familiar to our repertoire. It's important to realize that it sometimes takes awhile before a perspective can come in so we can absorb something new. It's interesting you mention Arnold Schoenberg. Was he a revolutionary? Or was he, in many ways, adhering, in a strong way, to a conservative form? It's interesting to look at that time in history. Brahms had finished writing his *Fourth Symphony*, and the relationship between Schoenberg and Brahms was very strong, as we know. Often, he looked back to that model. It seems he may have looked to the structural, formal models and set his new ideas in a tonal setting. One can see he revealed his deep, formal training within classical, so-called conservative forms. On the other hand, Mahler or Strauss began then to explore different kinds of systems and open forms. Are they conservative, or are they radically changing their direction? These questions have no answers. But it is important to realize, and admit, that if things are incomprehensible or difficult today, it doesn't necessarily mean that tomorrow we might not have a different perspective on them.

Did you accept the Bayerische Staatsoper invitation right away?

I thought about it months before I accepted, because it meant a lot of things. One, that I would stop traveling around the world as much as I had been. That I would want to sharply reduce the amount of ensembles with whom I was working, to have enough time to be here. It meant a strong amount of personal time dedicated to Munich. Without that dedication, I could not see a way that the job could be responsibly fulfilled. It meant a change of lifestyle, of professional working structure. It also meant preparing myself to be completely dedicated to the mission of the house, which was very much tied to its traditions. I was obliged to think about it very seriously. If you accept such an invitation, you accept the responsibilities that come with it. Otherwise, you shouldn't.

When you came you had to decide which operas to program. How do you approach this? Is it something that came up during discussions with your predecessor? Did you ask him why this or that particular opera wasn't done?

No, it's the result of three years of study and research, looking through the back libraries.

On your part?

Yes. I was fortunate in that I had three years, and took advantage of them, to study the history of the house. Part of that was a six-month sabbatical purely devoted to the Bavarian Staatsoper history. I just stopped conducting and retreated to libraries and to the piano.

Do people know this—that you took this research time off?

I don't talk about it that much. It was a three-year, intensive study period. And, by the way, it hasn't suddenly stopped! [*Laughs*] For me, the importance of this house was such that it would simply be audacious not to study. It would be wrong not to study. That also included stepping away from all performing, as I mentioned, for six months, the year before I came, and focusing on study. One person who was influential was Wolfgang Sawallisch, with whom I had many meetings. Speaking about the history of the house, having him comment on my sketches for what might be developed, asking for his perspective, his criticism. He's a beacon, a great guiding light. He was here for, what—twenty-five, thirty years? He helped put into focus what this vision is, a vision extracted from the tradition of the house, which hopefully will be an extension of the tradition of the house.

So you took this time off to visit libraries and research the history of the house and came up with these ideas that you're implementing now, to help make opera more relevant here.

You need an idea of what makes opera relevant for today. You have to ask the question with knowledge of what's taken place here for the past five hundred years. Otherwise, what's the point of asking? It takes time to develop awareness of the context before you can start dealing with these questions. Balance of repertoire is part of it. What hasn't been here in the past? What do the Munich people expect? What should they expect? What are the dynamics of the society in Munich today? Is it different from ten years ago? Are youth appearing in our opera series? Are families coming? Is the next generation being related to in a way that they feel the doors are open and the house belongs to them? These are all questions which are a part of what is the relevance of opera today.

Let's turn to a scientific subject that's also part of opera: acoustics. Depending on the opera house, or the work itself, the conductor can shift the orchestra around to improve the acoustics. Is this something you often do or are expected to do?

It is the conductor's responsibility to ensure the musical and artistic integrity of the performance. As a conductor, if you allow less than optimal acoustics, somehow you are not fulfilling your responsibility.

Who makes this decision?

In the broadest sense, the responsibility falls upon the leader of the performance to ensure the integrity of the performance. There are many influences and restrictions which come into play. One is the size of the orchestra pit. Another is the acoustics of the space in which you are working. Some acoustics are more favorable than others. There are acoustics which are sympathetic to certain periods or styles in music and less sympathetic to other periods. There are acoustics which favor the voice and acoustics which favor a larger ensemble. There are no perfect circumstances, is what I'm trying to say. So there is a constant need to try to find what the optimal condition is.

Can you hear how good they are from the podium?

No, you can't. You can have a certain awareness. But the only way you're really aware of what the audience hears is when you go out into the audience and listen yourself. Also, in most houses you need to think, "What is the audience?" because the acoustics change depending where you happen to be sitting. The acoustic experience is different if you're in the orchestra or on the extreme left or right, in the back, underneath a balcony or in an upper balcony. You have to know who and what you're defining as the public. Usually, it means moving around and finding a general sound you feel will best serve the score and the public.

And this is your decision?

It's the responsibility of the conductor. Some conductors elect to take that decision personally. Others work with a staff of assistants.

You altered the acoustics in the pit when you conducted Cardillac *at Paris's* Opéra Bastille, *which has been known for its problems.*

I've worked at both Bastille and Palais Garnier. The latter has wonderful acoustics. I wasn't that familiar with the acoustics at Opéra Bastille. The suggestion came, from past experience, since there had been a number of experiments, to try and find a more complete acoustic for the pit. I was having trouble having enough presence from certain instruments and sound frequencies. There are many ways you can compensate. You can ask your colleagues to adjust physically, to play less or more, to play in a different color. That's what's so remarkable about artists, and about people generally—we have this amazing spectrum of capability and flexibility. But there is a point at which you are no longer playing comfortably because you're playing in such an exaggerated way to help repair or balance a fundamentally flawed acoustic. This means you can't play to your full, because you're playing in an uncomfortable range of dynamics. In this case, we moved the physical setup of the orchestra to one where the instruments, since they were in a different physical position, had different projection capabilities.

Which instruments?

We moved the contrabasses.

Forward?

We moved them so they were playing out more, toward the audience. We also adjusted the height of the pit. Most pits have some hydraulic mechanism whereby you can raise or lower the level of the orchestra. Not all; in Munich we have a pit whose level needs to be assembled by hand, by putting in risers. At Opéra Bastille we found that the optimal position was a very high one, where there was a more intimate contact between the orchestra and the stage. Each player, through his or her own sensitivity, could adjust the dynamics and make the balance work. We also found that being up higher allowed certain natural frequencies from the instruments to come out into the house, which gave the orchestra a more colorful and full range of spectrum and possibilities. If the pit had been lower, some of those outer areas of the color spectrum were somehow dampened or less brilliant.

This solution was tailor-made for this particular opera.

That's right. It doesn't necessarily mean it's going to work for a different production or a different score.

Do you have any acoustical formulas that you'll have to change for Munich? You spoke about the risers.

The natural acoustic of the house is fantastic. It's one of the most wonderful-sounding opera houses I know. But because it's a wonderful, natural opera house doesn't necessarily mean it's the best-sounding stage for symphonic concerts. There are different acoustical properties for every form. In Munich, a number of acoustic shells, which fit onto the stage, have been designed over the past decades to try and give an optimal experience when the orchestra leaves the pit and assumes its role as the State Orchestra and gives symphonic concerts. It is a myth that there's a physically perfect acoustic. Still, there are ideals we can try and work toward. That's what we try to do collectively. Not just the conductor—any artist wants to be able to give his or her performance in a way in which it can be shared to the fullest.

What's your definition of acoustics?

Acoustics is an extension of your instrument. It's air vibrating in a cavity. From a violin or clarinet or trumpet, it extends out into the hall. It does need to be taken into account and needs to be assumed that it can have a major effect on how the experience is for the public. It's just as essential in opera as on the symphonic stage. We try to tune and set up our instruments in a way that can provide an optimal performance. We recently visited Paris's Théâtre du Châtelet with the Orchestra Symphonique de Montréal, and a large amount of time was spent adapting to the acoustics of that hall, which is radically different—it couldn't be more different—than our home in Montreal, which seats 3,600 and has open acoustics [the nineteenth-century Théâtre du Châtelet seats 2,010], where certain sounds are nearly impossible to focus and define. Acoustics is essential.

Would you say it's much on your mind when you go into rehearsals? Or just one of the things?

It's much on my mind.

Is there any special training conductors or musicians need in order to better understand acoustics? Architecture, for example? Architectonics?

The best training I've found, from people I admire, and in my own personal experience, has been sensitivity and experience. And to resist the urge to compromise.

You must compromise a little, if you're one conductor with scores of musicians.

Of course. But you have to keep searching for the optimum circumstances. With the full knowledge that from work to work, from ensemble to ensemble, from set to set, it needs to be readjusted and found anew.

How do you motivate the orchestra? Can you think of any qualities a conductor must have? How do you drive them toward that perfection without that compromise?

There's really no simple answer for that. Artists and performers are exceptionally well-trained, well-educated, intelligent, and sensitive. I suppose the only consistent thing I've found is that it's very important to be honest [*laughs*]. To simply honestly be yourself and not something manufactured. Colleagues find out if you're being mannered or artificial or trying to do something that's not real. They sense this in a millisecond. And of course it doesn't help the connection to the music if you feel you're having to work with something that's not true. There is a certain flexibility and ability to be able to accept different ideas in different ways. That's what makes our repertoire so great; it is open to humanity and interpretation. But part of that is being able to believe that your collaborators have prepared and studied and engaged themselves with a belief that under these particular circumstances, at this point in time, this interpretation is a reflection of the true and honest vision we have. I think that's about the only thing; I don't have a list of ten motivational points like you see on TV [*laughs*]. Simply being honest and true is the most consistent thing.

How do you do that?

I think that as long as one relates to musicians as a musician or to an artist as an artist—which is to say you focus priorities on the music making and on the score and the composer's intentions—in most cases you can find a way to work together. Because that's the one thing all of us share: devotion, dedication, and respect for the repertoire we've inherited.

That's how you work with them? Making music is the priority?

I don't know any other way to work with musicians. Sometimes aesthetic choices can be discussed. Most artists can accept an aesthetic vision, even if it may be unusual or not before thought of [*laughs*] as long as one feels there is respect for the music.

Would you say this happens most of the time—that your musicians are well-trained and committed?

Today, we live in a time when musicians are perhaps more educated, cultivated, well-trained, and experienced than at any other point in history. It's a very special moment.

Clashes are rare?

There can always be differences of opinion. One would hope for that. Sometimes a difference in opinion can be an opportunity to have a different look on things or can be stimulating. The goal—what we try to do—is to bring the composer's intention alive in a relevant way, in a way somehow meaningful. We try this every night. I use the collective "we." Every one of my colleagues and myself try as hard as we possibly can.

This is the interpreter's job?

There is a saying that composers are the creators. They look at the blank page and take their inspiration and feelings and, at a certain point, set them aside and abstract them into notes which are written on paper. Many composers have said the same thing in different ways; somehow, the source of their inspiration remains very personal. It's something almost impossible to communicate to someone else. That's why we use generic or mythological figures such as "muse" as descriptive forces. But it's nearly impossible to explain where that source of inspiration comes from. Through the abstraction and codification into notes, rhythms, you put that imagination onto a piece of paper. Olivier Messiaen often said that once these ideas or inspirations become a work, in a way it's not his anymore. It's meant to be performed and given life by people who fill it with their own experiences and inspiration. The saying is that performers are, in a way, re-creators. Of course, it's a creative process, but it's re-creating this work that has been left by a composer.

Some stage actors say that after the performance, they remove their makeup and leave their dressing rooms as quickly as possible. This is because they can feel the spirits of their predecessors, older actors who inhabit the theaters, who tell them if they have been good or bad that night. This spooks them. Perhaps not at a new hall like in Montreal, but is that something that crosses your mind in older European houses? Do you feel your illustrious predecessors here?

Yes, in a certain scientific way. It's true, if you think of wood as an organic substance. It responds to stimulus, vibrates and decays at various rates depending on the air and the acoustical sounds or phenomena taking place. In a certain way, the music making of great artists stays in the walls. It can be forgotten, particularly in our lifestyles today, where things move at such high speeds. Yet I think most of us, myself included, when given the time to be alone and quiet, can feel the nature of an acoustic. We can feel a personality of a hall. We can sense the differences in the physical feeling of the air that embodies a space. I'm the son of an architect. I would visit construction sites with my father as a boy. Being in the various structures that were being put up then, we're sensitive to shapes and spaces and environments. This is part of the skill of an architect's artistic expression; thinking how humans will fit into the space, whether they'll feel complete or full. What the feeling of a living room should be versus a reception room. So in that sense, yes, it's mysterious, but I'd say a quite normal experience for most of us to feel, and, yes, I do feel that. I wouldn't call it superstition, because that can imply all sorts of other things. Doing the same routine or having a special lucky pair of cufflinks.

Do you have any superstitions? Do you not shave or wear the same shirt for each performance?

[*Laughs*] Let's see. . . . That's interesting. I have friends who always wear the same cufflinks or try to wear the same shirt. One colleague only has one set of tails he's particularly fond of and has them laundered every day. I don't have anything quite so specific. But like a lot of artists, there are certain rituals or routines I try to keep as consistent as possible.

Such as?

It's important for me to be at the performance a long time in advance, to really sit. It is important for me to be able to walk onto the stage and sit on the stage; if it's a symphonic concert, to just have a quiet moment in the air and the physical space of the concert hall, to establish contact before I give a performance.

You clear the hall?

No, this is before anyone has come in. I really arrive at performances very early. I walk the stage, walk the pit, walk the house, just have it as a part of my awareness beforehand. That's part of a routine or ritual. It's also important for me not to have a series of administrative meetings beforehand, so I clear most of the day before a performance—even if it's an opera I've conducted many times. Just recently it was the eighth performance of one I'd done very often, and I still leave the day free for study, for reflection.

This is your way of making a connection with the environment, with the opera house?

Very much so. It's also having a chance to become more intimate with the musical ideas. Because the musical ideas are completely intertwined with the space in which they're going to be born and in which they're going to live and be shared.

This connecting with the time-space element would seem to come from a spiritual or religious person.

Music is very spiritual.

Everybody today seems to be trying to lure a new generation of opera-goers. Many younger opera directors have called it their number one goal. Is this much on your mind as music director?

One of the things that makes the arts so special is a universal language. We don't feel barriers or frontiers. We don't feel any age discrimination—young or old. Arts can appeal, they're so profound and multifaceted, to any age level. I had a group of elementary school children come to *Die Frau ohne Schatten*, and they left delighted. Many said what a wonderful libretto that was. That libretto puzzles adults! [*Laughs*] Arts open the door in a universal way. The thing we do remark on is that people, regardless of age and experience, are sensitive to quality. I believe that most people, if given the choice between something of superior quality or good quality, will choose the superior. Whether or not there's any cognitive understanding or not. It's about the only thing you can assume: if you perform something of exceptional quality—which brings the implications of the texts and subtexts involved, and the levels of refinement that come—people will respond. Especially young people.

This is what many opera directors are saying when asked how to lure a new audience: it's not a question of what will appeal to young people. Just put on a quality show, and they'll come.

I think that's what we are again discovering here in Munich. This house is obsessed with quality. Which is wonderful!

Are you obsessed with quality?

I've been called that, and sometimes in the most negative terms possible! [*Laughs*]

By critics? Or musicians?

By friends [*laughs*].

Meaning what?

That in a certain aspect I'm always looking for how to be better. Which is to say, never satisfied.

So where is the problem?

Yeah, I don't see a problem, either! [*Laughs*]

Seiji Ozawa, or the art of managing the orchestra

The mop of gray hair appears first, then under it the slight, sprightly conductor enters the pit, smiling. The audience erupts into thunderous applause.

As the maestro makes his way to the podium at Paris's Opéra Bastille, you realize it is not only the audience that is clapping. The orchestra members, too, are noisily welcoming Seiji Ozawa—tapping bows against music stands, stamping their feet, applauding. One doesn't often see such affection from the players in this house. Matter of fact, one never does.

Ozawa greets his orchestra, bowing, shaking hands, for a full three minutes before finally turning around and acknowledging the audience. It's another thing one doesn't see; conductors don't linger before their players —that's what rehearsals are for. Most prefer to turn directly to the paying guests.

But this extraordinary spectacle occurs before the curtain rises on each act: Ozawa enters and salutes his players. The identical long interval must pass while he completes this ritual of communion with them, before— almost as an afterthought—bowing in the direction of the audience. From the seats, operagoers realize they are not only witnessing the first Tannhäuser ever seen at Bastille this November evening; they are also being treated to what is clearly an exercise in effective team management. This could be a field trip for a business-school seminar in human relations or organizational behavior.

The tutorial doesn't end with the show. When the opera is over, the conductor bounds onstage, joining the cast for curtain calls. While they all stand and smile stiffly, he is nodding at his players in the pit, clapping, pointing to some like a politician at a victory party. They applaud him in return. Then, one by one, the onstage principals get the Ozawa thank-you treatment: he applauds, bows, and shakes hands with the soloists and chorus, hugging some of them.

Two weeks later, he appears in the lobby of his Paris hotel, visibly the Boston man. Faithful to the city where he's spent nearly thirty years, he's wearing a dark blue Red Sox baseball cap and bright red "World Champions" Red Sox parka. Two pairs of glasses dangle from his neck, along with an unidentifiable item which might be rubber goggles for the swimming pool. Black trousers, T-shirt, and shoes, dazzling yellow suspenders, and (what else?) red socks. The bright brown eyes give him a childlike air; the hair looks tame now that he's not working. He seems younger than his seventy-two years.

You are waiting with the question—have been waiting two weeks with it—but Ozawa declines to talk about any of the so-called team-leadership skills that appeared to be so visible a fortnight before. One takes the hint and can only suppose leadership is an instinctive quality; you have it or you don't, so there's nothing to explain.

He hastens straight to his boilerplate bio, perhaps as a way of getting started. Many oft-interviewed luminaries do, and it's a legitimate ploy for subjects who don't know what's coming, or who have—though this is rare —actually prepared some message to communicate. Quickly a clear picture emerges. Ozawa counts on family and fidelity. He talks of his children and repeatedly of people who have made a difference in his career: Herbert von Karajan, Leonard Bernstein, Mirella Freni. Numerous hand gestures accompany his words, which, despite three decades in Boston, do not stream out of him in what can by any stretch of the imagination be called completely fluent English. His tenses don't always match; his vocabulary deserts him today. There's something endearing about that, something human. It may help explain what makes a good leader.

You've been conducting a long time, but came to opera relatively late.

It's true. I started as a pianist in Japan. In those days, there was very little opera in Japan. My first teacher was Hideo Saito. He was a very important man for me—I started the Saito Kinen Festival in his memory twenty years ago—but he didn't teach opera at all. The education I got from him was playing piano, reading scores, conducting, intonation, ear training, all the ensemble things, violin, cello, and nuance, but nothing to do with opera. When I injured my finger, luckily, with a stupid rugby ball in junior high—I think I was fourteen or fifteen—I couldn't play piano for almost one year. The piano teacher said, "Maybe you should do a conducting-composition course." In those years, conductors came from outside Japan—Austria, Russia, America.

When was this?

The early '50s. I went to hear a real orchestra for the first time that year and thought, "This is fantastic." It was Beethoven's Fifth piano concerto, played and conducted by . . . [*thinks*] . . . a German, I always forget his name. . . . Anyway, it was a big shock. So immediately I decided to do this, but didn't know where to go. I hadn't been to music school yet.

You were in public school?

Private school. I was a member of the chorus. And rugby was very hot. My mother said, "If you want to start conducting, my relative, Hideo Saito, is a conductor." She wrote a letter, and I went to him. He was a close relative on my mother's side, but I had never heard the name. He said, "Usually, the mother comes with the child." But I was alone. I was the third of four boys. My mother was busy with the other three; we had no money, and she had to work. We lived far outside Tokyo, and she couldn't get away. That's when I started my life of conducting. And I went completely crazy about it. I think I was fifteen. For seven years, I worked under Maestro Saito as a student. But, and this is why I'm telling you this, I never did opera. We did all the ear training and score reading and string orchestras, big orchestras, but no opera. Our school didn't even have an opera section. Singers just did lieder.

They didn't make you listen to opera, or take you to any performances?

No. I never saw opera. I never heard an orchestra until I injured my finger.

How old were you when you saw your first opera?

It was maybe *Figaro*, in Vienna, 1959. When I came to Europe, Maestro von Karajan was conducting and playing cembalo together at the Staatsoper. It was wonderful. Then I started conducting and won an international competition at Besançon in France. That led to my meeting Madame Kousse-vitsky of Boston, Serge Koussevitsky's widow, and she invited me to Tangle-wood. So I went. But still I have no opera.

This is still 1959?

This was the summer of 1960. After the year, I came back to Europe. I be-came Maestro von Karajan's student that fall.

In Vienna?

Berlin. Then I received an invitation from Leonard Bernstein to be his assis-tant in New York. So I went to Maestro von Karajan. Everybody told me, "These two are not on such good terms." Karajan and Bernstein. Both big kings. I showed him the invitation and asked, "What should I do?" I was still his student until the following summer. He said, "Go. And come back later." So I went. I became Leonard Bernstein's assistant. After that, I became musical director of the Ravinia Festival—the Chicago Symphony's summer home—and the Toronto Symphony, then San Francisco and Boston. And meantime, I never conducted an opera! So Maestro von Karajan said, "Seiji, now you're conducting symphony, symphony, symphony." And he ex-plained: "There are two wheels on the car. One on this side, and one on the other. One is symphony, concerto, sonatas, string quartets. The other is opera. If you don't conduct opera, you cannot go forward in the car."

So how old were you when you conducted your first opera?

I was . . . [*thinks*] twenty-seven, maybe, twenty-eight.

And before von Karajan told you, did you feel anything was missing from your musical life?

I thought it was a different world.

Not for you?

Not for me, no. Because I never went to the opera house, I just went to concerts, concerts, concerts. I told Maestro von Karajan that I didn't know how to do it. Then I was thrown into it. I did Verdi . . . [*thinks*] this [*hunches over*].

Rigoletto?

Rigoletto. In a concert version. It was a very good cast. I enjoyed it very much. I did *Idomeneo*, in concert, in Japan. I enjoyed it. Von Karajan said,

"You want to do opera?" I said, "Yes." He said, "All right. Two summers from now, you do *Così* in Salzburg." I had never conducted *Così*! [*Laughs*] He said, "Next year, you'll come as my assistant to *Don Giovanni.*" He was doing a new production with Mirella Freni and Nicolai Ghiaurov. They met there, and they married. I was assistant to this for one summer. I was already musical director for the Ravinia Festival in Chicago, but they gave me one summer off. For most of it, I was in Salzburg, as pianist and assistant conductor. Maestro von Karajan not only conducted but did the stage directing and the lighting. The lighting, even! So he was busy, which gave me lots of chances to conduct. That same year, Claudio Abbado made his debut at Salzburg in the *Barbiere di Siviglia*, in Jean-Pierre Ponnelle's staging. And the next year, my *Così* was by Jean-Pierre Ponnelle. This is why Claudio and I are close friends. We spent both summers together.

How long did you conduct that Così?

I think two summers. Then I did *Idomeneo*. In the meantime, I had become musical director at Boston. And Boston didn't have any tradition of opera. But they did semi-stagings.

Why only semi-stagings?

We have no pit at Symphony Hall. The orchestra is onstage. We built a stage a little higher, behind the winds, and put lighting in. The orchestra has what we call opera lighting, for the musicians. And the house goes dark so they can use lights for effects. We did many operas that way. I was there twenty-nine years, and we did *Wozzeck, Elektra, Salome,* many Mozart operas, *Falstaff, Peter Grimes*, the Stravinsky opera—

Rake's Progress.

Rake, yes. Poulenc, *La Voix humaine.*

Any world premieres?

No. Because we didn't have a stage. We had no sets. But we did many operas. I don't know how many.

What do you like about opera? Why do you like to conduct it?

I like the voice. People used to ask me why I didn't do opera. When Maestro von Karajan asked me, I didn't have an answer. But already I had my own chorus in Japan. When I was a student, I built and conducted an amateur chorus, which is still going on—it's going to celebrate its sixtieth anniversary!

I was fourteen or something. I conducted a chorus before I conducted an orchestra.

So you like the voice.

Yes. I still sing in this chorus. Voice is, for me, so important. My teacher, Hideo Saito, never did opera, but liked to conduct the chorus, or a cappella, like the Brahms chorus piece. He said, "For a conductor, the most important thing is if he can conduct a cappella chorus. Because every note, every voice is so important. Every word is important."

More important than. . .

Than instruments, which sometimes can go boom-boom-boom. Brahms, for example, or Schumann or Schubert. He did a lot of Brahms. "Every voice has a nuance. They never play in one voice."

And you agree with that?

Absolutely. With the best vocalists, the voice becomes the most expressive instrument. For example, Dietrich Fischer-Dieskau, I conducted many years ago. Also José Van Dam in the Messiaen opera, I can never pronounce it . . .

Saint François d'Assise.

Yes. People singing like that, no instrument can compete. Last night, for example, in *Tannhäuser*, Matthias Goerne [German baritone who sang Wolfram von Eschenbach], when he comes in, he doesn't worry about accompaniment, he comes in alone. So much phrasing. Just one note goes to the next note. That's something. An instrument can't do that.

Are you referring to the emotional impact of the voice, or technique?

Not technique. I don't know technique. It's phrasing. My cello teacher used to tell me how much speed, how much pressure, how much vibrato, all combined, make the phrase. The voice is the same, only you don't see it. You just hear and feel it. Yesterday, I enjoyed very much this man Matthias Goerne. Fischer-Dieskau was the same, as was José Van Dam. And women like Mirella Freni. I'm very close to her. We did many things together. That was the link to opera, I think.

Can a conductor be tops in the field without doing any opera?

Yes.

Are there people today who are?

Yes, yes. I'm sure.

But it's possible that a conductor doesn't like opera.

Maestro von Karajan was absolutely right when he talked about the two wheels on the car. And now I say to everybody the same thing: I'm so happy I know opera now! I don't know many in the repertoire, like many opera conductors do. But—

Wait a minute. It seems to me that each time I see you, there's no score. You conduct from memory. So maybe you don't know many operas, but you seem to know them well.

When I conduct opera, I know the piece! [*Laughs*]

You're known for that. What is that? You have a colossal memory?

No, no!

You do that on purpose, to impress the orchestra?

No! [*Laughs*] No, no, no. When I study, I really study—slowly. I'm studying every morning right now. This Janáček opera, *The Cunning Little Vixen*, I'm doing it for the first time. And it's in Czech. I need a Czech teacher. When I did *Jenůfa* the first time, in Vienna, it was in German. I don't know why. A tradition. In Japan, of course, it was in Czech. I had a Czech teacher for one week.

When you study, are you at the piano?

Yes. Then I try to sing. Try to—how do you say?—pronounce. So I feel it. Messiaen [*laughs*] was terrible. *Saint François d'Assise*. Very difficult.

Because of the language?

Yes, and also . . . I don't know. You knew Messiaen?

No.

I knew him very well. And he never wrote opera before. Rolf Liebermann [director of the Paris Opéra, 1973–1980] asked him. And both came to me and said, "OK, Seiji, you do this opera" [*laughs*]. I accepted, I don't know why. I don't speak French. His wife and I got together when he finished one tableau. We played together and sang. Not together, but somebody had to sing because we taped it, and then gave it to the singer who would be doing the role onstage. It was very difficult.

Is that what happens for a premiere?

No; for him, yes. Because he never wrote opera. Before he gave the part to José Van Dam we had to do this. Van Dam is a genius. He devoted, how do you say, his concentration to this piece. He did not make a mistake, during rehearsal, even.

How does a conductor control an orchestra of one hundred members? I have a reason for asking, but I'll wait to hear your answer before I tell you what it is.

My teacher, Saito, has more up here [*points to his head*], how do you say—academically, in the head. He is very clear. For him, this was important. But then I learned from Maestro von Karajan. For me, the best conducting is, yes, conducting, but *inviting*. Inviting the orchestra player to play. So they don't feel [*slaps the table*] they have do it this way. Invite them, so they *want* to play this way. Maybe the conductor wants it that way. But they feel that they want to play it that way.

You don't impose your will on the orchestra.

I don't push.

You don't tell them, "I want this."

If a musician and I know each other well, and I understand he or she knows the notes, and if I study very well and know exactly the direction, then that could happen, with a good orchestra. It's happened many times. It's the same with opera. If a singer wants to do something one way, and I want to do it another way because of the way I've studied it, we meet halfway, and I invite the singer. Then it's good.

How does that happen, when you say you "invite" them? Do you suggest things?

No. I don't use words. I just conduct that way, I think. It's easier for them to sing that way. I've learned from orchestras that way. I think in Boston, because I stayed a long time and knew everybody. I auditioned 80 percent of the musicians. So I knew them and could invite them this way, and they came naturally. This works with a good singer. It won't work with a bad singer. Because the material must be there.

The reason I asked that question is because I was at the premiere of Tann-
häuser two weeks ago. Think back to opening night. Let me tell you what
I saw. You came out, into the pit, before the curtain went up. We in the
audience were applauding. You had your back to us. You didn't even look
at us, or acknowledge our applause, for at least three minutes. During that
time, it seemed you were first saluting every single orchestra member. Say-
ing hello, greetings, bowing, some sort of connection. You don't remember
doing that?

[*Laughs*] No.

Really? I ask because there was obviously a real connection between them
and you. And when you came back for the second act, same thing. We ap-
plauded you, but so did the orchestra. The string players beat their bows
on their instruments, others were clapping. They loved you.

Ah! [*Laughs*]

And again, you were connecting with them for what seemed to be another
three or four minutes before turning around and bowing to us. It's not only
unusual for Paris; I've never seen that, anywhere. And at the curtain calls,
you came onstage and were cheering, bowing to everyone, pointing, clap-
ping your hands, hugging some of them. It seems to me that, if you look
at it, not in musical terms, but in leadership, in terms of leading a team,
there's a lesson there.

Mm-hmm.

Do you do that consciously? Is it a method that evolved at Boston because
you knew everybody well?

Yes, I think so. I mean, I know everybody in Boston. Here I don't know
everybody. But we rehearsed this piece a lot. They did not know this piece
much.

It's the first Tannhäuser *ever done at Bastille.*

The older people knew it, but the younger ones never had a chance to play
it. We had lots of rehearsals.

Do you think that's the reason for the connection I saw?

I don't know. They played very well. You know, this piece is known as a hard
example. *Tristan* is even easier, intonation-wise. I don't know if Wagner did

not know, or if he did it on purpose, but some of the intonation is almost impossible to do. The same thing happened in the Messiaen opera. I conducted *St François*—this piece—in Boston, Berlin, Japan, with the BBC, Paris —maybe five orchestras. And this group here, Paris, for intonation, is the best. French people, if they want to be really good, they can be.

Are you saying they have a reputation for being difficult?

No. But many people criticize the orchestra in this country. For me, I love it. Maybe because I grew up here, in the competition at Besançon. I've conducted the Orchestre de Paris and the Orchestre de Radio-France quite a few times.

And with these orchestras, when you came onstage each time, did you greet every single member, like at Tannhäuser?

I don't remember.

It seems to be a natural thing with you. It doesn't seem to be studied, like you're out to seduce them. After the final curtain, you took about ten minutes to leave the pit because you were shaking hands with everyone.

[*Laughs*] I don't know! Maybe because this time it was difficult for everybody. We had the strike. Maybe that's why [a stagehands' strike meant half the performances went on sans décor].

All right. Is there anything more you'd like to say about that?

No.

You don't seem like you want to talk about it much.

No, no [*laughs*].

Okay. If I were to ask you to name the one quality, or the three or five qualities, that someone must possess in order to do what you do, to be a conductor, what would you say?

I think a conductor needs to read the score as much as possible. You know, the score is only paper. And behind that paper the composer wrote music. To read the notes, everybody can do that. But what important things can the conductor do? The conductor doesn't make sound. Pianists, violinists, or vocalists instinctively create a sound. The conductor cannot. So it's important that the conductor read and find what's behind the paper, what the composer wanted.

How do you do that? You read the composer's biography?

No. I learned that because many times I did premieres of works of live—how do you say—living composers.

Messiaen.

And Toru Takemitsu. I've conducted almost everything of his. I've conducted Messiaen many times. Lately, I conducted a piece by Henri Dutilleux. When he finished *Le Temps de l'horloge,* I conducted it. So I read, and I ask, Why this?

That's with a living composer. But how do you find out what a composer wanted who is no longer living?

Yeah, that's very difficult. You have to really read. Sometimes you have to conduct one time to find out. When the real, actual sound is there, you say, "Wait a minute. This doesn't work." Then you have to go back and read the score again. That happens when I do a piece for the first time.

You were born in China, of Japanese parents, but you've lived many years in the West. Is that important for a conductor today, the global under-standing or international experience, when dealing with artists, orchestras, and audiences in different parts of the world?

Maybe. I've never thought about it. I learned so much from my teacher Saito, from Maestro von Karajan, and from Leonard Bernstein and from Charles Munch. These four people—Saito, Munch, Bernstein, Karajan—were very important. I've also learned so much from working with different orchestras. I don't know how to explain it.

What did you learn from orchestras?

I learned so much conducting the Boston Symphony for a long time. And the Berlin Philharmonic. Karajan believed I needed to conduct the Berlin Philharmonic. And the Vienna Philharmonic; many times, he put me together with them. I don't know. I learn from orchestras when I work with them. I learned the French repertoire from the French orchestras, for example.

How about singers. Anything you can learn from them?

Yes. I cannot sing. I really learned from Mirella Freni. Or from cellists, like Rostropovich, I learned so much what the strings are. And what are the possibilities of a string player. I did not know these things before. If you only conduct an orchestra, you don't know this. Unless you conduct a cellist like Yo-Yo Ma or an Isaac Stern or Anne-Sophie Mutter. Then you learn so much. A singer like Mirella—I learned so much from her! How she makes her phrasing. How not to push. From Fischer-Dieskau, José Van Dam, and this guy yesterday, Matthias Goerne. Even Pavarotti. He had his own color. When I conducted *Tosca*, for example, I learned more about what is possible.

With the voice or with the character?

With the voice. I think he put his vocal technique, and his . . . how do you say it? . . . intensity. And that charm, it's unbelievable. Domingo, for example. How he controls. Unless you work together it won't happen. Just listening to a CD doesn't do it. You have to work with these people.

You've been working for a long time now. How do you maintain longevity in a career as a conductor?

I don't know.

No rules?

No rules. Passion, maybe [*laughs*]. But I've been very lucky. I've had very good orchestras. That's important, you know. I don't conduct low-standard orchestras. Only the best. Boston, Chicago, San Francisco, Toronto.

Do you choose the opera productions you conduct?

No. The production is not much me. Mr. Mortier [then director of the Paris Opéra], or before him, Hugues Gall, is responsible. I'm not a specialist about productions, you know [*laughs*]. I don't really know how it's possible to put one together or find the money or the timing.

So you don't do the lighting, like von Karajan?

No! [*Laughs*]

I read that after September 11, 2001, you started wondering what relevance a musician has in the world.

Yeah, that's true.

Do you mind talking about that?

Before 9/11, I thought music was very strong. But then, at that moment, I thought, "Ah! a musician cannot do anything. We cannot help the world." I really thought so. It was terrible. Especially in America.

Were you there at the time?

No, I was in Japan, at Saito Kinen. It was evening, I was having dinner with a friend. His wife was in New York. And I thought, "Oh, my God." I remembered then when the war started in Japan—the Second World War. I was very young; I was not a professional musician but was playing piano. And many people at the time said piano is, how do you say, not necessary. The war was more important. And I felt music was nothing. It was more important to do something politically.

And now?

Now I think that since the war is over and 9/11 is over, music—well, not only music, but something, inside of human beings—can go out, in music, or some hope or beauty or health or the spirit or the mind. How do you say? Individuality. I don't like the Olympics, for example. Because the Olympics is always concerned with how many flags—what do you call it, medals— one country gets. For me, it's more important how fast *this person* has run. One person. Not because of a country. I don't believe in groups and countries. This is why I've never been attached to any political group.

So you have returned to your original thoughts that music is important?

Yes. One month after 9/11 we played Berlioz's *Requiem* in Carnegie Hall, and people cried. And I felt their crying was not from depression or being down. They cried but they found life from there. And I thought everybody came out of the hall with more energy. Only music can do that. Music is so direct. And everybody felt—I felt—very positive. There must be a new life from here now.

You conduct all over the world. Where do you call home?

Tanglewood and Japan.

You still have a house in Boston?

Yes, I haven't sold it yet [*laughs*]. It's stupid I haven't. Too many memories in the Boston house. Twenty-nine years is a long time.

Do you travel too much?

[*Nods yes*] My problem—although it's a little better now that I'm no longer with the Boston Symphony—used to be that I'd be on U.S. time, European time, and Japan time. Three completely different time zones in the year, and all the time. Not only America-Europe, America-Europe, but America-Europe plus Japan. It was all mixed. I was doing too much.

And now?

Now it's a little better. It used to be much worse. But two years ago, I got really sick. I was in Vienna. And I learned. I canceled everything for a year and was hospitalized six weeks in Japan. My management and everybody got together and worked out a lighter schedule.

Do you mind talking about that illness? What happened?

They call it "shingles" in English. From here to there [*indicates from the right side of his neck over his head to his left ear*]. It almost went to my spine. And it went into this eye [*touches his right eye*]. I almost lost my eye. It could have gone to my brain, which happens many times.

Nature was telling you to slow down.

Yeah. So I did. My family were happy to have me home! [*Laughs*] My daughter said, "In the morning I wake up, and Daddy's here."

How old are your kids?

Big. Thirty-five and thirty-two. Girl and a boy. But not married. Daughter, not married. Son, not married.

You look a little disappointed.

I don't know why.

You want to be a grandfather.

[*Laughs*] My daughter is a writer. Novels. My son is an actor. He's more popular than I am. In Matsumoto, we were coming out backstage and saw a group of girls. My agent thought they wanted autographs. But they all rushed to Yuki, my son [*laughs*]. "I'm Yuki's dad!" I told them. People know me, but say, "That's Yuki's father." It happened in the metro in Japan, too.

How does that make you feel?

Oh, it's okay! [*Laughs*] He has more exposure than I do. They see him in movies and on a weekly TV series. About Samurai [*laughs*]. He's tall. But not so smart as I am, so it's okay [*laughs*].

Last question: What's your message to people who have never seen an opera?

You know, I was not close to opera at all. So I needed a kick, like the one Maestro von Karajan gave me. It shouldn't be difficult to get people into the opera house. The only problem is sometimes it's too expensive.

What kind of a kick can get them in?

If they know that with opera, each good singer, good composer and a good performance, and staging and music together, it is really, as people say, the art of, how do you say, many things together.

Multimedia.

Yeah, that's it. For that, opera is perfect. And a last word: I'm so happy I learned opera! From the audience's point of view, it could happen, too. But you know, some doctor or teacher or housewife, who can sing or play piano a little or the organ or the accordion or harmonica, that is more important. To sing at the bus stop. Where there are good acoustics. That's the best part of music. Instead of going to the concert hall or the opera house.

Doing it yourself, you mean?

Yes! I know because I'm an amateur chorus member. And amateur music making I enjoy very much. We sing silly things—gospel or hymns or folk tunes. Eight people singing together. Or amateur doctors playing a quartet. That is the best way of tasting music in life. I don't mean technique. When you hear harmony, when it's good, it makes you so happy. You know? So happy! As a professional, you're not so happy when you're busy. But when the harmony goes well, and we're together, it's great.

That might be the best way into opera.

Yes, because you are involved.

© Corbis

Samuel Ramey,
or the lion at twilight

Samuel Ramey looks fragile when we meet. It is during a brief warm spell in May, and the basso feared coming down with allergies. Though not overly sensitive, he says, he has had problems in the past when spring comes. "All that stuff in the air, I can have a reaction." With one more performance of The Barber of Seville *to go at Paris's Opéra Bastille, I worried he would want to save his voice and not talk. But the gentlemanly Ramey obliged—no, was happy—to answer questions, despite his pollen-induced problem.*

We settle in a vacant dressing room, where he sits, pliant, and since we are filming the interview, lets us move him twice until we get the light right, delighted to oblige.

His chiseled face, thick brown hair, and neat gray beard give him the look of a tough old lion—if you can imagine a lion with an earring.

Or a shy lion. He talks modestly about his career, appearing timid, simple, even humble. He sings for the pleasure of it, not for the gratification of being known by crowds, though known he is. With it all, he seems to have kept a small-town boy's (Colby, Kansas) wide-eyed look at opera. He admits to having idols. An international star, Ramey talks of how he collects autographs and memorabilia of other stars, his "heroes."

He wears a crew-necked sweater, no T-shirt underneath, black trousers, and low brown zip-up boots. The stud earring sparkles—as do the necklace, rings, bracelets, and watch—as he answers questions in his unhurried, rambling, rumbling basso.

The end of the Barber run also—by his own admission—reflects the approaching end of his career, which has spanned three decades and made him one of the most-recorded artists around. It didn't seem right to force the issue, but the laconic plainsman talks openly of it, lending at one point, a touching, nostalgic moment to the interview.

You've said that you were in an opera before you saw one. Tell us that story.

I decided in my senior year in high school that I would study music in college, but probably with the idea of becoming a teacher, because I'd had no exposure to opera. I really didn't know what opera was—I grew up listening to Elvis and Pat Boone. I'd always enjoyed singing and performing, but hadn't even thought about if I could have a career using my voice. I went to Kansas State University, where I studied music and was taking voice lessons. My teacher had me working on an aria from *The Marriage of Figaro*—"Non piu andrai." He suggested I go to the library or find a recording to listen to, to get an idea of the style. So I went to the local record store and was going through the bins and came across this album of Ezio Pinza singing various arias, one of which was "Non piu andrai."

Did you know who Pinza was?

No, I didn't. He later became one of my idols. I bought this album—still have it today, forty-some years later. I started listening to it, and something—I don't know whether it was his voice that drew me—but I became curious about opera. I started going to the library and listening to recordings. And that's how I got hooked. In junior high and high school I had always enjoyed being on stage, performing in plays and going to the theater. I thought, "This is cool—it's like a sung play. What could be better?" Meanwhile, a friend of mine knew I had developed this interest in opera, and told me about a small company in Central City, Colorado, that does a summer festival, uses young singers in the chorus and has an apprentice program for them. So I went to my local radio station and made a tape of a couple of songs and sent it off with the application, and, lo and behold, they hired me. I went to Central City that summer—it was 1963—and the operas were

Don Giovanni and *Il Trovatore*. So I was actually in an opera before I had ever seen one.

How much did it cost you to make a demo in those days?

They didn't charge me. It was a small town.

You say "a sung play." You had had no exposure to opera but enjoyed theater. Am I right in assuming you were more drawn, in those days, to drama?

Yeah. Growing up, I always enjoyed movies of Broadway musicals. That was my only connection to it—I had of course never seen a Broadway play.

The other thing you've talked about a lot is playing devils and bad-guy roles. Is there anything more you'd like to say about that, before we move on to what I hope will be new questions for you?

I don't know how it happened that I got so into them, other than the fact that these roles are great parts, written for the bass voice, and all fit my voice very well. It just sort of happened that I've done all these different operas with the devil and made my career playing him and his various operatic incarnations. I've done many here in Paris: *Faust, The Damnation of Faust, Robert le Diable*. They're more interesting roles, more challenging, with more dimensions.

There's no personal connection? You don't like these parts because there's something in you that fits?

[*Laughs*] No, I don't feel any real connection to the occult. All of them are great roles to play. I've played good guys, too: Figaro in *The Marriage of Figaro* . . . That's about the only one, I think, actually. But I've always said bad guys have more fun. I wouldn't want to be a tenor, even though they get the girl.

In this production of The Barber, after your big first-act "Calunnia" aria as Basilio, you fell down on the stage. It seemed to work with the audience. Was that your idea, or the director's?

That was [director] Colline Serreau's idea. She has a totally different concept of this part than I had ever done. In all the productions I've done, he's played as a slimy guy who makes it his business to know other people's business. He does anything for money. But her idea is that all the stuff he's talking about in his aria—spreading rumors about people and bad things, how rumors grow and eventually ruin somebody—all this has happened to *him*. He's really telling a story about what has happened to *him*. So her idea of me falling down at the end is that by telling this story I'm just done in, and I collapse into the fetal position.

Did she explain that to you in so many words?

Yeah, because in one of our early rehearsals we watched a tape of when they first did the production [in 2002—Ramey's was a reprise]. I saw this and thought, "Odd." She had to explain it. I was a bit taken aback, but I went with it, and it seems to work.

What happens if the director wants you to do something, and you're more than taken aback? If you really don't want to go with it?

In my long career I haven't had very many fights with directors. I've never been asked to do . . . well, I won't say "never," but when I have been asked to do something I wasn't particularly happy with, I've found that directors are willing to discuss, and most are usually fairly . . . what can I say . . . ?

Flexible?

Negotiable about finding a middle ground, about what they want and about what—not what you want, but what you feel you can do.

Any experiences come to mind?

Only one, and it really didn't have anything to do with staging. I was doing *Nabucco*. It was an off-the-wall production: modernized; we were all in modern dress. And the director's biggest concern with me was with my hair. I've always worn my hair on the long side. But he was so concerned about it, I told him, "It can be gelled down." He had a totally different thing in mind for the look. But after the fourth or fifth time of him coming back and saying, "Oh, your hair . . ." I finally looked at him and said, "Listen. I don't think the failure or success of this production is gonna hinge on what my hair looks like. I think you have more important things to worry about."

I heard a tenor say it was impossible for him to do a recital of Handel songs when he was singing a Rossini opera—like you're doing now—because of style, which he called "rules." Rules for Rossini, rules for Handel. He said, "I have to acquire the necessary musculature for one type of music before orienting it—slowly—toward another kind of music." What does he mean?

Every singer is different, of course. But I can understand that. Because doing Rossini is very different than doing Handel. I've had my experience with both. There was a time where I was doing a lot of heavier repertoire—Boito's *Mephistofele*—and at the same time doing parts like Don Giovanni and Figaro in *The Marriage of Figaro*, which have different demands on the voice than Boito. That's what's difficult for me. I can see where that could be a problem.

Can you be more specific?

[*Laughs*] I don't know whether I could explain it. There's a tiny little muscle in the voice box that makes the noise. It has to adjust to whatever you're singing. If you're doing two very different things, it's difficult to do them at the same time. You need a period of adjustment, shall we say.

Is that how you structure your career now? You don't do two very different things in a short period of time?

Exactly. Now it's not so much a worry. I'm not as busy as I was at the height of my career. But that certainly was in my mind at that time.

As long as you mention it, where would you say you are in your career now?

Well, sort of the twilight [*laughs*]. I'm probably in the last few years of my career. After all, I just turned sixty-six. One's voice, after you've been singing for forty-some odd years, is not what it once was. So you have to start thinking about it. You retire roles, and eventually you have to retire everything! [*Laughs*]

Are you considering a post-singing career in teaching, as you thought you'd do after college?

I'm on the faculty of Roosevelt University in Chicago. I've started to do a little teaching there, when I've had the time. That's one thing in the back of my mind. I hope I'll be able to do it. I'm not sure how good I'll be. It's going to be a frightening career change [*laughs*], but I think it'll be interesting.

Any other things in the back of your mind for after your singing days are over?

Not really. I have no interest in being a conductor or a stage director—I don't *think*—although that could be a challenge. . . . We'll see.

Is there an experience which has marked you, which you remember today as being very strong, or fundamental to the musician you became?

Hmm. Wow. [*Thinks*]

Or simply a strong experience that happened to you, either when you were a student, a performer, or a spectator? Pinza, some influence?

I've had so many. It's been a years-long process with lots of those kind of experiences, lots of different people. I think it's mostly people I've worked with that have given me so much: conductors, directors.

Anyone in particular?

There's quite a few. I've worked with so many wonderful conductors that had great influence on me. Riccardo Muti, James Levine, Claudio Abbado.

What do you like about opera?

Opera is the ultimate art form. It has everything. It has wonderful singing, in many cases it has ballet, wonderful orchestral playing. I feel honored and privileged that I've had such a good career doing it.

Is the theatrical aspect of it still as strong a draw for you?

It's always been a combination of musical and theatrical aspects, equally important.

Do you select a role because of the two aspects? The character's theatrical side, or because there's something in the lyrical, musical line you like, or for some other reason?

I've seldom actually chosen a role I want. When I was beginning, I'd be offered a role, then would have to look at it and see how interesting it was. All that goes into it if you want to do something: how interesting the character is and, of course, how interesting, musically, it is, which is equally important.

Are there roles you haven't sung but would like to?

There are roles I haven't done, and some that I've done not as much as I'd like to, that I'll probably never get to now.

For instance?

I've done quite a lot of Verdi, but some of the roles, like the bass part in *Ernani*—Silva—I've never done. That was one I always wanted to do and just never had the chance to. So that's one I missed out on. Fiesco, in *Simon Boccanegra,* I've done only one time. It's such a wonderful part, I hoped I would get more chances to do that, but it didn't work out.

If I were to ask you what's the one quality you need to do what you do, what would you say?

What quality . . . well . . .

Maybe there's more than one. I'm eighteen years old, say, and ask you, "They tell me the voice is there. What do I need to know? What do I need to do?"

First thing, you have to have a voice [*laughs*]. That would be number one. If somebody has a voice, it's a matter of taking the time and developing the voice and developing artistically. There are so many things that go into it. The work on languages. All those things.

Do you work on languages a lot?

I studied French, Italian, and German in college. That's one of the regrets, that I never really became fluent in any language. I can stumble by in those three, but I'm not conversational at all. But I have studied. When I was to do Mephistopheles in *Faust* for the first time, in New York—this was the summer of 1974—I spent a month, here in Paris, working with Janine Reiss, who was on the staff of the Paris Opéra at the time and a well-known vocal coach. Whenever I got a new French role, I made a point of trying to find time to come and work with Janine—on all my French repertoire.

You do that for Italian and Russian?

Yeah, you have to find somebody to help you with those languages.

So if I'm eighteen, you'd tell me to work on languages. What else?

Somebody that age, you have to study voice and you have to take it very slow, because that's very young. You'd have to be very patient.

Is there anything you could tell audiences about opera that they don't know about it that might enhance their enjoyment of it the next time they go?

Hmm.

Is that clear? Is it a stupid question?

It's a good question, but I don't know if I have an answer for it [*laughs*]. Sorry.

Can you confess to anything about opera that you really, really dislike? Or can you confess to anything in opera, or in your career, that has defeated you?

You know, I can't. I feel so lucky to have been involved in this business and to have been as successful as I am in this business. I've loved every minute of it! [*Laughs*] Of course, we all go through bad experiences, but I really . . .

Tell us about a bad experience then, if you don't mind.

[*Sighs*]

People love to hear this stuff.

[*Thinks*]

Have you been ill onstage?

Oh, yeah. I've had quite a few experiences where I've been sick and didn't know it. It's happened to me a number of times where I've gotten up in the morning on the day of a performance and maybe not felt quite right, but thought, that's okay. You vocalize a little and think it'll be all right. Then you start the performance, and the voice starts to say bye-bye. I've had that happen on a few occasions.

What do you do? You're singing in the first act and realize you're not going to make it till the end. What goes through your mind?

Well, that's probably the worst feeling a singer can experience. For me, anyway.

Worse than boos?

I think so, yeah. Although [*reaches for the table*] touch wood, I've never had the misfortune of being booed. But it's a horrible feeling, knowing that your voice is going. Especially if there's nothing you can do. On the occasions it happened to me I had to finish the performance.

But what if you can't finish? The person is making the announcement on-stage that "Mr. Ramey has been taken ill and is unable to continue; his part will be taken by . . ." You hear the crowd's disappointment.

I've gotten sick and had to sing through a performance sick, but never left a performance in the middle. On these occasions it just wasn't possible; there was nobody to go in. I've wanted to leave, but couldn't. I had to figure out a way to get myself through the performance.

What do you do? Do you sing down?

Yeah, you sing down an octave when you have to.

Then you read the critics the next day who say, "What was wrong with Sam Ramey last night?"

[*Laughs*] Fortunately, it wasn't at performances that were reviewed. At least, not that I ever saw.

Do you read the critics?

Sure. I read them. Good or bad. Somebody said once, "The good ones, you use them; the bad ones, you use them for toilet paper" [*laughs*]. In fact, there's a funny story about that. I think it was a famous pianist that played a concert and got a bad review, then wrote a letter to the critic, saying, "I am reading your review in the smallest room in my house [*laughs*]. Your review is before me. Now it is behind me." [*Laughs*]

Critics don't affect you?

Nobody likes to get bad reviews. You'd like to get nothing but good reviews. But everybody at some point in their careers is going to get not such a good review.

One singer told me that when you're young, you don't ever imagine getting a bad review. You think everything's always going to be perfect.

Well, I've never had that feeling. We basically know when we've given a good performance and when we've given a bad performance. We don't really need critics to tell us otherwise. That's why I've never let reviews bother me, good or bad. I've always felt that I've known when I've given a good or a not-so-good performance.

Has it happened that you gave a good performance but felt that it somehow didn't connect with the audience? Is that possible?

Yeah, that's possible.

That it sort of passes right by them.

Right.

You have a hobby of collecting opera memorabilia.

I do, yeah. I have a friend in New York who deals in photos and autographs, things like that. I've bought a lot of stuff. I have a huge collection of composer autographs. My favorite composers.

Any favorite stories?

My friend has a catalog, and one time in this catalog was a photo of Cesare Siepi as King Philip. It was taken from his Met debut. And in the catalog was a copy of the program of his Met debut. So I bought those. I have a photographer friend in San Francisco who is a real opera buff. He was friendly with Siepi and spoke to him periodically. So I called him and told him I had these things and would like to get them autographed. "Do you suppose that if I sent these to you, you could send them to Siepi and ask him to autograph them for me?" My friend said, "I'll give you his number. Call him yourself." I said, "Call him *myself*?" [*eyes go wide, and he looks petrified*]. He gave me the number, and with great nervous trepidation, one day decided I'd call him. His voice answered [*in an extremely deep basso*], "Pronto." I said, "Mr. Siepi, my name is Sam Ramey . . ." And he said, "Sam!" He knew who I was! He said, "Of course I'll autograph them." I sent them to him, and he sent them back with nice autographs and a couple of other photos as well.

Did you ever meet him in person?

I had met him, way back when I was just beginning and he was still singing at the Met. We were with the same management. Every year, in the fall, they had a big party and I spoke to him once then.

So you yourself, a famous opera singer, collect memorabilia from other famous opera singers.

Mostly composers—my favorite composers. Pictures of them, autographs.

Who are these composers, and what do you have of theirs?

Composers of all my famous parts: Gounod, Meyerbeer, Rossini, Verdi, all these people.

At home, do you have a special room or museum for them?

I have a music room, and all my autographs are on the wall. Siepi's are on the same wall with one of Maria Callas.

Is there anything missing from your collection that you'd like to own?

Gosh. Can't think of anything. I think I have all the composers. . . . No, actually—Mussorgsky. You can't find autographs of Mussorgsky, for some reason. I've asked my friend, and he says if they exist, they don't get out of Russia. He's never seen one.

So there is a catalog of stuff that's around? Are there several catalogs or is it a definitive one?

I don't know, I only get his particular catalog. He makes trips to Europe and buys stuff from all over, then brings it back and puts it in his catalog.

When you're singing in a show, like here, do you do the same sort of thing? Do you take home autographs and pictures of your friends in the cast?

I haven't done that much, no. It's more my idols [*laughs*].

When you're in the older opera houses in Europe, are you ever aware of, shall we say, the spirits of your illustrious predecessors, either onstage or backstage?

Oh, sure. You can't but help but think of the ghosts of all these great singers who have trod the same stage. One of my favorite stories about something like that, is I did a production of *Attila* at La Fenice in Venice, twenty years ago. The opera premiered there [in 1846]. They still had all the records and all the original designs for the costumes and the sets and everything. For this production they re-created the original, the very first production of the opera. That was eerie [*laughs*].

Do you ever actually hear the voices of these singers of the past?

No, I don't hear the voices [*laughs*]. That would be spooky! [*Laughs*] Doesn't happen to me, no.

How about seeing Verdi's birthplace, or Puccini's birthplace. Are you moved?

Yeah. I did visit Puccini's place in Lucca. Of course, Mozart's Geburtshaus in Salzburg.

Any fetishes? Rituals before you go onstage? Yoga?

No, I don't really have any. I know some singers do. Luciano Pavarotti—I never saw this, but they said he did it—always went out on the stage and looked around to find a bent nail for good luck. That was part of his ritual. I've never really had one.

You don't come at a certain time before the performance?

Well, I like to get to the theater early. When they're scheduling makeup and everything, I always tell them I have to be ready by a half-hour before curtain. I have to have that much time to vocalize and relax. Otherwise, I feel too rushed.

After the performance, you've just wowed twenty-five hundred people, it's 1 A.M. and you're in your hotel room, in a foreign town, alone. How do you feel?

If I'm alone, I feel lonely. When I perform, I like to have my wife with me, but it doesn't always work that way. Up until now, my family has traveled with me—my wife and child. But he'll start school next fall, so I'll be traveling by myself.

Sounds like a young family.

Yeah, very young. My son turns five the end of this month. I started late [*laughs*].

After a performance, do you go out with colleagues and have dinner?

Sometimes, not always. I do like going out and celebrating. It's never been one of my favorite things to just go home after a performance. I always feel that every performance is something special. Otherwise, if you just go into the theater and perform, then go home, it gets to feel sort of like a nine-to-five job, where you punch in and punch out. I've never felt that way about this job.

This Barber of Seville *is a reprise. How different is that than working in a new production?*

Putting together a new production is always very interesting, because that's where you have the idea that you're really creating something. You're doing something brand-new. Whereas if you're coming in for a revival, very often, in rehearsals, you're just told, "You enter here, you sing, then you go out here." That's basically the kind of rehearsals you get when you go to the opera house, say, in Vienna, where you have two days of rehearsal. You're left more or less to your own devices.

Do you like rehearsing?

Lots of singers don't. I've always enjoyed the process. I've always enjoyed rehearsing almost as much as performing. That's what makes doing a new production special to me.

You want to be present for the full four or five weeks of rehearsal in a new production? You don't like to arrive just a few days before it opens? Do singers still do that?

Yeah, lots of singers. And, I must admit, I have done that myself. But never for a new production. But in the past, lots of singers have shown up for a new production a few days before the final dress. The big stars.

You mentioned two days' rehearsal in some revivals. Is that a problem for you, two days?

You come to expect it. One would probably never go into a situation like that doing a part you've never done before. I have turned things down, at opera houses like Vienna, simply because they offered something that you would like to do, something you've never done before—but it's impossible to premiere a role with two days' rehearsal.

Again, any examples you care to remember?

I was offered Boris Godunov in Vienna, and it was a situation like that. With almost no rehearsal. I think I had done *Boris* once at that time. But I had never done the version they were doing, so I turned it down for that reason.

Was it the conductor or the opera house director who asked you?

The opera house director asked for me, but I couldn't do it.

How about festivals? That's a system that might be likened to a repertory theater; they often ask you to sing roles you've done frequently because they can't afford rehearsal time, either.

I haven't had a whole lot of festival experience, except for Salzburg. But Salzburg really wasn't like that. I did Don Giovanni and Boris Godunov there. I think I did the production of *Don Giovanni* there for four years. It was with Karajan. And every time I did it, they rehearsed it like it was a new production.

Was that because they had a lot of money or because it was Karajan?

It was Karajan the first few times, then the second two times it was with Muti. So a new conductor—and he would never allow somebody to just drop in.

Can you describe your typical working day? You have a performance at 7:30 P.M. When do you get up? What do you do?

I try to get as much rest as I can the night before. Like I said, I have an almost-five-year-old, and he gets up very early, but usually on the day of a performance my wife lets me sleep in; she gets up with him. I usually just have a relaxing day. I vocalize through the day to get my voice slowly going. Because the whole process takes longer than it did when I was younger! [*Laughs*] It's one of the things about getting older. It just takes you longer to get the voice up and running.

"Twilight" was your word when talking about your career earlier. Without being too personal, and you don't have to answer this, but do you have any other thoughts at this period in your career that you haven't mentioned?

[*Thinks*] I don't know whether I'd use the word "traumatic," but it's kind of a traumatic thing. I'm thinking, "In a few years, you're not going to be doing this." It'll be a big adjustment. It's kind of sad. I'm kind of sad now because these are probably my last performances in Paris with the Paris Opéra. I mean, it looks that way, anyway. It's been off-and-on for thirty years I've been singing here.

You say that because this is your decision, or you just feel it, or what?

Well, I have no plans right now to come back, and there will be new management taking over. Maybe I'll be asked to come back, but probably not! [*Laughs*] Too many good young singers, you know. They don't look to hire sixty-six-year-old basses very much anymore! [*Laughs*]

All the same, you've had a career that's spanned three decades. Any secrets to longevity?

I don't think there's any real secret to a long career, other than being careful throughout your career—what you do, when. With every singer, it's different. I've been fortunate that I've had good people guiding me. My voice teacher that I've been with almost forty years. I've always had good management. I've been very careful as to repertoire. I spent a lot of my early years, early in my career, doing Mozart and the bel canto repertoire, which I think grounded my vocal technique very well. I didn't do a lot of the heavier roles until I was ready, till I was older. I think that's sort of been my secret.

Do you have any tricks for memorizing lines?

I don't. I wish there was a trick for memorizing, because I've never been a real fast learner, as far as getting a role into my head. It's always a fairly long process for me. I just have to go over and over and over the text, repeating it, till it becomes sort of automatic. I don't really have a secret; I wish I knew one.

In the old days, they had the prompter's box to help you, but a lot of houses have done away with them.

A lot of opera houses don't have them anymore. It becomes an issue with designers. Because they don't like that little box sticking up and spoiling the line of their set.

How do you approach interviews? You know you're going to talk to the press. Do you have a message? Before the interview, do you think, "I want the reporter to take this idea away when it's over?" Does your management say, "Here's a message"? Do you come prepared with anything?

Not really. I just wing it. When I first started doing interviews, when I was beginning, I had a public relations agent in New York, and the first couple of times I did interviews, he would get calls from the interviewers, saying, "I can't get him to talk! He won't talk!" I've always been a very shy person, anyway. I've gotten better over the thirty-some years. But in the beginning, I found it very difficult doing interviews. I wasn't very verbal. I'd be, "Yep." "Nope" [*laughs*].

Your Midwest side.

I guess [*laughs*].

But you say you're better now.

I *think* I am. I don't think my PR guy gets any calls anymore about my not wanting to talk.

Looking at these kind of questions, I can understand. For someone who does it all day, these things might be hard to explain to someone on the outside. Whether you're verbal or not.

There are some hard questions here. A lot of interviews are, you know, "What's your favorite role?" And blah-blah-blah.

"Where do you shop?"

Yeah.

Last question. Say the score calls for you to sing four notes: A-mor, a-mor— I'm thinking of Rodolfo, end of act 1 of La Bohème*—G-E-C-high E, I think it is. You sing la-la, laaaaaa-la. A-mor, aaaaaa-mor. You swim, portamento up to the last high note. Is that cheating?*

[*Thinks*] It depends on. . . . It depends on the style of the music. It depends on what's going on in the orchestra. I wouldn't say it's cheating. Very often a portamento up like that is very much with the style. It depends on the whole context of what the piece is.

I'm told that in bel canto, for instance, it's allowed, and in Strauss, say, it's not. Is that what you're saying? There are rules—like that tenor said about Rossini and Handel.

That could be part of it. I've never sung Strauss, so I don't know.

But there's no hard-and-fast rule.

No.

And if you don't exactly hit that little black dot on the page, I have no right to say you're faking or anything.

No, it wouldn't be; it's not necessarily cheating.

It's an interpretation.

It's interpretation, and it could be that it's very much in the style of the piece.

Well, thank you for clearing that up.

[*Laughs*] Well, I don't really know if I have!

© Nicho Södling

Esa-Pekka Salonen, or new opera and festival opera

Music reporter: Have you conducted much Stockhausen?
[attributed to] Sir Adrian Boult: No, but I've stepped in some.

There is plenty of new music around today, and, unlike in the recent past, it seems to get a reasonably good hearing. Esa-Pekka Salonen is involved in much of it. The composer/conductor, who recently turned fifty, divides his time between the two professions, both in the United States and in Europe. As a conductor, he led the Los Angeles Philharmonic for seventeen years before moving to the United Kingdom, where he succeeded Christoph von Dohnányi as principal conductor and artistic advisor of the London Philharmonia Orchestra.

During his time with the L.A. Philharmonic, he world-premiered works by John Adams, Franco Donatoni, Anders Hillborg, William Kraft, Magnus Lindberg, Witold Lutoslawski, Bernard Rands, Kaija Saariaho, Rodion Shchedrin, Steven Stucky, Tan Dun, and Augusta Read Thomas, as well as his own compositions. We dwell on Kaija Saariaho's new opera, Adriana Mater, because Salonen was preparing its world premiere in Paris when we met.

Salonen the composer premiered his first piano concerto in New York at Avery Fisher Hall. This work, co-commissioned by the New York Philharmonic, the BBC, Radio France, and NDR Hamburg, was performed by the New York Philharmonic and conducted by Salonen. His recent orchestral *creations include* Foreign Bodies, Insomnia, *and* Wing on Wing, *a work for orchestra and two sopranos.*

All this makes him the proper person to explain conducting and composing new music, and especially new opera, anti-opera, and the future of opera. He describes himself as "curious," and clearly enjoys exploring such questions as what makes for successful new music; why one piece makes it into the repertoire, another not; and what makes a masterpiece.

He is a friendly but serious, dour Finn when we speak in his dressing room backstage at Paris's Opéra Bastille. As he is in full preparation for the first-ever performance of Saariaho's newest opus, commissioned for the house, this meant that our talk, understandably, is not the only thing on his mind. Rehearsals are going well, but he is worried about a potential strike at the opera house for its opening, among other things, but shrugs finally, admitting, "It's out of my hands." (The strike was avoided for the most part, although some performances were canceled.)

He is accessible and talkative, and the fact that he rarely smiles—when he does, it's a crack—doesn't mean he lacks a sense of humor. He actually laughs, but not till the very end of the interview. More on the quiet, sardonic side, his language is less fulsome than some of the more effusive opera professionals interviewed for this book.

We begin by talking about festivals, a specific side to the opera profession.

You've been running the Baltic Sea Festival for six years. How do you program opera in a festival?

Programming starts with the idea that a festival has to offer something new in its own environment to justify its existence. So festival programming has to be something that doesn't happen at any other time during the season. There has to be some kind of local uniqueness to the programming, either in the repertoire, the performers, or the productions.

How do you ensure this at the Baltic Festival?

We try to program operas that have not been performed in Stockholm. There has to be a newsworthiness, if you wish, that guides programming to a certain degree, because it has to be news in its own milieu. That's the most important thing: a festival, first and foremost, serves its local audiences.

It should enrich the artistic life in the city where it happens. Of course, we want to program great productions, with great singers and conductors. The Baltic Festival hasn't been particularly difficult to program.

Yours runs ten days and tours to Helsinki, Tallinn, Gdansk, Turku, and Stockholm. Have you encountered any particular problems?

Visiting opera, or touring opera, is a logistical nightmare because of the sheer volume of things and the number of people involved, plus the costs and the complexity of setting it all up in a very short time in a house where it was not originally conceived. There are endless problems. But in our case, the Mariinsky theater has a fabulous routine of fitting their productions into any theater, since they travel so much. Touring is such a big part of their life that they are incredibly flexible. The Russians are willing to compromise, and they are very good at it. This would be much harder for Western companies, I'm sure. We are so used to everything being meticulously prepared, with this bucket being right there, and this ax being right here, and so on, that if they are not there for some reason, then the whole thing comes to a grinding halt. And there's the unions. But the Russians go with the flow quite often, and the results are stunning.

Let's talk about new opera, then about commissioning a new work. What's the state of new opera today?

It's difficult to say anything in general about the state of new opera. The field is wide open. And there are so many different approaches to the idea of opera these days. By new opera, let's say opera written within the last thirty years. We have really seen the gamut of styles and approaches and textual and contextual aspects. There was a moment in the recent history of music when opera was considered to be a hopelessly bourgeois art form. And composers, when writing operas, usually ended up writing anti-operas. Like Ligeti's *Le Grand macabre*; that's an anti-opera in many ways. Luciano Berio's operas are anti-operas on many levels. But when I think of the new operas I've seen or worked with recently, the trend has changed. Composers are again interested in the idea of writing a grand opera in the tradition of using the bells and whistles of an opera house.

What changed things?

These things go in waves. I'm not capable of analyzing what exactly has made the culture change, but I do think opera is one of the last forums where you can speak about the big feelings. Where you can treat the deepest emotions, the most tragic, touching, moving, and exciting things, without having to resort to distance and irony. Opera is a deeply emotional medium where you don't have to be postmodern to reach audiences.

What do you mean by "postmodern"?

In many films—especially European art cinema; I'm not talking about Hollywood—you can see that postmodern thinking has come to a point where the idea of a direct, undiluted emotion is almost impossible. It has to somehow always be seen through something else. That's the postmodern way. But opera is an instrument where everything's possible. I also think that the idea of visual, musical, and theatrical elements coming together interests people more than maybe it did thirty years ago. I can't say exactly why this happened.

What's the last new opera you saw?

Dr. Atomic by John Adams. While completely different from Kaija Saariaho's opera *Adriana Mater*, it has one thing in common: it firmly believes in the art of opera and what you can do with it. It's a big statement. While I'm not saying some of the anti-operas aren't great pieces, like *Le Grand macabre*, I welcome this idea of being positive and optimistic about the future of the medium. Even though both operas I mentioned, *Dr. Atomic* and *Adriana Mater*, are not exactly optimistic works. But they firmly believe in opera as an art form.

You mean they respect the conventions?

They are not conventional operas by any means, but they are aware of the history and are not ashamed of it. They use opera conventions whenever it suits them, but it's not something they try to ignore. They refer to other moments in the history of opera. Not quotations, more like a dramatic gesture. There are times when you know that this moment relates to some other moment in another piece.

Where do you see twenty-first-century opera going?

I wish I knew. I have no idea. But I think that we are in a better place now, generally speaking, than we have been for a long time. We might even see a very fertile opera period.

Can we conclude, then, that twenty-first-century opera is in good health?

Yeah, I think there's more happening. And the fear that opera would become a completely museum-like art form has been abandoned. That's not happening at the moment. New opera is alive and well.

Is this due at all to the fact that maybe opera directors are more cognizant of the fact that they have to appeal to a new public?

Yes, but it's simpler than that. Every theater in the world needs to commission new work. That's what theaters have always done. Shakespeare's group did new work all the time. It would be totally absurd to have a theater or opera house where new work was not happening; where you only made new representations of old material. And the audience ultimately would not accept it. I think there have been some very resonant audience successes with contemporary opera recently. Kaija Saariaho's earlier opera *L'amour de loin* was a huge success everywhere and had an amazing following. Another powerful new opera that was very successful was Thomas Adès's *Tempest* that Covent Garden produced. Really wonderful; incredibly imaginative, delightful music that managed to communicate directly without compromising its integrity. John Adams's operas have been not only very successful with audiences, but they also became hotly debated. *Klinghoffer*, for instance, was on some level the most politically talked-about opera.

Some people might say that has nothing to do with the musical worth of the piece. One group or another took offense.

That was not a musical debate at all. But the fact that a modern opera can actually become a hot issue—on any level—is already great. *Dr. Atomic,* because of the subject matter, created quite a bit of debate. It generated a lot of articles in the U.S. press—not only by music and theater people, but by physicists and historians. The fact that opera can do that is a very good sign, because the risk and the drag has always been that opera is seen as entertainment for the upper classes and has no connection to the society and the world of our time whatsoever. Now we are seeing that this is not the case. If you think about *Adriana Mater*, the story is universal, but you can set it in five different countries today or this week. [Director] Peter Sellars has chosen to set it in Chechniya—sort of—but it could be just as well . . . [*thinks*] . . .

. . . downtown Los Angeles?

Very well, yeah, east L.A. Absolutely. Or northern Iraq or parts of Turkey, Afghanistan.

You mentioned Shakespeare's theater commissioned new works, and that all theaters do. Where does one start today? You know going in, I assume, that you aren't going to make any money on it—even if part of your budget is underwritten by the state. Does the composer call the librettist? Does a singer call an opera director? There must be many ways to get a project off the ground.

It varies. In this case, Gerard Mortier [former head of the Salzburg Festival, then of the Paris Opéra] had commissioned Kaija's first opera [*L'amour de loin*] for Salzburg already, so he knew what he was getting into. The Salzburg production was a huge success. It became a very famous piece right away. Mortier wanted to continue supporting Kaija's work. Peter Sellars has been working with both Kaija and me for years. I was an obvious choice, because I am Kaija's oldest collaborator.

You were supposed to be involved in L'amour de loin *but weren't finally. What happened?*

The timing didn't work. I took a sabbatical year, and Kaija's premiere fell right in the middle of it.

Then you came in on the Adriana Mater *project rather early.*

I've been on this for a long time—since the beginning—three years ago, maybe. I saw the bits and pieces when they started to emerge. I was always sent the latest development of the score. I have a huge pile of scrap material, first versions of this and that. So I followed the process. I also was in touch with Kaija, and from time to time we talked about it.

Why did Adriana Mater *interest you?*

First of all, it is a fascinating process to see how a big thing like this comes together. Also she's a friend, and I would have been in contact with her anyway. So to be in touch with her about this was natural. I'd ask how it was going, where are you at the moment, things like that. Because I knew the text, of course, by then. It was interesting to hear where she was going.

Did you have any influence on the development of the bits and pieces she sent you, as you knew then you would be conducting the premiere?

Not at that stage. But of course, once I got the final score I made some suggestions from a practical point of view. Some notational things, tempi, the normal stuff that always happens. But in Kaija's case, we've been working together for such a long time that it's very easy. There's no prestige, or problems about somebody being right or wrong. We're just together, trying to find the best solution.

Did you work together on other projects, prior to L'amour de loin?

We studied together, and I've done lots of first performances of hers over the years and commissioned work from her. I commissioned a piece for the L.A. Philharmonic almost fifteen years ago. Her work has been instrumental as well as vocal. There was a piece called *Château de l'âme,* which Dawn Upshaw sang. That was pre-*L'amour de loin*. I premiered that piece in Salzburg. Before that we did some orchestral work together.

You've written many works for orchestra and for the voice yourself. Do you write operas?

I haven't written an opera, but I might one day. So it does interest me. Absolutely.

What's the story of Adriana Mater?

In terms of what happens, it's quite simple; psychologically, however, it's complex. In a place where an ethnical civil war is raging, a young woman is raped by a warrior who turns out to be a war criminal. She gets pregnant, and her sister tries to persuade her to get rid of the baby, but she doesn't want to. That is essentially the first act. The second act is seventeen years later. The child, a boy now seventeen, has learned the truth about his origin—that his father was not a soldier who died heroically trying to defend his family but was a war criminal and rapist. He confronts his mother about this and learns that his father is back in the area, then goes to see him, intending to kill him. But he ends up not killing him when he realizes his father has gone blind. So he goes back to his mother, apologizing, saying "Mother, I'm a failure since I couldn't kill this man." And Adriana is incredibly happy and thanks him for that, saying, "Now I know that the blood in your veins is more mine than his, and you're not a murderer." So there's almost a

Wagnerian redemption quality, almost like *Tannhäuser*. It's a simple story, as I said, but the psychological layers of all this are complex.

Is that what you like about it?

I like simple stories in operas—simple enough, I mean.

What is a simple story in opera? Is there one? Rigoletto?

Yes. *Wozzeck*. Not simplistic, but straightforward. *Salome*, definitely. I like the arrowlike quality that goes from one point and arrives at a different point. And then of course the psychology of it may have lots of different layers.

Is that your personal taste, or does a simple story allow you as a musician to do certain things?

It's my personal preference. I have problems with incomprehensible opera stories.

A lot of people think all libretti are gibberish.

That's not the case, actually. Look at Da Ponte. He is great.

But the libretto of The Magic Flute *or some nineteenth-century operas just go all over the map.*

The whole of bel canto, where the love intrigue is impenetrable.

And Wagner?

Wagner is different. Take *Tristan*. It all happened before the opera starts. The opera is really a four-and-one-half-hour epilogue to something that already took place. We're not talking about action at all. We're talking about the psychological layers, which are endless. In modern or new opera, it's nice to have a story that is not all over the place. A story can be emotionally varied, deepened and complex, but I like one that has focus.

Let's conclude with your Baltic Festival. Do you commission pieces for it?

Yes. We do a couple of new pieces every year. But I don't commission opera for the festival. I haven't got the financial means to do that for the moment. I commission orchestral pieces.

Is it roughly the same procedure?

Yes, it's always a balancing act, commissioning new work. You want to encourage new talent, of course. You want to be the first one who gets a masterpiece out of a young composer. We want to be like a . . . [*thinks*] . . .

. . . an incubator.

Yeah, a midwife, that kind of thing. Of course, the other aspect is to commission from established people. It's also important that we try to get new music out of the best composers around. So we're trying to find new names, while encouraging existing talent to do what they've done before. These are the two roles of a festival director. I guess it's the same for an opera director or anybody who is in a position where they can commission new work. You want to maintain the balance between the new, unknown, not-yet-tested and tried with the established.

Tanya Niemann

José Van Dam, or humility, the elite, and the caddies

A stately gentleman of the old school, José Van Dam won't read newspapers, doesn't particularly appreciate outrageous stagings, and isn't a fan of much modern music (though there are exceptions, like Olivier Messiaen's 1983 Saint François d'Assise, which he created and helped make a big hit).

He's a simple man—and that's the first thing he tells you. There are none of the trappings of heady stardom with the Belgian baritone, who has been one of Europe's top draws for decades—longevity corroborated by the white hair.

He doesn't make much of an impression at the start. He's so calm and controlled that at first you think it's an Olympian distance, age, indifference, some sort of generation gap. But in reality, it's none of those. He's solid, terse and polite, but more than anything, he's shy—and he'll tell you that, too. He's also humble, he explains, because early in his career he learned the value of teamwork. This characteristic adds to the air of low-key, peaceful self-possession. He is not the star who wants to stand out.

Sitting in a makeup seat that looks like it came from a barber shop, Van Dam is dressed in an overcoat, red silk scarf, blue jacket that matches his eyes, and black polo shirt. He could be anyone.

He is another who begins with his own biography and the story he knows best—probably a result of too many reporters, or in hopes that the interviewer will be satisfied with plain facts and thus abandon any more probing queries he or she may have brought along.

The enormous hype and fury surrounding the opera business seem to strike him as devoid of any interest at all. Since he doesn't read the press, whatever the eventual printed newspaper story says about him really doesn't concern him much.

This is not to say he's dismissive. He's forthcoming, even engaging, with common, down-to-earth, old-style courtesy, as we chat in his sparse black-and-white dressing room at Paris's Opéra Bastille. The room is empty; he is in rehearsals, and the premiere of Gustave Charpentier's Louise *is one week away. The dressing room reflects his simplicity. On the shelves are makeup, cotton, three bottles of water. There are two chairs, two lamps, and one piano. That's all. Somehow, you get the feeling that the whole thing—singing, a career in opera—is much less complicated than you imagined.*

Why did you want to sing opera?

It's very simple. I started singing when I was eleven. I was just a kid. When I was thirteen, I met my singing teacher—the only one I ever had throughout my whole career—a Belgian concert tenor. At thirteen, I was saying I was going to be an opera singer. I didn't know what that meant, but because of that I always say it wasn't I who chose this profession; the profession chose me.

Since then, it's been one straight, steady path?

From thirteen to fifteen, my voice was changing, so I had to stop singing, but at fifteen I started again. I entered music school in Brussels with my teacher; at eighteen, I entered the conservatory and won my first prize a year later. After that, I did my military service—in Germany because at the time the Belgian armed forces were stationed there. I returned a year later and did another year at the conservatory to get another diploma in opera. At twenty, I entered a contest in Paris, where the artistic director heard me and asked me to audition for the Paris Opéra. I was hired. That's how it began.

When was this?

Nineteen sixty-one. I stayed four years, then left because I thought I was beginning to waste my time. I went to the Geneva Opera, where I stayed two years. The director there had heard me at a competition in Geneva. Before I had left Paris, in 1964, Lorin Maazel hired me to record Ravel's *L'Heure espagnole* with him. Maazel was at that time music director of the Opera at Berlin, and asked me to join him there. So after my two years in

Geneva, I sang in Berlin for six years, in the troupe there. Since then it's been freelance.

Is the contest route the normal one? Young singers can also hire impresarios.

There's no normal way. I did competitions because I wanted to. It didn't bring me much, career-wise—except perhaps for Geneva, because the director, Herbert Graf, heard me and hired me. But apart from that, competitions didn't get you much—at least at that time. Maybe it's changed now. Today you have Cardiff and all these contests which have become pretty important. But not in those days.

Was it better to have an impresario then?

A good one, yes. But there aren't many good ones. The good ones handle singers who already have careers. There are plenty of impresarios for stars, but impresarios who handle young singers, no. You know, impresarios today aren't what they once were. In the old days, an impresario was somebody who took a singer and said, "I'm going to guide your career. You're going to sing here, here and here. Before the Met or Covent Garden, you're going to sing in small theaters." Now they try and launch people you've never heard of; suddenly, they're singing at the Met or La Scala, and it's all happening too fast.

You managed to avoid those pitfalls.

I had the good luck to sing twelve years in troupes in Paris, Geneva, and Berlin. I sang important roles and less important roles. When I was at Berlin, for example, I sang Leporello or Figaro, but in-between did Colline in *La Bohème*, which isn't dangerous, or the Speaker in *The Magic Flute*, or one of the smaller roles in *Die Frau ohne Schatten,* which lasts three minutes. I sang a lot and learned a lot of roles—especially that—and worked with many good singing coaches and masters. I sang with Giuseppe Patanè, who was pretty well known at the time. Maazel, of course. All that was great. Maazel was preparing a new production of *Tosca* and asked me if I wanted to sing Scarpia. I was twenty-nine. I told him, "Maestro, it's too early for me." He said okay.

You understood it was too soon.

I told Maazel, "If I sing Scarpia today, what am I going to sing later?" I said I'd do Angelotti if he wanted me to. He said he didn't dare ask, but I did it with pleasure. I sang Scarpia maybe fifteen years ago, not at that age.

What do you like to sing most—opera or lieder?

I love melody, but when it's accompanied by an orchestra. Mahler's *Rückert Lieder* or *Kindertotenlieder*, Ravel's *Don Quichotte*. I like Franck Martin. These are melodic pieces with orchestra. I also like oratorios but am doing fewer of them these days. I just did Mendelssohn's *Elias* in Japan and in Florence with Seiji Ozawa. The music is superb, and I love singing it.

And in opera? What do you like to sing?

What I like about opera is that you're acting, too. I like being an actor on-stage. When people go to the opera, they always say, "I'm going to see *Carmen*" or "I saw *La Traviata*." They never say "I'm going to hear *Carmen*." People don't go to opera to listen—they go to see a show. And that's fine. That's what opera is. It's spectacle. What I love about melody and in song recitals with piano, and it's not that easy, is that you return to pure music. People come because they are going to really hear a singer, Mr. Terfel or Mr. Van Dam or somebody. But they're coming to hear them as musicians, as singers, not as singer-actors, like in opera. So the big difference is that on one hand you have the singer-musician, and on the other you have the singer-actor.

Your rapport with the audience must be different in each.

Quite. The difficulty I had, personally at first, was that when singing melody it was much more interiorized than opera. In opera, it has to go out. It's the same with gestures. If I make a small gesture with my hand, you don't see it. On an opera stage, and particularly here at the Bastille, which is very big, my gestures have to be big, too. That applies musically as well; you have to create musical effects that will work. In recitals the melody is more interiorized. The public has to understand this. That's one difficulty of recitals, at least for me: at first I was too interiorized. You can create certain effects, musical or vocal, but a lot less than in opera. Still, I enjoy doing both.

Who told you it was too interiorized?

I realized it myself. Musician friends told me. I'm not saying it was bad. But certain things were lacking in my interpretation because of it—first of all, because I'm a very timid person in real life. I've fought against this, and made some strides—or at least I hope I have, after nearly fifty years in the business.

How do you manage to go onstage at all, if you're that timid?

Because onstage, I'm not me. Here we're doing *Louise*. And in *Louise*, I'm the Father. I'm no longer myself. Despite my shyness, if the stage directors asked me—and they'd be perfectly within their rights—to perform nude on-stage, and if I felt the part called for it, I'd do it, no problem. Because it's not me. I'm Hans Sachs or Golaud or Boris. And at that moment my shyness disappears. That's how it works. I suffer more stage fright for recitals than for operas because I have to fight my shyness a lot more.

Do you have some sort of formula to do this, before going out onstage?

No. I do some breathing exercises, that sort of thing. That's all. Fortunately, I'm reasonably calm by nature.

You say you're timid. Would you say you're a very emotional singer? If so, how do you manage to channel or master your emotions onstage?

I am much more a master of my emotions onstage than in real life. I'll be watching a film with my kids, for instance, and I'll cry. But not onstage. Because like I said, I'm no longer myself. In *Louise*, the Father has a very emotional final scene, but I manage to control myself. The first time I ever sang *Kindertotenlieder*, at the very end when he picks up the lullaby again, I was crying onstage while singing it. It's terrible when that happens. I started thinking, "Hey, watch out!"

What did you tell yourself then?

It was too late! You have to keep singing. But you have to dominate your-self and your feelings. You can let the emotions go to some degree in the interpretation, but not inside, let's say—if you see what I mean.

It doesn't sound easy.

It isn't. You have to make others believe it. But that's the interpretation, the musical side. Mahler's music is so well written that it's not hard to commu-nicate the message without investing yourself to the hilt. You're helped out by Mahler, or Charpentier in *Louise*.

You mentioned crying. How about if you start feeling ill onstage—what do you do? What goes through your mind?

Knock wood, that's never happened to me. Some singers are known for being nervous or emotional, so it might happen to those with that kind of makeup. They might lack a sort of nervous solidity. Neil Shicoff and I sang *Tales of Hoffmann* in Barcelona, and he told me, "I don't see how you can stay so calm." It might also be a form of vocal or technical insecurity that makes you nervous.

It doesn't sound like you've had to cancel many performances.

Very few. In the forty-five years of my career, I might have canceled eight shows because I wasn't feeling good. But that's a question of nervous health that I get from my parents and all that. Also, from fourteen to twenty-one, I did a lot of judo. That taught me how to stay calm.

What are the qualities one needs most to be an opera singer? Apparently one can do it even if one is shy.

One of the greatest qualities a lyric artist can have is generosity. In expression, in the way you sing and in the way you are. That's very important.

Is one born with this, or does one have to learn it?

I think it's your nature. But in general, the great artists are generous artists. It's in a great artist's soul to be generous. At least I think so. Not always, of course. Another important thing is humility. Being humble in your relationship to the music. You can be a big star today, but when you look at the history of music, and see the names lined up behind you, you realize you're a grain of sand on the beach. It's the same for the greatest conductors, singers, or musicians. You've got to stay humble. Generosity and humility for me are the two main qualities you need. And the will to work. You have to work, of course.

And you are humble?

I believe so, because I come from a rather simple family. My father was a woodworker. I was the first musician in the family.

Were they for or against your career choice?

My father was for it, fortunately. He died, unfortunately, when I was eighteen. But he really helped me. That's a bit of luck that I had. But my father was also a generous man; I'd say noble in his approach to life, despite the fact he was a woodworker. There are noble people everywhere.

I've seen you in many roles. Do you like to sing a lot of different parts? Do you collect them?

I started in 1961, don't forget.

Do you consciously look for new roles?

I'm very curious, musically. When I was young, not when I was just starting to sing, but after about five years, I told myself there were certain roles
that I wanted to sing one day, and that I *would* sing one day. I told myself,
for example, that I would sing Masetto, then Leporello, then Don Giovanni.
There are three roles in *Simon Boccanegra*: Fiesco, Paolo, and Simon Boccanegra. I wanted to sing Figaro in *The Marriage of Figaro*. When I was
thirty, I knew I was going to sing Hans Sachs, even if I sang it twenty years
later. Boris Godunov. There are a lot of roles. Golaud in *Pelléas and Mélisande* is something I always wanted to do.

Why were you drawn to these operas?

I love *Pelléas,* it's one of my favorites. It's not an opera, it's a slice of life.
And so well done—but not everybody likes it. I've sung it, 250, maybe 300
times, and each time I hear something new.

What do you like about it?

Something remarkable about *Pelléas* is that there are duets the singers never
sing together. You ask a question, and I respond. But you never have two
voices superimposed. Except at one point: at the end, just before Golaud
kills his half-brother—when Pelléas says "I love you," and kisses Mélisande
—you have two voices together. It's the only moment in the whole opera.
There's no union of voices except when the two declare their love simul-
taneously. I'm convinced Debussy wanted it that way. It lasts maybe ten
measures, five or six seconds. Then Golaud kills Pelléas. Maeterlinck's text
is superb. The only thing I reproach in Debussy's adaptation is that we don't
see Golaud try and kill himself after murdering his brother. That's in the play,
but not in the opera. You see his remorse, and it changes Golaud's character
a bit: you'd understand things better if you knew that.

Are there roles you've sung and never returned to?

Many. *Les Huguenots*. Figaro in *The Marriage of Figaro*. I last sang that in
1991, I think, in Brussels, directed by Mark Morris. And I told myself, "All
right, that's enough. I'm too old for that part now." There are other roles:
Escamillo, the toreador in *Carmen*. You can't be a toreador when you're fifty,
it's too dangerous. On the other hand, there are new roles I'm taking on.
Germont in *Traviata*, which I'm singing here this year, I sang for the first
time last year in Brussels. For Germont, or Scarpia, I've always told myself,
"If one day it happens, fine, I'll do it." But it wasn't one of those pillar roles
I talked about. I sang Massenet's *Don Quichotte* because I wanted to. There
are other unexpected things that happen, like Messiaen's *Saint François*

d'Assise. When I was young, it hadn't been written, of course. I was asked to do it and accepted.

Is it an affinity, a connection with a role that you look for?

Yes. Because I'm not really a big singer of modern music. It doesn't interest me that much. There are exceptions, like *Wozzeck*, which is a fantastic work. Four years ago in Brussels, I created a part, *Le Livre sur la route*, but did it because I knew the composer, who was Belgian, quite well, and knew the man who wrote the libretto. When they told me they were going to make it into an opera, I was ready to do it, right there. For *Saint François d'Assise*, I had time to talk with Messiaen two or three years before; that's a different matter.

It was a big success; they say it'll enter the repertory.

I think it will. It's one of today's operas that can become part of the canon, despite the fact it's not really an opera. He calls it "Franciscan scenes in three acts and eight tableaux."

How do you approach rehearsals? Do you get enough time?

One thing that always amazes people is that when we mount a production like *Louise* here, we rehearse for five weeks. I'm almost always here for all those rehearsals. Rehearsals are important for me, because a show isn't one singer or one star. It's a group of people who work together. It's like if you cultivate your garden, and have something that grows which is the fruit of everyone's labor. In his memoirs, Marcel Pagnol said that in the theater, we speak about the troupe, just like in the army. I know what he means, because when I did my military service, I was a sniper, an elite shot with a rifle. I also used a machine gun. And the machine gun weighs seventeen kilos. But the rifleman doesn't carry it because he's not supposed to tire himself out. So you had a team. You had the snipers, and you had the caddies. Somebody else loaded the ammunition. When the squadron leader said, "Prepare to fire," in seven seconds that gun had to be loaded and ready. It's the sort of thing you can't do alone. You need everybody's collaboration. It's the same in theater. If you really want a good show, you're not going to get it with only one star coming to sing. It's not José Van Dam or Plácido Domingo, and all the rest are just riffraff. That's not a good show. Even the small roles have to play their part; they're important. This is one of the things you learn when you're part of a troupe, like I was in Paris, Geneva, and Berlin, in the early days.

Have we lost something of that troupe feeling, with stars who fly in for one performance and then fly out again?

Some singers arrive a week before the premiere, while the others have been rehearsing five weeks; that happens, but it's rare.

Would you say that you manage to express yourself satisfactorily in music? And do you choose roles around this criterion?

Yes. I've refused roles because they didn't correspond to who I am. I've often been asked to sing Wotan, and I've always refused. After I recorded *Die Frau ohne Schatten* with Georg Solti, he wanted me to sing the role at Bayreuth, but I refused. And he wasn't too pleased about it. I've never sung Wotan. It's a role I just don't feel. I also think it's dangerous. A lot of bassos have damaged their voices singing it. I'll sing his adieux from *Die Walküre* in concerts.

And you recorded Die Meistersinger.

But that's very lyrical. The three Wagner roles I told myself, at the beginning of my career, that I would sing are Amfortas [*Parsifal*], The Dutchman [*Flying Dutchman*] and Hans Sachs [*Meistersinger*]. They are more singable. Wotan often has a lot of orchestra, or duets or trios. It's a character that I just don't understand. I've never wanted to do it. There are others. Karajan once asked me to sing Pizarro [*Fidelio*], but I didn't want to do that, either. He also wanted me to sing one of the parts in *Lohengrin*, and I said no to that. He said, "You're right—you have too fine a voice to risk it." People often say nobody ever dared refuse Karajan, but it's not true at all. I turned him down for Sarastro [*Magic Flute*] also. I did the record with him, but recordings are different. You have the microphones and all that. "It's not really for me," I told him. It was for Salzburg, with Giorgio Strehler directing, but I said no; I sang The Speaker instead.

What was working with Herbert von Karajan like?

Karajan was very respectful of your wishes. I refused three roles. The problem was that when he had singers he liked, he wouldn't change them. He found a bass, a tenor, and a soprano and asked them to do everything. There were cases of a soprano and a tenor I can think of who sang everything Karajan asked them to, and it wasn't good for them.

You've refused roles because they don't correspond to who you are. Do you ever refuse a part because you don't like the staging?

I nearly did, a few years back, here in Paris, for a *Meistersinger* at the Théâtre du Châtelet. Afterward, I told myself, "Next time I sign a contract, I want to know who's doing the staging. Or the conducting." Those are important things. But that's very hard, and it's too late for me to start that now. Once the director of the opera house has signed the stage director, he has no say in the stage conception. It happened once in Geneva, for *Aida*. The stage director was an American. When she signed, her conception for the staging was to put it around the Suez Canal affair, in the 1950s. The opera director said fine. Two years later, she changed her idea: she wanted an *Aida* with cannons and American jeeps. It caused a scandal. But the opera director can't do a thing once it's signed.

You were Leporello in Joseph Losey's film of Don Giovanni *(1979). How does filmed opera differ from opera onstage?*

There are advantages and disadvantages. If you've ever been on a film set, you know the problem is that you shoot scenes out of order. Scene 2, scene 18, and scene 7 are filmed together because they take place in the same spot and have the same décor. You do those three. Then you do scenes 6, 9, and 14, which have a different set. It's not easy. What I like about being in an opera is, as the Germans say, *einen Bogen spannen*, stretching an arc. For me, a show should always start out *piano* and keep in crescendo mode until the end. This allows tension to build up. You don't have this when you make a movie. You might feel it when you watch it, but when you make it, it's hard to feel, "Right, now I'm doing scene 7." I think we succeeded in this film nonetheless.

Did you see it?

No. I don't like to see or hear myself.

And you said you don't read newspapers.

I haven't for the last twenty-five years.

Which means you don't read the critics.

No. Criticism is a very personal thing. The French term is *critique*. I prefer the English term, "review." That implies it's not a criticism. If I had to write one, I'd ask fifty people in the hall what they thought of the show. I'd condense that, add my own two cents, and then have an opinion of a portion of the public. I spoke of humility earlier. I think one person giving an opinion of an opera performance is not very humble at all. But it's a profession, like the others.

As a performer, what would you do with that review, once you had the opinion of fifty operagoers? Would it change your performance?

No. I'd just say, I asked fifty people, and here's what they said. So you have fifty who say it wasn't good, or fifty who thought it was great, or twenty-five who said one thing and twenty-five another. It wouldn't change anything. I have my own opinion. But I don't think my personal opinion should appear in the newspaper. A lot of people read the critics before going to see an opera and base their decision on buying tickets on what they read. A lot of people let themselves be influenced by what critics say.

Do you ever feel the presence of your illustrious predecessors in the older opera houses or dressing rooms?

There are certain theaters where I tell myself there's a soul here. I sang at the Bolshoi Theater and had Chaliapin's dressing room. I won't say his spirit was there, but the place is inhabited by these people. Or at La Scala. It's been redone, but in the old dressing rooms, five or six years ago, you sat there and said, "Gigli and Caruso were here." Again, I won't go so far as to say I felt their spirits, but it's impressive. And it goes along with what I said about humility. You realize there were others here before you who were more important.

How about in Paris?

There's a soul at Palais Garnier, the old opera. Here at the Bastille, no. It looks like the métro. I don't like working here much, and they know it. I'm glad the *Traviata* I'm doing after *Louise* is at Garnier. But I made my debut there. I sang there from age twenty to twenty-five.

What do you like to do after a performance?

I'm pretty respectful of the public. When you sing in places like Toulouse or Marseille, there are always 150 people waiting for you at the exit for autographs. And I always do that. It doesn't bother me. In Paris, there's less of it. What I don't like, on the other hand—and this goes with my shyness again—is when I go into a restaurant with friends after a performance, and people start clapping. I hate that. Because the show's over for me. I'll sign for people waiting outside the theater, but two minutes later it's another thing entirely.

After a performance, and the restaurant with friends, it's 2 A.M., when you're all alone in a hotel room in a foreign city. How do you feel?

Alone. It happens to a lot of artists. It's a problem. For a long time, whenever I sang here in Paris, I drove back to Brussels after the show, to be home. After a performance, you're all charged up. So to relax you go out, which is what most people do. You eat, drink, and talk, then go to bed, and that's how you get fat. That's why you see so many overweight singers.

I thought you had to be big so the voice could resonate.

No, no, no, no, no. Fat doesn't resonate.

But driving relaxes you?

Yes. In those days, I had sports cars and drove fast—often at 200 or 230 kilometers per hour on the highway going home. I drive more slowly today.

Did you listen to opera, to help you relax?

No. I listened to music, but rarely opera. It's the same at home. I listen to music, but usually chamber music, quartets. Right now I'm listening to Beethoven's last quartets, which are extraordinary. Symphonic music, too. There was a period when I listened to a lot of that, but not much anymore. Now it's calmer music, more intimate music.

Jazz?

I like jazz a lot. Not modern jazz. I discovered George Shearing not long ago. Oscar Peterson. Another music I like is tango, Latin music. Not sung, especially the bandoneon. There's a nostalgic side to that I like very much.

Do you ever sing jazz? Some opera artists do.

I brought out an album of Christmas songs last year, things like "White Christmas," but no jazz.

We're seeing a rise in Asian opera singers in the West these days. Do you see any particular reason for it?

These people are curious about our Western culture. There's not that much opera in South Korea or China where they can express themselves, so they come west. That's great. The problem, I think, is that, physically, they haven't got the same build as we have, which can sometimes mean they have a different sound. It's interesting, but not everybody likes it. Because we're used to hearing a Rodolfo [*La Bohème*] with a nice, round tone, for example, and instead of that, suddenly you get a more metallic sound, or a silvery sound. You have to get used to that sort of voice. I think this different physical build

© felixbroede

makes it harder for them to sing well—harder than for us, I mean. It's similar with black singers. As soon as you hear a black singer on the radio, you know it's a black. You hear the sound coming out of the high cheekbones. You hear it with Oriental voices, too. It's good—but it's not easy for them.

Is there anyone you would have liked to work with but never did?

One conductor was Carlos Kleiber. It almost happened, but didn't work out. I liked him very much. I heard him conduct *La Bohème* at the Met, and thought I was hearing a different opera. He's the only one.

Can you tell operagoers something they might not know about opera that would enrich their experience the next time they go?

That's a hard question. A lot of people who go to the opera see a finished product. But we've rehearsed it for five weeks, and they've seen none of that. I think it would be interesting to let them see a bit of the show as it is put together. They do that sometimes; they let schools backstage. I think certain rehearsals should be open. But rehearsing before the public isn't easy; the conductor stops you, the stage director stops you, and the artists don't always like outsiders seeing that. But it might be the most interesting part of an opera—understanding the amount of work that goes into it, to reach that finished product the public sees on opening night.

How about preparation? Some people think operagoers should study the work before seeing it, while others believe you should come to opera with your feelings only and not worry about the plot, the libretto, or the history of the work.

I think both are possible. I tell people who have never been to the opera to see something easy for their first experience. *Carmen, La Bohème, Tosca.* I don't recommend seeing *Lulu* or *Wozzeck*, because they'll come away disgusted. You have to facilitate the approach to what you're going to see.

Does facilitating mean some sort of preparation on the spectator's part?

Yes; I feel spectators rarely inform themselves. They could read about the operas they're going to see, educate themselves a bit beforehand. That might help them understand it a bit better. Most people go, pay for their seats, and they like it, or they don't. That's their right, of course. But I think that if you're really interested in the work you're going to see, you should find out about it first. Anybody who's in the market for a new car is going to look around and learn. People should do the same for opera.

Rolando Villazón,
or the paradox of the performer

People rave about Rolando Villazón much as they gushed over Luciano Pavarotti a generation ago. People seem to appreciate the Big Tenor voice.

They've certainly got one in Villazón, who won Plácido Domingo's 1999 Operalia international singing contest (three awards) thanks to it. But his Big Charisma also played a part in that victory.

Peter Katona, director of casting at London's Royal Opera House, Covent Garden, was part of the Operalia jury that year (he still is). Of the Mexican tenor, Katona recalls, "You look for good singers, interesting singers, strong personalities. Villazón is proof of that. He wasn't that outstanding in the competition at the time. But this quirky, lively chap, who was excited and excitable—there was something special in the personality. You always have South American tenors. But the way they stand and deliver, slightly awkward—you don't see them rising in a similar way. It's really the whole person, what comes from inside. Villazón is able to exude that and pass it on to an audience."

He's lively, all right. And boy, does he exude. When the charisma operates —and it rarely takes a breather—it rivals the voice for bigness. He's passionate about music, literature, painting, his family. English is one of the many languages he speaks, and it has its special flavor. He's as bubbly speaking as he is singing and acting onstage. And if at times, while talking, he bubbles over the top, and you think you're listening to Roberto Benigni, you don't mind. Villazón is walking champagne. Charming, full of stories, you forgive him everything.

He's on a promo tour for his new CD of zarzuela (Spanish operetta) arias and has come (late) from a radio interview at the studio across the street. He finishes a run of Tales of Hoffmann *at the Opéra Bastille, here in Paris where he lives, before moving on to Munich and* La Bohème. *Both are sold out.*

A vivid striped jacket contrasts with a shirt of different-colored stripes, a uniform which has become somewhat of a trademark. His hair is waxed and wavy. He's excitable and laughs easily, but is also, unexpectedly, quite focused on what he says. The hands are in constant action to the end— waving, drawing in the air, stabbing it constantly, fleshing out his stories.

What kind of family background do you come from?

If we go back, back, back, I have a great-grandmother who, for reasons I don't know, emigrated from Austria to Mexico. Her son, my grandfather, continued to live in Austria for a while, but when the persecution of the Jewish people by the Nazis began, he was forced to leave Austria.

You have Jewish blood in you?

Yes, from my grandfather's side. He flew from Austria to Mexico with a fake Mexican passport. It's a whole adventure. He came to Mexico and became a star in football. He was the top scorer in the Mexican League, on the most important team. He met my grandmother, and she got pregnant. They never married. The name of my grandfather was Emilio Roth, like the writer. So my last name should be Roth. But my grandmother later married Hector Villazón, and she changed my father's name and named him Rolando Villazón. He was named in papers as Roth. Everyone was amazed, but in Mexico everything is possible.

Quite a story. Can we . . .

I first heard it five years ago. My father told it to me on the phone. I don't even know if my grandfather is still alive.

Villazón is a town in Spain.

In Asturias. When I sang in Oviedo, people came to me and said, "You're Asturiano, you're one of us!" [*Laughs*] When I sing zarzuela, in Spain I pronounce the "z" as "th," like a Spaniard. In Mexico, we don't.

You never went to Austria to look for family members?

No. But I was very close to my great-grandmother. She used to speak about her husband and how he fought in the First World War. She had his medals. We used to visit her twice a month—she lived in Cuernavaca. She had this beautiful house. There was something that always called to me in that house. Something European. I was very curious about Europe because of her. I loved something about the way she cooked the chicken with the potatoes and the way she played cards; they were not typically Mexican things. She didn't watch TV. Everybody watches TV there; we have a big American influence. This was another way. I remember the importance of wood in her house—of real, strong materials. She had many Mexican things. I remember the way she saw Mexico. Sometimes we see it in a way like we try to look more modern. But she adored the culture, the Mayas. So I saw my country from her eyes, and it was different than the way I looked at it from my own environment. I entered a German school because she wanted me to. She told my father, "I want them [Rolando and his sister] to get something from my culture, and the only way that'll happen is if you put them in the German school."

Was she musical?

She liked classical music, and I think that's my first memory of it. But it wasn't something really important. It was more about the whole ambiance. At one point, she was feeling very ill, and everyone thought she was going to die. This was a strong motivation for my father, I guess, to put us in the German school. It was a mess to get in there, by the way. To enter you had to be German, but there were no real German roots in my family. My great-grandmother was too distant. So there was no way they were going to accept us.

How did you get in?

My grandmother came to the school and made herself up to look like somebody working in the Education Ministry. She went to the principal. She told us the story: "I had this suitcase full of papers and was playing with them all the time. And that was very important, because it was a distraction. I said,

'I need to speak to the principal.' 'He's busy,' they told me. 'Well, you tell him that I come from the Education Ministry, and there's a huge irregularity in this school. My children, who are Mexican, are not allowed to enter. We're going to launch an investigation.'" The principal saw her, and she started going through the whole routine again. He said, "Don't worry. Would you be happy if we accepted your grandchildren?" She said, "Sure. If you're accepting Mexican children, I'll look the other way." So the performer was already there in my grandmother!

What do you remember about the school?

Nine years later, they kicked me out; but I still remember quite a bit of German. But, meanwhile, my great-grandmother didn't die! The end of my great-grandmother is like something out of Garcia Márquez! She called everybody, all the people who loved her, and said, "This time, I am going to die. But I don't want you to go through the process, so I'm calling to say goodbye. I love you all, you've meant a lot to me." She was really old, I don't remember how old. "Be happy," she said, and hung up. That weekend we went to her house to see her, but she was gone. Nobody knew where she went, and we don't know what happened to her. She simply went off and died like the elephants.

How does the family deal with you now? Do you still see them or are you in another universe?

Sure, I see them. My father lives in the U.S., and my mother in Mexico. When I'm in the States my father goes to my performances. He comes here to Paris. They don't travel that much, though.

But you do. Having an international career hasn't changed your relationships with them?

There is the physical distance, but we try and stay in contact. The career has not been a problem for the relationship with the family.

Let's turn to something that apparently doesn't travel—zarzuela. Why has it remained pretty much a Spanish thing?

It has traveled to Spanish-speaking countries, like mine, but it's true that it has remained kind of closed. I think one reason is some zarzuelas speak of very traditional aspects of Spain, or of regions, like Aragon. They speak deeply to the people there who know these traditions. And it might be only charming or interesting if you know the places they're singing about. Maybe the main reason is that they have dialogue between the sung numbers. Some of the roles are written for actors, and they add some singing lines for these actors. So it doesn't matter if you have a lyric voice. Sometimes you hear voices with no training singing alongside the lyric voices, and it's strange; we don't hear that in opera or even in operetta. There are many small reasons. Maybe it's a cultural thing. Perhaps there's a cultural wall that people erect between themselves and Spain in certain things.

It's big in Latin America, so that proves it can travel.

I think it could be universal. *Carmen* talks about Sevilla, even though it was written by a Frenchman. It's not a problem presenting that story in New York; on the contrary, it enriches the whole thing. There's a lot of dialogue in zarzuelas, and maybe some needs translation or rewriting. There haven't been people interested enough to do that. There was lots of dialogue in *opéra comique*, but people cut it, added music, and made it opera. You can do *Carmen* with or without dialogues—normally, people prefer it without. In zarzuela, that hasn't been done. And nobody has written music to link all the arias together to make it a big opera. Also, unfortunately, it's seen as a minor repertoire, like operetta. So no important opera theater has been interested. I think this is starting to change though. Because of Plácido Domingo, who has always been a champion for this repertoire. Also because of artists like Carreras and Berganza, or others who have performed it. I hope that my own recording of zarzuelas has also made a contribution and can help spur a revival.

So in addition to facing cultural problems, it hasn't really been properly packaged for the international consumer?

Maybe, yes. You could or couldn't do it. It might not be necessary. You could present it the way they present *Die Zauberflöte* sometimes, with the dialogues in translation. But I guess it's not the same effect. And, of course, it's not Mozart.

I read where you said, "I sing for the public. But I'm not trying to please them. That should be a result of what I do, but I never lose sight of the fact that only the music, the drama and the text matter." Can you elaborate? Does that mean you're not trying to educate the audience?

No. I hope they like it. In opera, it's not me; it's a whole team of people. If somebody goes to the opera for the first time and wants to continue going after that initial performance, that's fantastic. But if they don't, if they just found it a fantastic evening, that's also great.

Does that mean you don't have the audience in mind?

Yes, and that's the paradox of the performer. Of course you have the audience in mind, because you're performing for these eyes and ears out there. But when performing, you have to try and unify all the members of the audience into just one set of eyes and ears.

You mean an ideal spectator?

No. Let me explain. We go into rehearsals. And the rehearsal period is the time of searching, the time of testing and making mistakes. It's the time of finding reassurance, knowing what works. You make a whole map that will become the performance. There you are creating your character; let's say Hoffmann or Rodolfo or Alfredo. But Hoffmann or Rodolfo or Alfredo will only come alive when there's an audience in front of you. But still, you are doing for them what you were doing without the audience. You made certain decisions with the others in the cast in terms of your relationships with your colleagues, and with props on stage. In theater everything has a spirit. You make the stage move, but you don't move alone. The whole thing is moving. But for that to happen, we need an audience.

That doesn't happen during rehearsals?

When you rehearse, you can find an emotion, but it's not enough. You have to make sure the emotion can be seen and grasped. So you have to choose the right movement. It can be a big movement or a small one, like this [*waves his hand slightly*]. It can be a reaction of your colleague. So the audience gets the emotion and the impact. That's why you're always thinking of that somebody who will be looking. It's a question of energy. Also, during a performance, a colleague can change something after hundreds of rehearsals, make a movement that takes us in another direction. That's fantastic. Coughing in the audience might generate a feeling that you have to use something onstage for the character, and maybe it will make you do something in one moment. That is a key aspect of the relationship between performer and audience: the audience performs with me. Their spirit and energy, their active presence in the hall, is an integral part of my performance.

It's not a question of trying to please the audience?

If you do something to please the audience, you will never be free. Because then, the audience can say, "I think you moved too much," and it was a decision you made after weeks of rehearsal, and you decide not to move because that particular part of the audience or that critic didn't like how you moved. You have to stay as you are. I'm conscious of that; it's a decision, and I will continue to do it. Of course, you listen to everything. It's a distorted mirror, what people can tell you about yourself. It's an opportunity to analyze. But at the end of the day, trying to please the audience is trying to make the audience like Rolando Villazón. When I go onstage I don't care about Rolando Villazón. We shouldn't care about him. We should see Alfredo and his story with Violetta and his father. We should see the story of these characters.

When you do concerts, do you want the audience to see this, too?

Concerts are different. Because in concerts people come to see the performer. They want to see the *tenor*. What I like to do is establish communication. There I would like to feel like I'm singing to you, you, and you—not to a bunch of people, but to each one of you. When I sing opera, I very rarely look at the audience. If I do, it's an accident.

You can't see them.

No, you can see some faces, but I look at the faces when I do concerts, not opera. I look at the people. And I react to them. You can see somebody who is very serious, and someone else is smiling, and this generates a reaction in you. I like to say that for me, concerts are like a big hug. It should feel like, thanks to music, souls are coming together.

And you're saying this doesn't happen in opera because you're more inside the character?

No, and that's the paradox. The audience is there, and you're acknowledging the fact that there's an audience watching the story. You don't close that fourth wall. It's open. You know they are there, and you're telling the story to them. It's like if you're writing a novel, and you're in your room, and suddenly you realize there are people watching you. The door was open, the family came in, and they're watching. It doesn't bother you. But it is going to influence the way you're writing and the way your body is putting it together. It's different, maybe, because when you write you are not performing, but a performer acknowledges the audience, but you still want to be the character. It's hard to explain. The important thing is not to go out there and say, "Look how beautiful I'm singing." That shouldn't happen.

Doesn't it happen in rehearsals that everyone settles on something that works, but then doesn't work in performance?

Yes. Sometimes you expect something is going to be very funny, and it's not. Or sometimes you do something very serious, and people start to laugh. You have to react to that. Normally you try to avoid all that; a good stage director has a good eye for it. But there are realities that you will only know when you have an audience. That's why the dress rehearsal is extremely important. There you have an audience, and you have to perform. Then you can feel the audience's reaction. And you adapt to certain things. It might look like I'm contradicting myself, and in a way I do. Because it does influence you, but on an artistic level. If this movement [*waves again*] didn't cause a reaction, then you look for another. But you don't change things in order to be liked, to be adored by the audience. You have to change things to create the impact, so you're still serving the music and the drama. You change them so this becomes a more powerful moment.

Can you give an example?

Sometimes it might be better to stay in the shadow. You're in the shadow, but it makes for a stronger image. The wrong example would be, "Oh no, they don't see my face here, I'll go to the light." Because maybe it was more powerful when you were in the shadow, so you stay there because that's what the whole thing needs. What your vanity would need is to be in the light, thinking the audience will want to see you, to be seen how strong you are performing this movement. In the end, in the world of opera, who cares who is singing, really? If it's sold out because Villazón is singing or because Alagna or Domingo are singing, that's fantastic for opera. But ultimately, what you see there is the character that Verdi or Puccini put together. And everybody is as important as everybody else. Nobody is more important. Whether you have CDs or interviews or not doesn't matter. Opera is about the story and the characters.

This relationship with the audience is important. But you also said it's important where you sing. You said you would never sing Don José in New York.

I would take the "never" out. I meant today I would not sing Don José in the Bastille or at the Met.

Because of you or the house?

Because of me. I don't know if the theater would agree—maybe they'd like me to do it—but there are certain roles I prefer to sing in smaller houses.

It's a personal question, then—nothing to do with acoustics or buildings?

Yes. Also because I feel more secure if I sing *Carmen* like I did in Berlin, where there are maybe not even two thousand people. Opera was made for that. Today we have theaters with three thousand or four thousand; the Met has, what, four thousand seats? Opera was not made for a theater like that, although the acoustic at the Met is amazing, and I love to perform there. But on the other hand, the guy who is sitting in seat number four thousand up there, he can hear; but does he feel the things, does it reach him from the stage? I'm not sure. For me, it's very important what we do onstage and how it comes through. In these theaters, there's a moment where some people can just feel the power of music, which is already fantastic, but they'll miss the power of the connection between the artist and all that you do get in smaller houses. I always feel that I have to reach that person. So I know if I sing Don José—which is already a role that has a big orchestration in certain parts and is dramatically very powerful—I will try and make all that go into that particular place. But if I'm singing it in Berlin or Palais Garnier in Paris or Staatsoper in Vienna, I know what I do will reach the last row without forcing. Because I can see the faces of the people up there. I know my voice will reach them. Maybe it's a psychological thing. I see this infinite space, and I know there are people way up there, and as much as you tell yourself it's the same, and it's not about the voice, it's not about singing louder, it's about the energy, there's still a feeling of . . . I don't know. I know if I sing Alfredo at the Met, or *Roméo and Juliette*, it will travel. But with other operas, I feel I don't reach those people. And I want to reach everybody.

Let's talk about Plácido Domingo. You once said that you learn more from him over one lunch that during years of singing.

The question I'm asked is, "Is Plácido your teacher?" Because I call him "maestro." The answer is yes and no. No, he has never given me lessons in a classroom. He has never told me what to do with my voice. And yes because I have learned so much from him.

What have you learned?

He is, for me, the best performer that opera has and one of the best artists ever in the history of humanity! [*Laughs*] This doesn't come out of love; I say this as an objective artist myself! He once invited me to see him rehearsing. And it's fantastic, to see—that now, at his age, with his fame and his stature—the love and humility with which he comes to the art form and toward music, and the enthusiasm. He could come to rehearsal, snap his fingers, and say, "No, no, no, you go here, you stay there, I'm not going to take this now, I'll take it later." He comes, he sees what the structure is, then comes to the stage director and asks, "What do you think if I do it this way?" He's a real collaborator. And things don't always work out, the car didn't arrive or something, but he stays cool. He says, "Okay, we'll call another car." And he's the busiest guy in the business! I've never seen him explode, or holler, "Get these people out!" or this kind of thing that could be normal. With the pressure and the amount of things he has to do, it would be justified. But never. He still takes this as the most wonderful thing that has happened in his life! That's one side. And from the other side, the artist, he is for me the one person who has put together the drama and the music. I remember seeing his *Pagliacci*; I saw what was happening to the character. And the beauty of that voice. And the emphasis on his technique. He's huge. So yes, what I said is correct. We sit down and tell jokes, but if I ask a question he answers me completely freely.

Your relationship has been going on since Operalia in 1999?

It started then. But in Spanish I still talk to him using the formal "usted," not the familiar "tu" form.

Really?

Yeah, of course. And he has told me, "Come on, you can say *tu*," but I say, "Maestro Domingo." He says, "Call me Plácido." I say, "Never."

Does he use the "tu" form with you?

Yes. And that's the way it should be. But in Spanish it's different. In French, it would be disrespectful if he addressed me as *tu*. But in our culture, when you find somebody you respect, you can love them. For example, I say *usted* to my in-laws. And with them I get drunk, and we have a fantastic relationship, I've known them for years. It's a cultural thing, and that's fine, nobody's offended. With Maestro Domingo, we play tennis together, we go for beers together, and I keep calling him Maestro Domingo and you know what? I'd feel very weird if I said, "Hey, Plácido, how are you?" Because this admiration and this respect remain with me. I have the chance to speak to one of the gods in the opera Olympus. And he is a friend to me. And I want to be a friend to him. We've worked together, and it's fantastic. I'm not intimidated; I love to work with him. We've sung concerts together, and I don't feel shy, quite the contrary. It's inspiring to sing with him. Yet, he's still a god in Olympus, so I don't treat him like a normal mortal walking in the street.

People say you are his protégé, this generation's Domingo.

Journalists say that. To me it's a great compliment to be compared to him, but on the other hand, I know it's not true. I'm not trying to be the next Domingo, of course, I'm trying just to be Villazón. The main reason is that Domingo's career is unique. Nobody can do what he has done. And if you try and follow that career, you'll break into pieces.

He's singing baritone now.

He's continuing to sing tenor repertoire, but he's also doing *Simon Boccanegra*. He can do whatever he wants, and it'll be fantastic. He should, and I hope he does. I hope he sings *Rigoletto* one day. I hope he continues to give portraits of these roles. I'm not following any footsteps. I'm doing my career and I'm happy with his friendship. We already have very different repertoires. At my age, Maestro Domingo was already singing *Otello*. And that's something that's not even in my future yet. It's not something I can even think about. Different careers, different repertoires.

Do you want to talk about your future?

I used to think about the big roles, like *Otello*. But recently I sang Monteverdi with [*conductor*] Emmanuelle Haïm, and I want to explore more baroque. She made me discover a whole new world. So I prefer to go there, to Mozart, *Idomeneo*, maybe.

Handel?

I have recorded a CD with Handel arias, together with Paul McCreesh and the Gabrieli Consort, and it has been one of the most enriching and wonderful experiences of my artistic life. It was, of course, a learning process: I had to get in tune with the very specific style required for this repertoire, to work on my coloratura technique, adapt my personal style to complement this music without giving up what defines me as a singer. It was hard work, but in the best possible way. To be able to perform this music—Handel's music is like balsam for voice and soul. I can't wait to perform this music in concert, too, and to explore more baroque repertoire, also in opera.

What do you like about baroque?

It's very modern. I thought while singing these melodies that a pop singer could be singing them with a guitar. Rhythm is extremely important there, as are the words; baroque operas are extremely dramatic. They are theater pieces, but very strong, very psychological, very rich in what they demand from the performer. It's just fantastic. And singing baroque, I discovered some colors in my voice I didn't know I had. I had to use them because Emmanuelle kept telling me, "I want your voice. Don't change." But of course we worked a lot on the style and positioning of the voice because it's so different from what I do in the romantic opera repertoire.

Can you think of something to tell people who go to opera, romantic or baroque, that they don't know about it—something to listen for, or watch for—that might enrich their experience the next time they go?

I would say when you go to the opera, don't think you have to learn about it before. You don't have to study it. You don't have to know the libretto. Just the music will tell you a story, even if you don't have the supertitles. Don't think you have to understand everything that's happening. Don't receive opera through your brain. Receive it through your *feelings.* Be amazed at the human voice that is capable of filling an opera house without microphones. And the harmony. Be amazed at the teamwork, at what a bunch of human beings can do with a genius's music. Humans do so many terrible things to our world and to ourselves, but this is one bright, luminous thing we can do! They can come together to create something beautiful. Not only beautiful, but powerful. Something that can open the soul. This is what I would say. I'd say, Don't go thinking it's a smart thing, that you have to understand it and try to explain everything that's happening onstage. With modern productions, people try to get the meaning of everything. Don't. Sometimes it's just an aesthetic experience. Let it hit you, like a Kandinsky painting hits you. Don't think. The composer and people had the thoughts; you sit down, and you receive it. And they speak about universal emotions. You're going to be moved, just the way the person was who saw it for the first time. The first time *Bohème* was played, nobody knew it. But they sat down and were amazed. Or not. You might not be moved; that's okay. Don't worry. Try another opera. Don't think that just because one opera didn't move you, opera is not for you or no good. Go to another opera and maybe you'll be moved this time.

Is this something people have told you? "I don't go to opera because I don't understand it"?

Yes, a lot. People are kind of afraid. They say, "I've never been, I don't know anything." As if they are ashamed when they don't know. You don't need to know anything about opera! Just go! It's true that maybe if you go to *Parsifal* for the first time, you might find it long. But that's fine. Fall asleep for one hour, then wake up and listen to it. Really. It's fine. We do. Everybody does. When I went to see my first *Walküre* I thought, okay, five hours. I'll sleep three. But I still want to hear the music. Because even if you sleep, the music will have an impact on you.

How old were you when you saw your first Walküre?

This was very recently. I was doing *Don Carlo*, I think three years ago. It was my second Wagner experience. And I didn't know anything about the opera. It was supertitled in Dutch. I speak German, but Wagner uses a complicated German, though not hard to follow. This was after a long day of rehearsal for *Don Carlo*. So I thought, I'm very tired, I might sleep. *I was moved to tears!* I was overjoyed! I didn't follow the titles, I couldn't follow the story word by word. I was completely ignorant. I just let the story go. And I thought, this is what people should be open to do. To sit down. Don't worry. It might happen that you don't like it. It's okay. Try again another time. Don't be afraid of opera. It's not such a smart, huge thing.

People also say it's expensive.

There are prices for everything. I paid two hundred euros for four people to go to the circus. For two hundred euros, four people can go to the opera and have good seats. For sixty euros each you can have good seats—maybe a little more. And if you want to go alone and pay that, and give yourself a present, that's good. If opera is expensive, it's because it's worth it. Then again, there are other opportunities. Last-minute tickets for five euros, standing room, student seats. How much does a football match cost?

Is there any difference between your generation and previous ones? Any opportunities you think you have that they didn't, or any drawbacks? Are there any comparisons you can make?

Opera singers today have the opportunity of reaching a bigger audience. The price for that is you have to give a lot of interviews.

Sorry about that.

I wouldn't do it if I didn't like it! I *want* to do it. Maybe it's also a necessity. I think the classical field has learned some strategies from the pop field.

Marketing?

For marketing, yes. That's changed completely. And opera has changed in terms of time. It's easier to travel. It's easier to know what's going on. You crack a note, and it's on YouTube. You leave the stage, it's on YouTube. If you sing wonderfully, it's there or on a CD or already on the Internet, and everybody has a copy of it.

Does that bother you?

I don't think so. It's part of our times. Before, news that happened in the States stayed in the States, and nobody else knew about it. Even Caruso, if he was singing in Italy, maybe in France, they didn't know or care what was going on. But today, everybody knows what's happening everywhere in the world of opera. And when you go to each country, you have interviews. You're on TV, you're on the radio, you need to invest a lot of time in non-artistic things. I don't think it's wrong; I'm not saying that. But they say speaking isn't good for the singer, so we shouldn't give a lot of hours to interviews. It tires the voice. Maybe that's the difference. It has both pros and cons. I'm sure Renata Tebaldi didn't have to do these things. I don't even think Callas had to do this amount of interviews and things like that. But today we have to, because of the evolution of the CD, the Net, and the ease with which people get copies of recordings.

You have to promote.

You have to promote and make it special. Before, everybody recorded everything. Today, that's very rare. I feel lucky to have made DVDs of *Traviata and Elisir d'amore,* but on CD, *Traviata* is the only opera I have. I'm happy that I'll soon have a *Bohème,* and a *Werther* and a *Carmen.* And that these are projects that work. But they only work because of talented artists and because of marketing. Because now they are reaching other audiences who think, "Hey, they said it's fantastic, let's buy it." If not, it would just stay in the opera world. And in the opera world you already have, what, five hundred *Traviatas*. But when marketing tells you this is the *Traviata* of today, or this is the tenor you have to listen to, you say, "Okay, I have my CDs of Domingo, but I have to listen to this." It's important. I'm not bothered by that. It has changed the investment of time and how you arrange your time; the time you give to performances has changed. I don't know if, in the past, people had to think, "This is my time for concerts, this my time for opera, this my time for vacation, this my time for promotion and this my time for recording." Today, you have to reserve time for promotion.

Does your generation have more access to singing competitions than previous generations had?

Maybe, but honestly I think competitions are good to get some money and recognition. The most important thing about Operalia, and Domingo knows it, is that in the jury he always invites opera theater directors. Prizes there are very good; they give a lot of money. And that's fantastic to start a career. Because if you're starting, you have at least that money to concentrate on your career. You don't have to wash dishes or something to support yourself. That's one thing. The other thing is, say, a theater says, "I want to support this guy and give him the role of Alfredo because I saw him, and he won." That's why it's important. To win first, second, or third prize is not important in this business. Even today. Who's the best tenor today? It's not tennis; it's not a competition. In opera, it depends on who you are. Who is the best writer ever? Tell me what you read, and I'll tell you who's the best for you.

Last question. I can't believe this is a true story. It sounds like something out of Hollywood [Villazón puts his hand over his head and dangles his fingers, mimicking a shower]. Yes. When you were twelve, you were singing in the shower [he laughs]. You know what I'm talking about? That's how you were discovered? That can't be true. You made that up.

No, it's true! I was eleven or twelve. I recently said this, and now they ask it because everybody says, "Nah, come on, that's bullshit, you're making that up! He was discovered in the shower!" [*Laughs*] But it would be an exaggeration to say I was discovered in the shower. I wasn't singing opera. What I was singing in the shower was Baloo, from *The Jungle Book.*

Isn't that a basso part?

Yes, but I was doing it. There was no accompaniment. And I was dancing. It was very alive in that shower. What you heard was somebody going "babadabadabadaba" [*drums his fingers on the table*] and clapping his hands and splashing and all that. And my neighbors were having a party. And one of the guests, a good friend of theirs, had been appointed director of the Academy of the Performing Arts in Mexico City, a place called Espacios. They were later bought by Televisa, the big TV chain. As he was coming in, he heard that noise from the shower. I think he found it funny, and he knocked on our door. My mother opened it and he asked, "Who's singing up there?" And she said, "I'm sorry. I'll tell him to shut up." And he said, "No, no. We're starting a program for young people, and maybe he'd be interested in singing." Maybe our neighbors had told him that their neighbor liked to sing. So I went and performed and stayed in this academy. But it had nothing to do with opera. It was not like one day I was singing opera in the shower, and the director of the Theater of Bellas Artes heard me and invited me. But it is true that I went to this academy, and that's where I discovered that the stage was heaven for me. I spent almost two years there, and that's why I was kicked out of the German school. Because I didn't care about chemistry and those other subjects. I used to go to German school from 7:15 to one in the afternoon, then went to go to the Academy from four to ten in the evenings, so I didn't even have time to do homework or study for the other subjects.

So you got your big break in the shower?

Yes. It was like a seed that was planted in me, and made it clear for me that this is what I really wanted.

Index

Names of operas and other works appear in italics; opera roles are not in italics; arias are unitalicized and within quotation marks.